SARAH'S
STORY

Gary Tatem

ISBN 979-8-89485-462-5 (Paperback)
ISBN 979-8-89485-463-2 (Digital)

Covenant Books
11661 Hwy 707
Murrells Inlet, SC 29576
www.covenantbooks.com

INTRODUCTION

Sarah was born in a medium-sized city. She has red hair and a sprinkling of freckles. Her mother worked in a grocery store not far from
the house. It was not one of those chain stores; it was a small mom-
and-pop shop. She was the store's produce manager and sometimes
filled in at the checkout register. Sarah's dad was a supervisor at a
manufacturing company just outside of town. He had worked his
way up in the company, where he started as a laborer. It was hard
work, and the company had lots of turnover. He liked his job and
was very good at it. He liked what he was doing so much that he
passed up a couple of promotions to be a section manager and above.
He said that dealing with people was hard enough, and he didn't like
doing a bunch of paperwork too. They are both retired now.

Sarah is an only child. Her mother developed female problems
and could not have any more kids. Growing up as the only child of
a father who wanted a boy, Sarah was it. She and her dad did everything together. They fished, hunted, and if anything needed to be
fixed or build, they were side by side. That's probably why Sarah is
such a tomboy.

When she was not with her dad, Sarah was with her best friend,
Ben. Ben lived just around the corner from Sarah's house, and he was
an only child too. If they were not out and about, they were together
either at Ben's house or Sarah's house. They were more like brother
and sister than friends. One of their favorite things to do was watch
the freeway being built. It was a few blocks from their houses. They
sat for hours on the hill overlooking the construction site, watching
all the different operations going on.

Waiting for the workers to finish work for the day, and after the
last worker left, Sarah and Ben would climb up on the bulldozers and

motor graders and pretend they were driving them. That was back when parents didn't worry about their kids like they do today. The kids knew they were to be home before dinner. If they went back out after dinner, they had to be home as soon as the streetlights came on.

Sarah was very athletic. She even made the varsity fast-pitch softball team as a freshman in high school. She played either second base or in the outfield. Her greatest asset was her batting. She never fell below a .650 batting average. She was voted the most valuable player both her junior and senior years. Sarah was also a good student and got straight A's, except for one B she received during her freshman year. She missed an A by one percentage point. She still thinks it's because the teacher didn't like how smart she was and wanted to make her feel humble.

Sarah was also involved in other school activities. She was on the school's debate team and was the team captain. They even went to state and won first place. Ben, on the other hand, was at best a B student. He didn't like playing sports, but he did like watching Sarah's games. Sarah thought it was so he could watch all the girls play. Later, she found out it was just the love of the game.

Early on, Ben and Sarah went to some of the school's functions together, but as their time in school went on, guys would ask Sarah out on dates. That was okay with Ben as he, too, felt they were like brother and sister. He loved Sarah, but not romantically.

A boy named Dan transferred to Sarah's school from out of state at the start of their senior year. Dan's father had taken a job in town. It wasn't long before they were dating. Sarah's dad didn't like Dan from the get-go. There was just something he could not put his finger on. Sarah's mom thought Sarah's dad didn't think Dan was good enough for his little Sarah. Sarah's mom liked Dan because he made Sarah happy.

Sarah and Dan got married right after they graduated from high school. Everyone thought they had to, but Sarah was not pregnant. They just loved each other and didn't want to wait. It was a fancy wedding with lots of people in the wedding party. Her dad reluctantly walked Sarah down the aisle. He did it but was not happy about it. He was against them getting married so young. He preferred that they wait a few years to see if they still loved one another. The straw that broke the camel's back was when Sarah and Dan moved six hours away. Dan had gotten a sales job working for his uncle. Sarah's dad didn't talk to her for a long time after that.

After the move, Sarah got a secretary job and went to night school at the local state college. She had two scholarships, one for academics and the other for softball. Even though she went to night school, she was allowed to play on the team. Her boss gave her time off to practice and play games, but that was without pay. Luckily for Sarah, the season was not long, so she didn't miss much work. Her boss at the time did come to her home games from time to time.

Dan had a gift for persuasion and was doing a good job at selling. He was on a base salary plus commission and making good money. With both of them working and Sarah's school being paid for, they could afford a small two-bedroom house. At first, it was hard making ends meet, but they did.

Sarah finished her first year of college. She made very good grades and was well-liked by her teachers and fellow students. She thought that after she got done with the standard required classes, she would start working toward being a lawyer. She was sure she was smart enough to pass the hard classes it takes to become a lawyer.

It was soon after she started her second year that disaster struck. Her husband, Dan, was killed in an accident. Sarah was devastated. She went into a deep depression and even went into grief counseling. She quit school and her job. She just couldn't do it. She received money from Dan's life insurance policy and a wrongful death settlement. She didn't date and basically didn't do much of anything.

The money was starting to run low. She didn't want to lose the house and knew she had to do something. Sarah was not going to return home, even though her mom begged her to do so. Sarah was determined to go it alone and needed a job. So she started looking. There was a job ad in the newspaper for an administrative assistant to a vice president. Sarah didn't know if she had the qualifications for the job but was going to give it a try anyway. She applied for the job and got an interview. Bill saw lots of potential in Sarah and offered her the job. She started her job a few days later.

CHAPTER 1

How They Met

Karl and Sarah worked for the same company, but in different departments. Karl was a CPA and worked in the accounting department. The company hired Karl right out of college about six years ago. He was twenty-nine years old and stood five feet, eleven inches tall. He had light brown hair, blue eyes, and weighed around 185 pounds. Karl worked his way up to his current position as one of only two senior accountants the company had. Karl was the pitcher on the company's men's softball team. The team was in one of the city's softball leagues, where the teams were made up of employees from companies around the area.

Sarah was an administrative assistant to one of the company's vice presidents. Sarah had just turned twenty-seven years old. She had shoulder-length red hair, a sprinkling of freckles, and blue eyes. She was five feet, eight inches tall, with a petite frame and legs that went all the way to the floor. Sarah had been working for the company for about three and a half years. She was a hard worker and well respected by the people she worked with. Bill, one of the company's vice presidents, was her boss.

Karl and Sarah only knew each other from their paths crossing from time to time. Karl liked seeing Sarah but never thought he had much of a chance dating her. Sarah gave Karl a warm smile but didn't say much more than "Hi."

It was a warm Saturday, the day of the annual company picnic—a time for the employees to enjoy all kinds of fun with their families and fellow employees. For the kids, there was face-painting, a bounce house, various contests, and a variety of kid games. One of the employees of the company was a Simon Says master and volunteered to conduct a Simon Says game. He made an announcement, "Anyone want to play Simon Says?"

A crowd of kids soon surrounded him. He said, "So you want to play, do you?"

The kids cheered and yelled, "Yes!"

He reminded them, "A quick reminder of the rules: If Simon says, 'Put your hands on your head,' you put your hands on your head. The ones that didn't—you're out. If Simon DIDN'T say, 'Put your hands on your head,' and you did, you're out. Okay, let's play."

He gave a bunch of Simon Says commands, and mixed in were some that Simon didn't say. The game went on until there was one little boy and one little girl left. They both were excellent players and didn't make a single mistake. It was declared a tie, and both were given first-place ribbons.

For the adults, there were horseshoe and cornhole tournaments, a watermelon eating contest, and more. The winners got first, second, or third-place ribbons. They had all sorts of carnival-style booths, and one of those was a dunk tank. You know, where someone sits on a bench above a tank of water, and people throw a ball at a target. If they hit the target, it caused the person to fall into the water. Sarah's boss, Bill, was one of the people who volunteered to be dunked. Sarah did not dare try to dunk him, even when he said, "Come on, Sarah, give it a try."

Sarah, having been on her high school and college softball teams, had a good arm and could easily hit the target. Even though it was all in fun, she thought it best not to do it.

There were some food trucks at the picnic, but most people brought food to feed their own families. The highlight of the picnic was the tournaments—horseshoes and softball. By far, the softball tournament was the most popular. A couple of weeks before the picnic, teams were formed. Here at the picnic, the teams played against each other, with a trophy going to each of the team members of the first-place and second-place teams. Karl was picked as the team captain for the team he was on.

As the day went on, the losing teams were eliminated. Karl's team had not lost any games and were the winners in the winners' bracket, and the team they were about to play had only lost one game. They were the winners in the losers' bracket.

This last game would determine the first and second-place teams. These two teams were fairly evenly matched. One team would be ahead, then the other, as the score bounced back and forth. It was the bottom of the last inning, and Karl's team was down by one run. There were two outs with one guy on second base. All the other team had to do was get this last out, and they would win. It was Karl's turn at bat.

Karl let the first pitch go by, and the umpire called out, "Strike!" The next pitch was way outside—one ball and one strike. The next pitch was the one Karl had been looking for. Karl connected, and the ball went sailing. Karl had hit the ball out over the fence. A home run, and with the guy already on second base, Karl's team went ahead, winning the game. The trophies were awarded, and handshakes were exchanged. Karl collected his equipment and was walking to his car to put his equipment and trophy away and then return to the picnic.

Sarah had been watching the game. Karl looked up and saw Sarah standing in the middle of the sidewalk. Sarah said, "That was quite a home run you hit."

Karl had a big smile on his face and could not believe she noticed him, let alone was talking to him.

He said, "I was just lucky."

They continued talking, mostly about how exciting the game was. Karl was feeling really good. He decided to go for it and asked Sarah, "Would you like to have dinner with me tonight?"

Sarah thought for a second and said, "Yes, that would be nice."

Karl said, "Is seven okay with you? That would give me time to go home and take a shower."

Sarah agreed to the time and gave Karl her address.

*****

Karl drove up to Sarah's house right at seven. Sarah met Karl at her front door. Karl thought Sarah looked fantastic. Her beautiful red hair fell just past the collar of the white sleeveless blouse she was wearing with a very short skirt.

Karl said, "It looks like you're ready to go. I picked a local steak house not too far from here. Is that okay with you?"

Sarah said, "That would be great. I'm in the mood for a nice steak dinner."

At the restaurant, they were seated, and the server asked, "Would you care for a drink?"

Sarah said, "I would like a glass of wine."

Karl said, "I'll have a beer. I have eaten here several times before, and I'm going to order the rib eye steak."

Sarah looked at the menu and said, "I will have the New York strip."

The server returned with the drinks and asked, "Are you ready to order?"

Sarah ordered the garden salad with ranch dressing, the New York strip cooked medium, and a loaded baked potato. Karl ordered the garden salad with ranch, the rib eye medium rare, and the mashed potatoes.

Sarah told Karl, "I really enjoyed the picnic and watching you hit that home run. I'm looking forward to next year's picnic. Maybe they will have a coed softball tournament too."

The server came with their salads. As they ate, they talked some more, and Sarah told Karl, "I've been married. My husband was killed in an accident."

She did not say what kind of accident, and Karl didn't feel comfortable enough to ask.

Karl said, "I'm sorry to hear of your loss. I have been in a couple of relationships but never got married."

The server delivered the rest of their dinner. Karl asked Sarah, "How is your steak?"

Sarah said, "It's the best. How is yours?"

Karl said, "It is better than the last time I had one here."

They finished their dinner, and it was time for Karl to take Sarah home. It was a quiet ride back to Sarah's house, neither having much to say. They arrived at Sarah's house, and Karl walked her to her door.

Sarah asked Karl, "Would you like to come in?"

Karl said, "Yes."

Sarah lived in an small two-bedroom older home in a well-established neighborhood. The inside was very nicely decorated. Sarah said, "I'm going to have a glass of wine. Would you like one or a beer?"

Karl said, "Yes, please, a beer would be great."

The two sat on the couch and sipped their drinks. They talked and got to know each other a little better. Karl felt things were going well and was feeling very comfortable with Sarah. They kissed a few times. Sarah stood up, took Karl's hand, and said, "Let's go to the bedroom."

Sarah led the two of them down the short hallway to her bedroom. They kissed and kissed some more and then had sex. After the day at the picnic, a wonderful dinner, and the activity they had both just experienced, they both fell quickly asleep.

*****

The next morning, Karl woke up to an empty bed. He smelled coffee. He put on his pants and followed the smell to the kitchen. Sarah was in the kitchen, wearing a short robe tied around her slender waist. The robe just hung below her firm buttocks.

Sarah said, "Good morning, sleepyhead. Did you have a good night's sleep? How about some coffee?"

Karl said, "The best, and yes, I would love a cup."

Sarah asked Karl, "How about I cook us some breakfast?"

5

Karl said, "That would be great. I usually don't eat breakfast, but for some reason, this morning, I'm hungry."

Karl was hungry for more than just breakfast, but he thought he'd better not press his luck.

Sarah said, "I put some clean towels out for you in the bathroom. Why don't you take a quick shower, and I will have breakfast ready by the time you're done?"

Karl finished his shower, and the smell of bacon had filled the air. He quickly got dressed and returned to the kitchen. Sarah asked him, "Are scrambled eggs okay?"

Karl said, "They're my favorite."

Sarah said, "I will be finished cooking here in a minute or two. Help yourself if you need to refill your coffee."

Soon, Sarah sat down with two plates of scrambled eggs, bacon, and toast. Sarah's cooking was excellent.

Karl said, "I like your cooking, and the eggs are just how I like them."

She said, "Thanks. I had so much fun yesterday. I enjoyed the dinner and would like to eat there again someday."

Karl agreed with her, a big smile on his face. Karl said, "I have some things I have to do today," which was a lie. He wanted to spend the entire day with Sarah.

Sarah said, "I have things to do too."

She knew those things could be done anytime, and she too would have liked to spend the day with Karl.

Sarah walked Karl to the door. They kissed, and Sarah stood at the door until Karl drove off.

CHAPTER 2

Jill's Arrival

They talked on the phone every day and were now dating on a regular basis. They agreed that they should not be seen together at work, not knowing how that would be accepted.

Karl invited Sarah to his apartment for dinner. He had put a roast in his slow cooker several hours ago, and the apartment was smelling great. It was about time for Sarah to arrive. As he waited, he was thinking about all the things he had left to do to prepare for the dinner. He wanted everything to be just right. Yes, he wanted to impress Sarah.

There was a knock at the door. Karl looked at the clock hanging on the wall, and Sarah was right on time. He opened the door and said, "Come on in."

He gave her a kiss and a big hug, and she kissed him back. She was wearing a light pink blouse, very short shorts, and sandals. Her red hair had a little curl to it.

This was the first time she had been to Karl's apartment. It was a small place, just one bedroom. Karl was trying to save up enough money for a down payment on a house. The apartment had a simple open layout. The front door opened to the living room. The kitchen had a half-wall counter and was just big enough for a small table. Karl gave her another kiss and said, "Welcome to my place. Have a seat. I need to get back to my cooking."

Sarah said, "It sure smells good. I can't wait to see what kind of cook you are."

Karl was a good cook but not a fancy one. He cooked basic dishes and left the fancy stuff to restaurants when he ate out. Karl asked Sarah, "Would you like a glass of wine?"

She said, "Yes, that would be nice."

He poured her a glass and handed it to her.

For the few weeks they had been dating, Karl had really fallen for Sarah, and Sarah for Karl. Not only was she smart and beautiful, but she was also the best sexual partner he had ever had.

The roast was done, and the gravy was made. Dinner was almost ready to be served when there was a knock at the door. He thought to himself, *Who in the world could that be?*

Karl went to the door and opened it. Standing there was Jill, Karl's ex-girlfriend. He had stopped dating her about a month before he started dating Sarah. There were tears running down her face. He asked her, "What happened?"

Jill said, "I was on a date and was eating dinner at the restaurant just around the corner from here."

She went on to say, "The guy I was with was drinking a lot, being a jerk, and getting verbally abusive to me. I got really scared, and I'm afraid to go home because that guy might be crazy enough to go there and possibly hurt me. I didn't know what to do, so I came here."

It was about then that Jill saw that Karl had company. Karl introduced Jill to Sarah. Jill started to apologize for barging in on them. Sarah, hearing Jill's story, said, "It's okay, come on in. The three of us will figure out something for you to do."

Karl offered Jill a glass of wine.

Jill said, "I sure could use one."

Karl had to get back to fixing dinner or everything would be burnt and dinner a total loss. Jill and Sarah sat on the couch, and Karl could hear they were talking, but he couldn't make out what they were saying. Every once in a while, he could hear a bit of laughter from the two of them.

Jill told Sarah, "Karl and I dated, and it's over. Karl was good to me, but things never worked out. I haven't seen Karl since the breakup. We've remained friends. I've talked to him on the phone a couple of times, and he said he was seeing someone. I guess that someone is you."

Sarah said, "We have been dating for a while. I have fallen in love with him."

Jill said, "It's not hard to do. He is a fantastic guy."

Karl mashed the potatoes as the asparagus sautéed in butter and olive oil. The dinner was coming together nicely. Karl said, "It's dinnertime, come and eat."

Jill said, "I'm not hungry, and if it's okay, I would just like to sit here for a while. The two of you go ahead and enjoy your dinner."

Sarah said, "Don't be silly. At least join us at the table."

Jill agreed.

Karl asked Jill, "Would you like some more wine?"

Jill said, "Yes."

He refilled Jill's glass and Sarah's glass too.

The roast was so tender you could cut it with a fork. The gravy was not Karl's best thing to make, but it turned out to be the best he had ever made—not too thin and no lumps. The mashed potatoes were stiff and easily held the gravy. The asparagus had a bit of cara-melization to it and was very tender.

The talk during dinner was very pleasant. Sarah said, "Karl and I work at the same company but in different departments."

She told Jill what her job duties were and how much she enjoyed working there.

Jill said, "I moved from a town about the same size as this one. I moved mainly to put a bit of distance between me and my mother."

Jill explained, "I love my mother very much, but my mother is overbearing and controlling. I felt I had to move away or I would be smothered and controlled the rest of my life. I found a job very similar to the one you say you have, Sarah. I love my job and where I work."

As Karl and Sarah finished dinner, Karl said, "Why don't you two go into the other room while I clean up this mess."

They both offered to help clean up the kitchen.

Sarah said, "After all, you cooked this wonderful meal."

Karl said, "Thanks, but this kitchen is too small, and we would be bumping into one another."

Sarah gave Karl a quick kiss, and she and Jill went into the other room, leaving Karl to clean up. It was not too long before he had put all of what was leftover in containers and into the refrigerator, and the dirty dishes in the dishwasher. One thing that Karl really liked about his tiny apartment was the dishwasher.

Karl walked into the living room and sat down in his chair. They talked some and watched a movie on the TV. It was getting late, and Jill asked, "Would it be okay for me to spend the night? I just don't feel safe going to my place tonight."

Karl looked at Sarah, and she nodded her head to indicate it was okay with her. Karl gave Jill something for her to sleep in.

Although Sarah had not planned on spending the night, she decided that now she would. They had slept together several times before, but this was the first time she had slept with Karl in his bed. Karl had fixed a place for Jill to sleep on the couch.

CHAPTER 3

The Next Morning

Karl was the first to wake. He took a shower and got dressed for the day. He walked into the living room, where Jill was folding up the sheets and blanket.

"Good morning," said Karl. "How did you sleep?"

Jill said, "I slept well," and then jokingly added, "You should have bought the hide-a-bed couch. Thanks for letting me sleep here last night. You are a good friend."

"Where's Sarah?"

Karl asked.

"She's still in bed," Jill replied. Then she asked Karl, "Do you think it's okay to go ahead and take a shower?"

Karl said, "I think that would be okay."

Karl went into the kitchen and got the coffee going. Jill finished her shower, got dressed, and peeked in on Sarah.

Jill said, "I hope me staying here last night didn't interrupt any plans the two of you had."

Sarah said, "I hadn't planned on staying the night, but after the late night watching the movie and the several glasses of wine, I was too tired to go home."

Jill said, "The shower is all yours."

Sarah asked, "Is there any hot water left?"

Jill said, "There was when I got out."

They both laughed.

Jill went to the kitchen and told Karl, "Sarah is getting up and going to take her shower now."

She asked Karl, "What are your plans for breakfast?"

He said, "I have bacon, some eggs, and pancake mix."

Jill said, "Sounds great, let's have all three. I'm starving."

She poured herself a cup of coffee. Karl started emptying the dishwasher and putting everything away.

A few minutes later, Sarah walked into the kitchen wearing one of Karl's softball jerseys. She said, "The coffee smells great."

Karl handed her a cup of coffee and a spoon and said, "There's milk in the refrigerator and sugar on the table."

Sarah asked, "What have you two come up with for breakfast?"

Karl said, "We decided on bacon, eggs, and pancakes."

Sarah said, "Sounds great. Why don't you let Jill and me cook?"

Jill said, "I like that idea," and she gave Karl a little push out of the kitchen. Karl refilled his cup of coffee and went into the living room, turned the TV on, and sat down in his chair.

Karl could hear the girls talking and laughing, along with the opening and closing of cupboard doors and drawers and the rattling of cookware. Soon, the sound of bacon frying and that wonderful smell filled the apartment.

The girls worked out who would do what for the mixing and cooking. They decided that scrambled eggs would be best, and Jill would be the one to cook them as soon as the bacon was done. Karl didn't have many skillets or pots and pans, for that matter, either. Sarah mixed up the pancake batter and found another skillet to cook the pancakes.

The girls were hip to hip, cooking away, enjoying each other's company, and seemed to be becoming friends. The pancakes and eggs finished cooking, and they even made some toast. A call to come and eat was made.

They all sat down and started to eat. Jill said, "I have gotten many text messages and a couple of voice messages from that jerk."

She asked, "What do you think I should do?"

Karl said, "You should send a text message saying you don't want to ever hear from or see him again."

Sarah said, "Don't delete the texts or voice messages anytime soon, just in case you need them for some reason later on."

Then both Karl and Sarah said at the same time, "Block his number on your phone."

They all laughed at how Sarah and Karl had said it at the same time.

Breakfast was done, and the kitchen was a mess. Karl said, "I guess since you two cooked, I should clean it up."

Everyone's spirits were high, and again, laughter filled the room. Despite Karl's small kitchen, all three of them managed to work together to get it cleaned up.

Karl said, "I'm going to drive Jill to her place."

And he asked Sarah, "Would you like to go along?"

Sarah said, "I hadn't planned on spending the night and really should be getting home."

She was still wearing Karl's softball jersey and was planning to wear it home. It was long enough to cover her nicely shaped butt, but that was just about all. She gathered up the rest of her clothes and gave Karl a big kiss goodbye.

She said to Jill, "It was a pleasure meeting you, and I enjoyed the time we all had together. I hope to see you again. I think we two could become friends."

Jill responded, "I, too, enjoyed the evening and working with you in the kitchen this morning. But I don't want it to become a regular threesome. I like you, too, and would very much like for us to become friends. Thank you for being so supportive with the problem I'm having with that jerk."

Sarah said, "You're welcome. Goodbye."

Karl walked Sarah out to her car. They kissed, and Karl said, "Thanks for being so understanding and supportive with Jill."

Sarah said, "Just remember who your girlfriend is" and gave Karl a wink. She got into her car and drove off. Karl waved goodbye and walked back into the apartment.

When he got back to the apartment, Jill said, "You are so lucky to have a girlfriend like Sarah."

Karl said, "I agree. I love her. Get your stuff, and let's get you home."

Jill and Karl walked to his car. As they drove to Jill's place, neither said much of anything. When they got there, Karl looked around and didn't see anything out of the ordinary.

He said, "It looks like no one is around here or has been here either. Maybe the guy sobered up and decided to leave you alone."

Jill said, "I can't thank you enough for your kindness. You have always been so nice to me. I enjoyed dating you, and I miss what we once had. I like that we can still be friends. I know you are happy with Sarah, and both of you are very much in love with each other. I wish you the best. Invite me to your wedding. You two make such a great couple."

Karl said, "Thank you. Let me walk you to the door."

The two of them got out of the car and walked to Jill's front door. Standing at the front door, Karl gave Jill a hug and a kiss on her cheek and said, "Goodbye."

As he was walking to his car, he turned halfway around and waved to Jill as she stepped through her front door. Karl got into his car and drove back to his apartment.

CHAPTER 4

Have You Ever Been Camping?

Midweek, Sarah called Karl and said, "Have you ever been camping? I have all of this camping gear that my husband and I camped with."

Karl said, "I did a long time ago when I was in the Boy Scouts. I did enjoy it back then."

Sarah said, "Why don't you come over on Saturday, and let's go through this stuff and make plans to go camping?"

Karl said, "Sounds good to me. What time do you want to do it?"

Sarah said, "How about two?"

"Okay, see you at two on Saturday. Bye, love you."

"Bye, love you too."

*****

At two on Saturday, Karl was ringing Sarah's doorbell. Sarah answered the door. Karl stepped in, and they kissed and held a nice, long hug as she held herself close to him.

Sarah asked Karl, "Would you like a beer?"

And he said, "Yes."

They walked to the kitchen, and Sarah got two beers out.

Sarah said, "Let's go out to the garage, and I will show you what I have. The tent is a four-person tent, more like two adults and two small kids at most, but it is just right for two people."

They laughed at that.

There were two sleeping bags, a large cooler chest, a lantern, an air mattress, a cook stove, dishes, forks, knives, spoons, and a variety of cooking pots and pans.

Karl said, "Don't you think we should set up the tent to see if all of the parts are here? I would hate to get camping and find out a piece or two was missing."

Sarah said, "I think everything is here, but that sounds like a good idea."

They gathered the tent and all of the tent poles and took it into the backyard. The setup instructions were nowhere to be found. After some trial and error and working together, they got the tent up.

Karl said, "I saw an air mattress in the garage. Maybe we should air it up to see if it will hold air."

Sarah went back to the garage and returned with the air mattress and the pump. Karl attached the pump and began to fill the mattress. It didn't take long before the mattress was inflated. They both lay down.

Karl said, "This is nice. I think a camping trip will be a lot of fun."

Karl leaned over and gave Sarah a kiss. They kissed several more times.

Sarah said, "Let's pretend we are camping right now."

They both lay there as they fantasized that they were out camping. They imagined they could hear the water in the stream flowing over the rocks. It was nighttime, and Karl had built a fire, and they could hear the crackling.

Sarah said, "It's going to be fun camping with you."

They took the tent down and folded it up, let all of the air out of the air mattress, and put all of the other equipment back in the garage. They had worked up a sweat in the afternoon heat and had gotten a little sweaty.

Sarah said, "I think we should go take a shower."

That was an activity they had done before and enjoyed very much. They both ran through the garage and then into the house. There was a debate between the two of them as to whether Karl enjoyed washing Sarah or Sarah being washed by Karl.

CHAPTER 5

Moving In Together

That next week, Karl was over at Sarah's house, telling her that his apartment lease was just about up. He said, "The rent is going to increase a lot."

The two talked about it for a while.

Sarah said, "You are here most of the time. Why don't you just move in here with me?"

They had been dating for over six months now, and he was spending a lot of time with Sarah at her house. Sarah and her late husband had purchased the house a couple of years before his death. The house was a little over fifteen years old, and it was getting to the point it needed some maintenance. Just last week, Karl replaced the hot water heater. Sarah said, "I would like to paint the inside of the house, and I would help you do it."

Karl said, "That sounds like we could have fun while we do it." He added, "The outside could stand to be painted too."

Karl put in his notice that he would be moving out of the apartment, and the following weekend, the two of them moved Karl's stuff into Sarah's house. Karl, living in a small apartment, didn't have a lot. The only things of value, besides his clothes and personal items, were his bed, TV, and that old beat-up chair that Karl loved. If you asked Sarah, his chair had no value. It had definitely seen better days. Karl's mattress was fairly new and was in better shape than the one in Sarah's bedroom. They moved that mattress, along with the bed frame from Karl's bed, to the guest bedroom and then put Karl's mattress in Sarah's bedroom bed frame. The guest bedroom had a very uncomfortable day bed in it. Sarah was happy to see it go.

Now for that old beat-up chair of Karl's. Sarah knew how much Karl loved sitting in that chair and wondered how she was going to tell him it really was not going to be an addition to the living room. For now, she decided to go with it and later see if she could talk Karl into getting a new one. That discussion would best be at a future time.

For a small house, it had a lot of closet space, and with a little rearranging, Karl had a place for all of his clothes. It felt nice to be living together. As the weeks went by, Karl and Sarah painted the outside and the inside of the house. Karl was a bit of a handyman and could do most anything that needed to be done around the house. The house did not have ceiling fans, so they bought one for the living room and one for the bedroom. Since there was a ceiling light already in both rooms, it was not hard for Karl to remove the lights and install the fans.

Sarah had kept in touch with Jill since they first met at Karl's apartment a while ago. They did some shopping together and had a few girls' days out. One time, they went and had a spa day, which they both really enjoyed and wanted to someday do again. Jill had not heard any more from that jerk. She had found a new boyfriend and had been dating him for just over a month now. Sarah said to Karl, "Now that the house is looking really nice, if it's okay with you, I would like to invite Jill and her new boyfriend, Jack, over for the evening."

Karl said, "I think that would be nice. We have been working a lot, and an evening of entertaining would be nice."

Sarah called Jill to invite them over on Friday night. Jill said, "That sounds great. Let me see if it's okay with Jack, and I will call you back."

It wasn't but a few minutes later that Jill called back, and the visit was all set.

*****

Friday night came, and Jill and Jack arrived at Sarah and Karl's house just a few minutes late. They came in, and introductions were made. Sarah said, "Come on in and sit down."

Jack said, "What a comfortable-looking chair."

Sarah thought to herself, *It must be a guy thing.*

The girls had wine, and the guys had beer. They sat around and made some small talk. Jill told how she and Jack had met and a few of the things they had done together. Karl said, "Do you guys want to play some cards?"

They all agreed, and they decided to play Hearts. Karl knew Sarah was very competitive. She showed no mercy and had no problem playing the queen of spades on him several times during the game. Of course, Sarah had the lowest score.

It was getting late, and Jack and Jill said their goodbyes and left. There was not much to clean up. Putting away the uneaten chips and dip, throwing away the empty beer bottles, and washing out the wine glasses was about all.

Karl said, "Remember, I have a company softball game tomorrow."

Sarah said, "I'm planning on going."

Sarah and he went off to bed.

Karl said, "Good night. I love you so much, even though you dropped the queen on me several times."

Sarah said, "Twice."

They both laughed, and Sarah said, "I love you bunches, and I'm not sorry for dropping the queen on you. Besides, you did pass it to me that one time."

They both laughed again and fell asleep in each other's arms.

CHAPTER 6

The Softball Game

The softball season was almost over—only a couple more games left. The league was made up of nine company teams. A company could have more than one team, but once a player joined a team, he could not switch. All players had to be full-time employees of the company they played for. That rule was to prevent any team from having a ringer or two. Large companies had a slight advantage due to having more employees to draw from. Karl's company was medium-sized but had some good players. His team was in second place. Karl was considered the best pitcher in the league. Today's game was against the number one team. They had not lost a game all season. Karl was determined to change that tonight. Company teams were a big thing in this city. Company executives would brag to one another about their team winning the season.

The last time they played this team, they lost by only one run. Karl liked playing under the lights. He felt it added a bit of magic to the game. Sarah was in the stands as she liked watching Karl play. He enjoyed playing the game and usually played on another city league team too, but this year, with moving in with Sarah and all of the work they were doing on the house, he decided it would be best to only play on his company's team. Karl heard that the city was going to have a coed softball league next year. Karl liked the idea of playing softball on the same team with Sarah. Sarah, in her own right, was very athletic and very fit. She played fast-pitch softball in high school and in college too. She played second base and sometimes in the out-field. She was a good batter. She also liked the idea of playing on the same coed softball team with Karl.

One of the best players on Karl's company team got hurt in the last game and could not play in tonight's game. The game got off to a bad start. Karl was on his usual game, but the other team was really good and had run up the score early on. It was the bottom of the last inning. The score was 7 to 4, two outs, and there was one man on base. It was Karl's turn to bat. The first pitch was a called strike. The second one was a ball. Another pitch, a swing, and a miss. Now the count was one ball and two strikes. It was like déjà vu; Karl's eyes lit up on the next pitch.

It was just like the one at the company picnic when he hit that home run. The bat came around, struck the ball, and the ball shot off the bat deep into right center field. It seemed to float deeper and deeper; it cleared the fence by a good six feet. Home run.

Both the runner and Karl rounded the bases. The score was now 7 to 6. The spirits of Karl's team just got a whole lot higher. There were still two outs, but the game was not over. Karl could hear Sarah yelling from the stands. The next batter hit a single and got on first base. The following batter got up to bat. He swung at the first pitch—strike one. The next pitch was a called strike. Two outs, two strikes, and no balls. The pitch was thrown, and the batter hit a bouncing shot between first and second base. The second baseman caught the ball and tossed it to the first baseman. The batter was out, and that ended the game. Both teams came out on the field in support of the game. They shook each other's hands, and one player said, "Great game," to Karl.

Karl went back to the dugout to get his equipment. Sarah met him at the gate, and they left the field for the parking lot. "Great homer you hit, Karl," someone shouted from the stands.

Karl said, "Thanks."

It was a tough loss. Both teams had played a good game; the other team just played a little better.

Sarah and Karl walked to his car. Another person said, "You played a great game, Karl. See you at work on Monday."

Karl said, "Thanks. See you Monday."

Sarah told Karl, "I really enjoyed watching you play. I really get turned on, and when you hit that home run, it reminded me of the homer you hit at the company picnic. Let's get you home, and you can take a nice hot shower."

They drove home, and Karl reminisced about the game.

*****

When they got to the house, Karl parked the car, and Sarah said, "I'll race you to the house."

She had a bit of a head start on him, but he caught her just as they got to the front door.

Karl said, "Let's call it a tie."

Being the competitor that she was, she said, "No, I beat you fair and square."

They opened the door and stepped in. Karl grabbed Sarah and turned her around. They kissed and had one of their long hugs. Sarah stepped back and said, "You are sweaty—go get that shower, and I will fix us a snack."

Karl said, "That is an excellent idea."

CHAPTER 7

Bill's Retirement Announcement

Karl and Sarah had a routine for getting ready for work in the morning. Karl would shave while Sarah showered, and Sarah would put on her makeup while Karl showered. After getting dressed, they went into the kitchen for breakfast. Karl didn't normally eat much of a breakfast before he moved in with Sarah. Breakfast was simple on workdays. On the weekends, they would have a fancy breakfast or sometimes go out.

Today, they were going to have cold cereal. Yesterday, Sarah had made them oatmeal. Not a big deal—just add some water and put it in the microwave. They bought a coffee machine, the one that makes one cup at a time. It was more convenient and quicker than making a pot of coffee. Plus, they could choose the flavor they wanted. They finished eating, and after a quick cleanup of the kitchen, it was off to work.

They drove together most of the time. Upon arriving at work, Sarah went to her desk, and Karl went to his. Lots of people knew they were living together now. Sarah and Karl made up their own code of ethics. They would never visit one another at the other's desk during business hours. They would not hold hands or kiss while at work, nor would they have little get-togethers. It was okay to text one another, but only once in a while and to keep it short.

When Sarah got to her desk, Bill, Sarah's boss, called her into his office and said, "Close the door. I have something I want to tell you. I'm going to be retiring soon, and I wanted you to hear it from me and not through some rumor mill. The higher-ups want to make some kind of big formal announcement, so I'd like for you not to say anything until you hear the official announcement."

Sarah said, "I won't say anything. I will miss you. You have been a wonderful boss."

Bill pulled out a check and handed it to Sarah. Bill could see the blood flow from her face. Bill said, "No, this is not a severance check. It's a bonus check. I'm going to see to it that you are well taken care of before I leave this place. You have quite a reputation here in this company, and there are several executives fighting over who will hire you after my retirement."

Sarah asked, "When are you retiring?"

Bill said, "At the end of next month."

That would be in just about five weeks from now.

Sarah told Bill, "You have taught me so much. I have enjoyed working for you."

Bill said, "You've been a wonderful administrative assistant. Now get back to work."

Sarah stood up and floated to the door with her bonus check in hand. Bill said, "Remember, not a word until you hear the official announcement."

Sarah said, "I promise."

Sarah went to her desk and started sorting through all the projects that Bill was responsible for. She knew that Bill would want to finish as many of them as possible before he retired. She was trying to prioritize them so that Bill could start working on them as soon as possible and get as many of them completed as he could before he retired.

Sarah and Karl had lunch plans to eat out today. Sarah said, "My boss, Bill, is retiring," and she showed Karl the check. Karl said, "Is this a severance check? Are you out of a job?"

Sarah said, "No, it's a bonus check. Bill said that he was going to see that I was taken care of. He said that I have quite a reputation and that a bunch of the executives are fighting over who is going to hire me after he retires."

Karl said, "This is quite a bonus check. You must have been really doing a good job."

Sarah said, "You know I work hard and do a good job."

They finished their lunch and drove back to the company. As they were getting out of the car, Sarah said, "Remember, not a word about Bill's retirement until you get the official notice."

Karl said, "I promise."

As the two of them were walking to the building, one of Karl's teammates yelled, "Hey, when are you two going to get married?"

Karl just waved and said, "See you at practice tomorrow night."

They went into the building, Sarah to her desk, and Karl to his.

CHAPTER 8

Jill's Wedding Announcement

Sarah's cell phone rang. She looked at the caller ID and saw it was Jill. Sarah answered the phone and said, "Hi Jill, you never call me at work. It must be important. How are you doing, and what's up?"

Jill said, "Jack asked me to marry him, and I want you to be my maid of honor."

Sarah was taken aback by the news. She said, "I would be most happy to be your maid of honor!"

Jill said, "I was counting on you to say yes. I will need you to help me plan my wedding."

Sarah said, "You can count me in, but what about your mother? When are you going to have the ceremony?"

Jill said, "The date has not been set yet. We have to find a place and see when it would be available. That was one of the things I want you to help me with."

Jill went on to say, "It will be a small wedding—only a dozen or so attending. I have another piece of news to tell you. I just came from the doctor's office. I'm pregnant. That's why I don't want my mother to help. I don't want her to know I'm pregnant. I would never hear the end of it."

Sarah said, "Wow! That's a lot to process. I'm so happy for you."

They talked for a few minutes longer, and Sarah said, "Sorry to end this so quickly, but I'm really busy and have to get back to work. I will talk with you more later this evening. I will call you. Bye."

It was getting on to lunchtime, and she and Karl had planned to eat together in the company cafeteria. The cafeteria food was not bad, and eating there was very convenient, especially on days when they were busy. Sarah sent a text message to Karl: "We need to go out to eat again today. I have more news to tell you."

The two met at the elevator and went down to the ground floor and out to the car. They drove over to the restaurant, got their food, and went to a booth in the back.

Karl said, "So what's the more news? Is it about Bill?"

Sarah said, "No, it's about Jill. She called and said that Jack asked her to marry her, and she asked me to be the maid of honor. Jack's brother, John, is going to be the best man. Jill wants me to help her find a dress and help with the arrangements for the wedding. I told her I would help her as best I could. I'm so happy for her that she and Jack are getting married. There's more."

Karl said, "There's more?"

Sarah said, "Glad you are sitting down—Jill is pregnant."

Karl said, "She always wanted to have kids, and I guess she's getting the opportunity. She is a good person. I'm happy for her."

Sarah added, "I think Jack would make a wonderful dad."

*****

After lunch and back to work, Karl wasn't at his desk long before his cell phone rang. It was a call from George. George and Karl had gone to the same college and were together in most of the accounting classes. They both took the CPA exams at the same time. George had gone to work for an accounting firm just about the same time that Karl got his job here at the company. George said, "How are you doing, old man?"

Karl said, "Doing just fine. Everything's going well."

George said, "Our firm is growing and could use another senior accountant, especially one with your talents. I can guarantee you'll make a lot more money than what you're making now. How about setting up a date where we can meet and talk about it? I want you to meet Janet. She is one of the senior partners in the firm and my boss."

Karl said, "Give me a little time to think about it, and I will get back to you."

George said, "Don't take too long. They want to fill the job opening soon."

They said their goodbyes, and Karl went back to work but couldn't stop thinking about maybe it was a good time to change jobs. What Karl was doing every day was much of the same.

It was now getting on to quitting time. Karl texted Sarah, asking, "Are you ready to go home?"

Sarah sent a message back, saying, "Cleaning up my desk. Meet you at the elevators in just a couple minutes."

They went out to the car and started the drive home. On the way, Karl told Sarah about the phone call he had with George. Sarah asked Karl, "What are you going to do?"

Karl said, "I have thought about it all afternoon, and I'm going to meet with them."

Sarah said, "Boy, there sure is a lot going on."

CHAPTER 9

The Call from Sarah's Mom

The next day at work, Sarah's cell phone rang. She answered it.

"Sarah, this is Mom."

"Hi, Mom," said Sarah.

Her mom said, "I want you to come home this weekend. It's a three-day weekend, and I really need to talk with you."

Sarah said, "What's up?"

"Oh, honey, I don't want to talk to you about it over the phone. I will tell you when you get here."

Sarah knew that her father had dementia and was thinking that her mother wanted to talk to her about that. Sarah texted Karl, "My mother invited us to come home over this three-day weekend. It's about time you meet my parents."

Karl texted back, "Okay."

*****

Saturday rolled around, and by nine o'clock, they were all packed, the car was loaded up, and they were ready to go. It would be a six-hour drive but an easy one—mostly freeway. Sarah could not stop thinking about what her mom wanted to talk about and didn't like it when she didn't feel prepared. Sarah had not said anything about this to Karl. Sarah said to Karl, "I hope you like my parents, but more importantly, I hope they like you."

Karl said, "I'm a likable guy."

Sarah said, "My dad didn't like my husband. He didn't feel he was good enough for me. It really got bad when he got a job some six hours away from my folks' house and we moved away. My father didn't speak to me for some time after that." Sarah added, "My father wanted a boy and treated me as if I was one. That's probably why I'm such a tomboy today. We did everything together—built and fixed things, went hunting and fishing. My mother couldn't have any more kids, and that probably made me more special to her. My dad has dementia. He still has good long-term memory, but his short-term memory is getting really bad. Not too long ago, he drove to the grocery store, and on the way home, he got lost."

Karl said, "I'm sorry to hear that. How did he finally get home?"

Sarah said, "They have a handyman/gardener guy. Mom sent him out looking for him. Dad almost made it home. He was only a couple of blocks away, very much in a panic attack mode. That was the last time he was allowed to drive."

It was getting on to lunchtime; they were about halfway there. Karl started looking for a place to eat. They liked eating at local places. They could eat at the chain restaurants anytime. They pulled into the parking lot of a place that looked locally owned. There were a lot of cars in the parking lot, so they thought it must be a good place to eat. Besides, there was a gas station next door, and Karl wanted to fill the car up with gas before going on. They went inside and sat down at a table. The server came by, gave them a menu, and asked what they would like to drink. They both said, "Iced tea."

Looking over the menu, Karl decided on getting a cheeseburger, and Sarah ordered a bowl of soup. Sarah said, "A place like this, the soup has got to be homemade."

The server took their order, and it wasn't long before the food was delivered. Sarah said, "This soup is delicious, just as I thought—homemade."

Karl said, "The cheeseburger is very good. We need to remember this place on our way home and eat here again."

After finishing lunch, Karl paid while Sarah took the opportunity to go to the restroom. They got in the car, drove next door, and Karl filled up the car's gas tank. It was then back on the free-way. They listened to the radio and sang along to some of the tunes. Neither one of them could carry a note, let alone sing, but that didn't stop them. If they had a dog, it surely would have been howling.

They were getting close to Sarah's folks' house. Sarah said, "You will want to take the next exit."

Karl followed Sarah's turn-here-and-turn-there instructions, and before long, they were entering her folks' neighborhood.

It was the neighborhood and the house that Sarah grew up in. The houses had to be at least seventy-five years old or more. Sarah said, "All of the city's growth was on the other side of the freeway. I watched them build the freeway as a young girl. After the workers left for the day, my friend Ben and I would go play on the equipment. We would pretend we were driving the big equipment."

Sarah then said, "That's the house right there on the right."

Karl pulled up and stopped the car in front of the house Sarah pointed to.

Her folks came out of the house and were standing on the front porch. Sarah said to Karl, "Just leave our stuff in the car for now. We can get it later."

They walked up the sidewalk to the bottom of the steps lead-ing to the rather large front porch. As they were climbing the stairs, Sarah said, "Hi, Mom, hi, Dad," and gave them both a big hug. She turned around and said, "This is Karl."

Karl said, "Happy to finally meet you."

Sarah's mom said, "Come on in."

As they entered the house, Sarah said, "The old porch swing looks different."

Her mom said, "That old thing got so old I was afraid to sit on it anymore. Your dad and Pete, our handyman—you remember Pete—he and your dad built a new one."

Her mom asked, "Would you like something to drink? I made some fresh iced tea."

They both said, "Yes."

They all sat around, and Sarah caught her mom up on all of what was going on at the company and what she and Karl had been doing in and around the house. The conversation was light. Karl said, "I'm going to get our things out of the car."

When he returned, Sarah's mom said, "Sarah, you can sleep in your bedroom, and Karl, you can sleep in the guest room."

Karl thought to himself, *Is this a sign of things to come?* He was thinking maybe her mom didn't like him. *What have I done?* he thought. *I'm a likable guy.*

Sarah said to Karl, as he was putting the suitcase in Sarah's childhood bedroom, "That's just my mom. I know she will warm up to you soon. Maybe I will sneak in for a visit later tonight."

*****

It was getting on to dinnertime, and Sarah said, "Mom, can I help you make dinner?"

Her mom said, "That would be nice, just like old times."

While the ladies were cooking, Karl and Sarah's dad sat in the living room watching a baseball game on TV. Her dad asked Karl, "Do you like baseball?"

Karl said, "Yes, I played baseball in high school and college. I was never good enough to go pro, and that was just fine because my love was accounting."

Sarah's dad said, "So you are a bean counter."

Karl chuckled and said, "Yes, I am, and I can account for every one of those beans."

That answer made her dad laugh out loud. He then said, "Go get us a beer, and let's watch the rest of the game."

Karl felt he and Sarah's dad were hitting it off nicely.

The house was smelling great. The girls seemed to be having a good time cooking dinner together. It was time to eat, and the call to come and get it was given. They all gathered around the table, her mom pointing to where each should sit. Fried chicken, mashed potatoes with cream gravy, and fresh green beans picked from the garden. After dinner, Sarah, seeing that her mother looked tired, said, "Mom, you sit. Karl and I will clean up the kitchen."

When the kitchen was all cleaned, they went to the living room. Sarah said, "Tomorrow night, we are going to take you guys out for dinner."

Sarah's mom said, "You don't have to do that."

Sarah said, "I know that, but we want to."

They all gathered around the TV set and watched a movie. When the movie was over, Karl went to the guest bedroom, and Sarah went to her childhood bedroom. Her bedroom was left just the way it was when she lived there. Her dolls were on full display. Some of her old clothes still hung in the closet. She was tired and still wondering what it was that her mother wanted to tell her. She was thinking of Karl lying in bed in the room next door. She really wanted to sneak in there and climb in with him, but knew she better not. It had been a long day, and soon she was asleep, as was Karl.

*****

The next morning, her mom was already up and had the coffee made. Sarah poured herself a cup and said, "Mom, what is it you want to talk about?"

Her mom said, "Let's go out and sit on that porch swing, and I will tell you."

They went outside and sat down.

Karl came out to the kitchen, found a coffee mug, and poured himself a cup. Sarah's dad came out of the bathroom and said to Karl, "Come with me. I want to show you my workshop."

Karl followed Sarah's dad out back to where his workshop was located. It was full of old tools and various woodworking machines and equipment. Sarah's dad was telling Karl about the memories he had working there with Sarah by his side. He spoke clearly, and Karl thought, *Does he really have dementia?* Karl remembered her dad was drawing on long-term memories, which he still had. They must have been out there for over an hour. Her dad went on and on, telling stories he and Sarah had. Some of the stories he repeated more than once.

Karl knew then he really did have dementia. Karl really enjoyed this time with her dad. It was interesting to Karl how Sarah's dad could tell him about the tools but could not remember that he had told Karl the same thing a few minutes ago. Karl enjoyed hearing stories about the things her dad and Sarah had built and the times they had together.

While the guys were in the workshop, Sarah and her mom were having their talk. Sarah started off by saying, "Is this about Dad? His dementia doesn't seem to be that bad."

Her mom said, "You are seeing him on one of his better days."

She went on, saying some of the things her dad had done. She said, as a tear rolled down her cheek, "I just can't take care of him anymore."

Sarah said, "We can get someone to come in and help you take care of him."

Her mom said, "Sarah, you don't understand. I have cancer, and the doctors say I have about six months left to live."

There was a big silence, and Sarah started to cry. Her mom said, "Don't cry, honey."

Sarah said, "Can't there be something that can be done?"

Her mom said, "I'm not going to have them cut on me, then radiation and chemo, taking what quality of life I have left just so I might live another four or five months longer. No, thank you."

Sarah asked, "What can I do to help?"

Sarah's mom said, "Your dad can't take care of himself, let alone me. Find us a place where we both can be cared for until I die and for the rest of your dad's life."

Sarah said, "I will start working on it as soon as I get back home. But for now, let's enjoy the rest of our visit."

Karl came out onto the porch, saw the two of them sitting on the swing, and said, "So here you guys are."

Sarah stood up and said to Karl, "Let's go for a walk."

Right away, Karl saw that Sarah's eyes were all red and she had been crying. Karl waited until they got away from the house before asking, "What's wrong?"

Sarah told Karl about her mom and what her mom wanted her to do. Karl said, "I'm so sorry to hear it. What do you want to do?"

Sarah said, "I'm trying to process it. For now, let's go for a walk and let me think."

It was nice out and a good day for a walk. They rounded the corner, and Sarah stopped dead in her tracks. She turned to Karl and said, "I have an idea. Someone who could really help."

Sarah started walking up the sidewalk to a house. Karl followed along. Sarah rang the doorbell, and a guy answered the door. Sarah said right away, "I'm so sorry for barging in on you, Ben."

Ben said, "Sarah, don't be silly. You are always welcome here. It's been a while. Come on in. So good to see you. You look wonderful."

This was the house of Ben's parents. They had moved to Florida, and Ben bought the house. Ben and Sarah had grown up together. You hardly saw one without the other. Everyone was sure they would get married someday. After high school, Ben had gone off to college to become a lawyer, and Sarah got married and moved away. Ben had gotten married, but the marriage didn't last long. It turned out Ben was gay. Ben was now working for the largest law firm in town. They all went into the house, and introductions were made. Ben said, "I just made a fresh pot of coffee. Can I get you a cup?"

They both said they would like one.

Sarah said to Ben, "This is not actually a social call."

Sarah told Ben about her mom having cancer and not going to be living long. Sarah wanted Ben's help on any and all legal matters that would be needed.

Ben said, "You will need to have power of attorney. That's not hard to do. Mostly drawing up the paperwork and filing it. What are your plans for the house?"

Sarah said, "I'm not sure, but they will most likely want to sell it and use the money to help pay for their care for the rest of their lives."

Ben said, "We have tax attorneys and real estate attorneys in the firm. I will see what is the best way to handle the house. Can you think of anything else right now?"

Sarah said, "I don't know. I can't tell you how much this means to me. Thank you."

Karl said, "I think I will step outside and let you two have a visit."

Sarah and Ben talked about old times they had together and caught up on what they had been doing the last few years. Soon they came out of the house, and Ben said to Karl, "It was nice meeting you. Take good care of this girl. She's a keeper."

Karl and Sarah both thanked Ben for the help he was going to give and continued on their walk.

Sarah knew she had a lot of work to do and felt a great burden lifted from her shoulders after talking to Ben. They passed the day away until it was time to get ready for dinner. They were going to eat early and planned to have dinner at one of the nicest restaurants in town. Dinner was excellent. Everyone was stuffed.

Sarah's mom said, "I haven't eaten like that in a long time."

Sarah's dad said, "Thanks, that was some meal."

They drove back to Sarah's folks' house. Sarah said, "I'm going to change into something more comfortable."

When she came back out, her mom had set up the Scrabble board. Sarah remembered that she and her mom had played that game for hours on end, probably why Sarah was such a good speller. On the other side of the room, her dad sat. He had set up a checkerboard and made a challenging motion for Karl to come play. Karl thought, *Why not?*He had not played checkers in a very long time. They played, and Karl had to remind her dad, "It's your move" on several occasions.

It was getting late, and they had that drive back tomorrow. Sarah said, "I sure am tired. If it's okay with everybody, I'm going to bed."

To Sarah's surprise, her mom said, "Why don't you sleep in the guest room with Karl?"

That put a smile on Sarah's face, and she and Karl went off to the guest bedroom for the night. Karl knew everything was going to be all right between her folks and him.

*****

The next morning, her mom was already up and had the coffee made. Sarah poured herself a cup and sat down at the table. Sarah said to her mom, "Everything will be taken care of. Don't you worry. You need to save your energy to care for yourself."

Karl came out to the kitchen and got himself a cup of coffee. He said, "We are all packed."

About that time, Sarah's dad said to Karl, "I want to show you my workshop."

Karl didn't say anything about seeing the shop yesterday and spending a couple of hours listening to his stories. They all knew he was having a bad memory day and were thankful for the good day they had with him yesterday. Karl said, "Thanks, I will have to see it the next time I'm here. We need to get on the road. We both have to go to work tomorrow, and it's a long drive home."

They all said their goodbyes, and they started their trip home.

It was getting close to lunchtime, and they were about halfway home. Karl said, "There is the place we ate at on the way up. I'm hungry, how about you?"

Sarah said, "Let's stop."

They said, "Maybe we should call this place the Midway Café."

They had their lunch, Karl filled the car's gas tank, and they were on their way.

CHAPTER 10

Bill's Retirement Party

Sarah was at her desk, and in her in-basket was Bill's official retirement announcement. It was now full speed ahead on both the projects and the retirement party. Sarah and Bill had been working on Bill's outstanding projects. They knew they would not be able to finish all of them in the time left before his retirement date. Sarah could now officially start working on Bill's retirement party. She had done a lot of planning, and now it was time to implement her plan. As she had promised Bill, she had not said anything to anyone.

Her phone rang, and Sarah answered, "Bill's office, Sarah speaking."

No one ever called Bill by his last name. On the phone was Ms. White. She said, "I would like for you to come to my office and speak with me."

Sarah replied, "Yes, Ms. White, right away."

Sarah poked her head into Bill's office and said, "Ms. White just called and wants to see me immediately."

Bill said, "I'm sorry, I was supposed to tell you she was going to call this morning. With everything going on, I got sidetracked and forgot. She wants to talk to you about coming to work for her after my retirement. Hurry on up, go see her. Don't keep the lady waiting."

Sarah went to the elevators and pressed the button to the executive floor. She found her way to Ms. White's office. Sitting in the outer office was a nicely dressed young lady.

She said, "Hi, my name is Tammy. You must be Sarah."

Sarah said, "Yes, I am."

Tammy said, "Ms. White is expecting you, go right in."

Sarah stepped into Ms. White's office. It was the biggest office she had ever been in. Off to one side of the office was a sitting area with a couch, a coffee table, two large overstuffed chairs, and a side table with a huge lamp on it. On the other side was a small conference table with six chairs. In the middle was a large hand-carved desk with two high-back chairs in front of it. On the floor was a thick carpet, and floor-to-ceiling drapes hung to the sides of a big picture window. Behind the desk sat Ms. White.

Ms. White said, "Come on in and sit here," as she pointed to one of the high-backed chairs. Ms. White's father was the founder and president of the company. He still came to work most every day, and Ms. White would someday run the company. Everyone thought she was running the company now as her father was getting up there in years.

Ms. White was known for being direct, to the point, a bottom-line leader. She said, "After Bill's retirement, you are to report to me. Your title will be Executive Administrative Assistant. We will have business cards printed up for you. They should be here by the time you start work. You come highly recommended by Bill. Your salary will be increased to your new position grade level. At six months and every year thereafter, you will be reviewed, and you can expect a salary increase—if you have done a good job. The outer office will be yours. You work for me and me only. Don't take any SHIT from anybody. What you do and how you do it will be a direct reflection upon me. Tammy is from a temporary employee service and will be here until you start. Do you have any questions?"

Sarah had heard Ms. White was direct and to the point and felt the full force of Ms. White from what she had just said.

Sarah said, "I do. There will not be time enough to complete all of Bill's current projects before he retires. I don't want any of them to fall through the cracks. After he retires, I would like to see that the outstanding projects get reassigned and any information I have gets communicated to the ones who will be taking over those projects."

Ms. White said, "That is very responsible of you."

Sarah continued and told Ms. White about her mother. She said, "I would need to take some vacation right around the time I would be starting."

Ms. White said, "Family is very important. I'm sorry to hear about your mother. Cancer is a terrible thing. We will just have to work around it. When you know the dates, you will need to call the temporary employee service and see if you can get Tammy to work while you are gone. Is there anything else I need to know?"

Sarah said, "No, I don't believe so. Thank you for this opportunity. I will work hard for you. I better get back to work. I've taken enough of your time."

As Sarah walked to the elevator, she looked around at the people working on this floor. She thought to herself, *I better spend some of the bonus money on upgrading my wardrobe.* The elevator door opened, Sarah stepped in, and pressed the button to take her down to her floor where the cafeteria was located. She thought, while she was away from her desk, it would be the best time to try to make some arrangements for Bill's retirement party.

Sarah knew Lisa, the head of the cafeteria.

Sarah said, "Hi, Lisa. Do you have a minute?"

Lisa said, "Sure."

Sarah said, "I guess by now you have heard that Bill is retiring soon."

Lisa said, "I read that this morning."

Sarah said, "Well, that's why I'm here."

Lisa said, "I've known Bill for a very long time and will do whatever I can. What did you have in mind?"

Sarah went on, "I would like to have the party here in the cafeteria. I'm thinking of doing a 'Let's Roast Bill.'"

Lisa said, "Like the idea already."

Sarah continued, "Some finger sandwiches, maybe some other type of hors d'oeuvres."

Lisa said, "If it's okay with you, why don't you let me take care of everything?"

Sarah said, "That would be so helpful. I have so much on my plate, trying to get as much done as possible before Bill retires."

*****

Sarah returned to her desk. Bill asked, "How did it go?"

Sarah said, "Beyond my wildest dreams."

Bill said, "Are we still on for our two o'clock meeting?"

Sarah said, "Sure thing, boss."

Sarah and Karl had already had plans to go out to eat lunch today. Sarah was bursting at her seams to tell Karl what had just happened. They met at the elevator and walked to the car.

Sarah said, "I have news to share with you."

Karl said, "I have news to share with you."

Sarah said, "Okay, you first."

Karl said, "A private courier delivered to my office the offer letter to go to work at the same place George works. The offer is half again more than what I'm currently making, and I would be eligible for bonuses after six months. I went ahead and signed the letter and faxed it over to George. Then I went to my boss and gave him my notice and letter of resignation."

Sarah said, "That's quick, and a big pay raise too."

Karl said, "It's your turn. What's your news?"

Sarah said, "No sooner than I got to my desk this morning, I received a call from Ms. White."

Karl said, "The Ms. White?"

Sarah said, "Yes, THE Ms. White, in person. She is just as direct as everyone says she is. I went up to her office and will start my job as soon as Bill retires. Come to think of it, we both will be starting our new jobs about the same time. I am going to have the outer office to hers, and my new title will be Executive Administrative Assistant. I'm going to have to use some of that bonus money to buy some new business suits. Got to look the part."

Karl said, "I, too, will need to buy new suits, as I will be meeting directly with clients."

They finished lunch and returned to work. Sarah had that two o'clock meeting with Bill and needed to finish up a few things in preparation for the meeting. She had just finished what she had to do right before the two o'clock meeting. Sarah stepped into Bill's office and said, "Are you ready?"

Bill said, "As ready as I can be. What do you have for me?"

Sarah laid out her plan to maximize the number of projects she thought could be completed before his retirement and the priority order to do them in. Bill and Sarah spent the rest of the afternoon going over the projects and the plan that Sarah had come up with. Together, they made some changes. At the end of the meeting, Bill said, "It looks like I will be working right up to the last minute."

They both smiled. Sarah said, "In the meeting I had with Ms. White this morning, I mentioned that we would not be able to finish all of the projects you had. I told her I felt responsible that none of them would fall through the cracks. Ms. White said she would support me in handing the projects off to whoever is going to work on them."

Sarah asked Bill, "Do you know if they are going to replace you?"

Bill said, "I've heard several different things. None of them I can talk about. You going to work for Ms. White is the best thing that could happen to you."

Sarah was contacting people to be roasters for Bill's retirement roast party. Just after a couple of calls and the word got out, people started calling her wanting to be part of the roast. Sarah made a list of the names and email addresses of the ones she had contacted and the ones that contacted her. She sent out an email to all of them and said there was an overwhelming response to the ones that wanted to roast Bill. She said, "A limit of four roasters is all that time would permit. If you are still interested in being a roaster, send a brief explanation of why you should be the one selected, and the four will be picked from your responses."

Sarah reviewed the responses, picked the four best, and let them know to be prepared for the party.

Sarah called Tammy to book an appointment to see Ms. White.

Tammy said, "Ms. White is available at ten o'clock for 15fifteeninutes."

Sarah said, "Please add me to her calendar."

At ten, Sarah was in the outer office saying "Hi" to Tammy.

Tammy said, "Good to see you. Is everything okay?"

Sarah said, "I will let you know after I speak with Ms. White."

Tammy said on the intercom, "Sarah is here to see you, Ms. White."

Ms. White said, "Send her in."

Sarah opened the door and walked in and up to Ms. White's desk.

She said, "Thank you for seeing me."

Ms. White said, "Sit down. What is it that you want to talk about?"

Sarah said, "Remember I had told you about me moving my parents to a care facility and needing to take a week's vacation?"

Ms. White said, "Yes, go on."

Sarah continued, "I am supposed to start on Monday. I figured it would be less disruptive if I started the following Monday. I would take my vacation the week before coming to work for you. This way, I would have my parents moved and not need to leave shortly after starting to work for you."

Ms. White said, "Sounds like you have thought this out, and it makes perfect sense to me. See if Tammy can extend another week on your way out. I know it will be stressful. Please take care of yourself."

Sarah said, "Thank you, and I look forward to being here the following Monday."

Tammy asked, "How did it go?"

Sarah said, "It could not have gone any better. Would you be available to stay one additional week? I have personal business that I have to take care of and need to start a week later."

Tammy said, "Give me a minute, and I will call the office and see." Tammy made the call, and after hanging up, said, "No problem, done deal."

Sarah said, "Thank you" and left to return to her office.

When Sarah got back to her office, she wrote a quick text to Karl: "Things are all worked out, and I will be taking vacation next week so we can take care of my folks. The week that you are unemployed. HAHAHAHA."

*****

Time passed quickly, and today was the day of the retirement party. The party was to start at three o'clock. Sarah went down to the cafeteria around two-thirty to get ready for Bill's Roast Party. When Sarah walked into the cafeteria, she was blown away. The place was so well decorated she hardly recognized it as being the cafeteria. Lisa and her team did an outstanding job. The tables were all set up. There was a head table, and it had a sound system on it so the people could hear the roasters clearly. Sarah went looking for Lisa and found her in the kitchen.

Sarah said, "Lisa, when you said leave everything to you, I gave up a lot of control, and that is hard for me to do. You and your team have done such an outstanding job. Thank you, and I know Bill will really appreciate it too."

Sarah went back out to the dining area. People were already gathering. Some of Lisa's team were bringing out the food and setting it up. Sarah met with the roasters and asked, "Are you people ready?"

They all said, "Yes, can't wait!"

Bill came walking in with his wife. Sarah was hoping she would come. Sarah went over to greet them. They exchanged hellos, and Sarah escorted Bill to his seat.

The roasters were already seated. Sarah stepped to the microphone and said, "My name is Sarah, and I'm, at least for the next few hours, Bill's administrative assistant. Thank you all for coming to Bill's retirement party and the roast. Bill has been the best boss anyone could have, but we are not here today to praise him. We are here to roast him."

That brought a roar of laughter from the crowd, many of them eating some of the snacks that Lisa's team had prepared.

Sarah introduced the first roaster, then the second, third, and fourth one. They all told stories or memories they had about Bill. By the time they were done, Bill was laughing so hard tears were rolling down his cheeks. Sarah took the place at the podium and said, "It's time to bring the man of the hour up here to give his side of the stories. Ladies and gentlemen, I give you William Everett Livingston."

And with that, Bill stepped to the podium.

Bill said, "I would like to thank everyone for coming. I heard there was a long line of people that wanted to roast me. I'm thankful that Sarah only allowed four. I want to say thank you to my wife of thirty-seven years, who gave me three wonderful kids—none of whom are in jail. Just kidding, they are a great bunch of kids. She has stood beside me when I had to work late night after night and many weekends too. I want to thank this wonderful company for the opportunities they have given me. I want to thank Sarah, who saved my butt on many occasions. The greatest administrative assistant one could have. Lastly, I want to give a big thanks to my friend, Lisa, and her team who helped to put this party together."

With that, Lisa came out pushing a cart with a huge cake with "Happy Retirement Bill, We Will Miss You" written on it.

As Bill stepped away from the podium, people started coming up to him, shaking his hand, congratulating him, and wishing him a happy retirement. Bill walked over to where Sarah was standing next to Karl. Bill gave Sarah a big hug and a kiss on her forehead.

Bill said, "I hope you are not going to file a sexual harassment complaint against me for hugging and kissing you without asking."

Sarah said, "Oh no, I wouldn't do that. I would hope we could settle out of court."

With that, she gave Bill a big hug and kissed him on the cheek. They both got a kick out of that and had a laugh.

Bill turned to Karl and said, "When are you going to ask Sarah to marry you?"

Karl just smiled as he did every time he heard that question.

Bill, his wife, Sarah, and Karl all got a piece of cake. Sarah thought, *I hope the cake we get for Jill's wedding tastes this good.*

Bill said to Sarah and Karl, "We have dinner reservations and would like you two to join us."

Sarah said, "Thank you very much. How nice of you to invite us, but we need to get home and pack and get ready to drive to my folks' house in the morning."

The party was over, and the people were leaving. Lisa's team started to clean the place up and take down the decorations. Sarah went over and thanked Lisa one more time.

Sarah said, "The cake was delicious."

Lisa said, "There's some leftovers, let me get you some to take with you."

CHAPTER 11

Taking Care of Sarah's Folks

It was Saturday morning. Sarah and Karl were all loaded up and ready to go. On the way, they talked about the plans to get her folks moved over to what will be their new care facilities. Sarah had been working with the care facility people for the last few weeks. Everything was in place, and Monday was the scheduled move-in day. Sarah and her mom had been talking every day since her and Karl's visit. Her mom had been sorting through things, selecting items she wanted to take to her new home and packing them up.

To lighten things up a bit, Sarah and Karl talked about how fun Bill's Retirement Roast Party was. The things that were said about Bill and what a good sport he was. They commented again on how good that cake was.

Sarah said, "I packed the cake that Lisa gave us for us to eat later."

Karl said, "I wondered what happened to it. I was looking for it to have as a snack last night and couldn't find it."

Sarah said, "I figured you might eat it, so I hid it. Don't worry, you will get some later."

They were coming up to their halfway point and their Midway Café at the next exit. They stopped, had lunch, and Karl filled the car's gas tank. Soon they were back on the road. The afternoon ride seemed to go quickly. It was not that long ago since their last trip, things were familiar, and they were enjoying the drive. Traffic was

47

moving along at or above the speed limit. Coming up was the exit to take for Sarah's folks' house. Karl took the exit and remembered the turns to get to Sarah's folks' house. Karl got his and Sarah's things out of the car, and the two of them started up the walkway to the house.

They were met at the front door by Sarah's folks. Hellos, hugs, and kisses were exchanged.

Sarah's mom said to Karl, "Go ahead and put all of your things in the guest bedroom."

Without hesitation, Karl took their small suitcases and put them in the guest bedroom. They visited that afternoon, and when it was dinnertime, they ate the casserole that Sarah's mom had made for them earlier that day. Sarah and her mom played Scrabble while Karl and Sarah's dad watched a game on TV. While playing Scrabble, they talked about the plan to get them moved. It was getting on to bedtime, and everybody headed to bed. Karl and Sarah were lying in bed, and Karl asked Sarah, "Are you sleepy?"

Sarah said, "Not really."

With that answer, Karl and Sarah began to kiss. One thing led to another, and soon they were making love, but very quietly.

*****

Everything that Sarah's mom packed was placed in Sarah's old bedroom. The next morning, the plan was for Sarah and her mother to make sure everything she had packed to be moved to the care facilities was there. Karl was to spend the time occupying her dad.

Karl said to Sarah's dad, "You said the next time I came here, you were going to show me your workshop."

Sarah's dad said, "So I did. Come on."

It didn't matter to Karl if her dad had remembered or not; he got him out of the house, and that was what he was to do. Knowing that Karl was welcome to take any and all of the tools back home, it gave him the opportunity to see them again. Sarah's dad showed Karl the tools. He started with the woodworking lathe. He said, "I made all sorts of things on this machine, from bowls to table legs."

Some of the stories he told Karl were the same ones he had told the last time Karl was here.

Karl said to Sarah's dad, "I have to go to the bathroom. I will be right back."

Karl really didn't have to go; he just wanted to check to see how Sarah and her mom were doing.

Karl said, "How are things going?"

Sarah said, "They are going well. I'm sure we will be able to take their things over to the care facilities late this afternoon as planned."

Karl said, "I'm going to take your dad to a sports bar, have some lunch, and watch whatever games they have on their TVs."

Sarah said, "That's an excellent idea. I don't think he has ever been to one. Remember, we need to have enough time to get my folks' things over to the facilities and back in time to go out to dinner."

Karl said, "I will watch the time. You can always text me or call me if we are not back when you want us to be."

Sarah's mom gave Pete a call to help Sarah load the things that were to go to the care facility into the car. Pete came straight over. Sarah said to Pete, "You have been so good to my folks, mowing the lawn and generally helping with whatever. I can't thank you enough for your kindness."

Pete said, "Your folks have been very good to me over the years. It's my pleasure to have worked for them."

Sarah and Pete carried the few boxes, and it didn't take any time at all to get them loaded. She really didn't need his help, but it was nice to have it as it gave her the chance to thank Pete for all he has done over the years.

Karl returned to the workshop. Sarah's dad was rearranging some of the tools.

Karl said, "Are you hungry?"

Sarah's dad said, "I could eat."

Karl said, "Let's go."

They got into the folks' car and drove to the sports bar. Once inside, Karl asked, "Have you ever been in a place like this before?"

He said, "I have never seen so many TVs showing so many games at one time. I think I could really get used to a place like this."

49

They found an empty table in an area where they could see lots of TVs. A server dressed in a T-shirt and tight short shorts gave them a menu and asked, "What would you gentlemen like to drink?"

Karl and Sarah's dad both ordered a beer and started to look over the menu. A few minutes later, the beers arrived, and they ordered lunch. As they ate, they watched a game on one TV and then another game on a different TV, switching from one to another.

Sarah's dad said, "This is better than flipping channels on the remote."

Sarah's dad was like a little kid in a candy store. They watched bits and pieces of several games. They finished eating, and Karl said, "You think we should be getting back?"

Sarah's dad said, "And leave this place?"

Karl said, "Don't want the girls to worry about us now, do we?"

While the guys were gone, Sarah and her mom went to the bank, and Sarah was added to the banking accounts. This way, Sarah would be able to write checks and pay for what her folks needed and take care of their financial affairs.

The guys returned to the house. Sarah said to Karl, "Your timing is perfect. Everything going to the care facility has been put in our car. It's good that you took the folks' car. Pete helped me carry the boxes out and put them in the car."

Karl and Sarah left and were on the way to the facility. Sarah asked, "How was your outing and lunch with my dad?"

He said, "I wished you could have been there to watch your dad. He was as happy as one could be. He couldn't believe there were that many TVs showing that many different games at the same time."

They parked the car and went inside to the administration office. Sarah had called earlier to say they would be there soon. Sarah introduced herself. The person at the desk said, "Please be seated. Someone will be with you in a moment. We have been expecting you."

They sat down, and within a few minutes, a person came out and said, "Hello, I'm Linda. I am the one you have been talking with over the last several weeks. So happy to meet you, Sarah. I will be giving you a tour, and after the tour, you can then put your folks' things in their suite."

Sarah said, "I was hoping to meet you in person. You have been so helpful and easy to work with. Being Sunday, I didn't think you would be working today. This is Karl."

Linda said, "Pleased to meet you, Karl. This Sarah is quite the woman. I don't usually work on the weekends. My job is in the administration office, but after working with you over the phone, I just had to meet you face-to-face."

The three of them walked over to the building where Sarah's folks will be living.

Linda said, "This is our newest building. The place your parents will be living has never been lived in before. They will be the first ones."

The outside has lots of landscaping and is well kept. Lots of walkways and little places to sit. There is a small pond with a fountain spraying water about twelve feet into the air.

Linda said, "At night, the fountain is all lit up."

Linda opened the building's door, and they all stepped in. The entry opened to a hallway that went to the right and to the left.

Linda said, "We need to go to the right."

There were a couple of small meeting rooms down the hall. At the end of the hall was another door. This door has a security keypad. Linda pressed a few keys, and the door unlocked. The door opens to a huge common room. The residence rooms were along the perimeter of this room. The common room has a dining area and two sitting areas—one with a big screen TV, and the other with a fireplace. In the very center was the care center station, where the staff member could see everything. It was staffed twenty-four hours a day. The meals were prepared in the facility's kitchen and delivered to each of the residence buildings. The staff in each building area then served the meals and cleaned up afterward.

Linda said, "This is your folks' place."

Linda opened the door. Inside was a small living room with a sizable TV hanging on the wall. The bathroom had a walk-in tub and a shower, a sink, and a toilet. Grab handrails were all around the room. Next to the bathroom was the bedroom. In there were two hospital-style beds. When Sarah and Linda had talked, they thought that would be the safest way to go. The closet was big and had plenty of storage space.

Sarah said, "Linda, this is unbelievable. The online pictures—they are good, but seeing this makes me so happy. I know my folks will be happy here."

Linda said, "That makes me feel good to hear you say it. Also know the staff here has access to medical personnel 24–7. So, as your mother's cancer progresses, we can provide the care she needs. As we spoke on the phone, we have licensed hospice personnel that will take care of your mother when she needs it and until she passes. Your father will be cared for as long as he stays here."

Sarah said, "That is the major reason I picked this place. Linda, thank you so much. You have been so helpful. This gives me such peace of mind."

As they walked out, Linda gave them the access code to get back into the area. Linda, Karl, and Sarah said their goodbyes, and Linda went back to her office.

To Karl and Sarah's surprise, they were met at the car by a person dressed in the uniform of the care facility. He asked, "Are you Sarah? Linda sent me over here to help you move your folks' things inside to one of our new residence rooms."

Both Sarah and Karl thought this was unbelievable. Sarah said, "Yes, I'm Sarah, and we would love some help."

They loaded the cart with her folks' things and wheeled them to her folks' suite. Karl said, "Thanks. Can I give you something for helping us?"

The guy said, "No, thanks. It was my pleasure to help you."

Sarah and Karl unpacked the boxes and placed the clothes in the dresser and closet. Sarah put the keepsakes her mom wanted around the room. The people in the care facility said they would take care of the empty boxes.

Karl and Sarah returned to Sarah's parents' house. Sarah's mom said, "Are we still going out to dinner?"

Karl said, "Yes."

Sarah's mom said, "Let's get with it. We are about to miss the early bird special."

Karl and Sarah looked at one another and smiled, then Sarah said, "It's hard to argue with that."

They had a nice dinner and returned to the house. Sarah's mom took Sarah aside and again said, "I want you to take anything that is left in the house, and if Karl wants any or all of your dad's tools, they are his."

Sarah said, "Yes, Mom, you have said that to me several times already."

Then, jokingly, she added, "Mom, you are getting as bad as Dad, repeating yourself."

With that, they gave each other a big hug and had a bit of a chuckle.

They sat around the living room watching TV. It was still early, and Sarah's mom said, "I'm really tired. I'm going to bed and read a while. Come on, old man, you are coming to bed too."

It was too early for Karl and Sarah to go to bed, so they stayed up and watched a movie. Karl said, "What happened to that cake?"

Sarah said, "After that meal you ate, you are hungry?"

Karl said, "That was hours ago. What did you do, eat all of that cake and leave none for me?"

Sarah said, "No, I will get us some. Stop acting like a big baby."

They ate the cake, watched the rest of the movie, and then went to bed.

*****

As usual, Sarah's mom was up first and had the coffee made. The smell of coffee got Karl and Sarah's attention, and they both got up. Karl headed to the bathroom to take a shower. Sarah, still in her pajamas, went to the kitchen. She gave her mom a hug and said, "Today's the big day. How are you feeling?"

Her mom said, "I know this is the best for your father and me. It gives me peace knowing that both of us will be well cared for as long as we live. I also know I have a tough time ahead of me as my cancer continues to consume my body and my life. Sarah, I love you very much, and it must be hard on you too."

Sarah said, "Mom, you will always be here with me" as she placed her hand on her heart.

Sarah's mom said, "I hope your dad can adjust to not living in this house."

They hugged, and Sarah said, "I'm going to take a shower. When I'm done, I will help you cook breakfast. Now don't you go and start without me."

Sarah walked down to the bathroom. Karl had finished taking his shower and was dressed. Sarah took off her pajamas and stepped into the shower. Karl asked, "Do you need me to wash your back?"

Sarah said, "No, I can manage just fine."

Karl went to the kitchen. He said, "Good morning."

Sarah's mom said, "Good morning, Karl. Sarah told me I was not to start cooking breakfast until she finished her shower and would come back out to help. I'm just waiting on her."

Karl said, "That's Sarah for you. I tell you what, I know how to cook. I would be honored if you would allow me to help you."

Sarah's mom turned around with a big smile on her face and said, "Let's do it."

It wasn't long before sausage was cooking and pancake batter was being mixed. They were kidding around and having fun. Soon the house was filled with the smells of breakfast. Sarah stormed into the kitchen with just a towel wrapped around her. She said, "Mom, I told you not to start cooking without me."

It was then that Sarah saw Karl wearing one of her mom's aprons, flipping sausage. She laughed and said, "You two! I'm going to go get dressed."

Sarah walked down the hall and passed her dad. He said, "Sarah, go get dressed. You can't go around with just a towel wrapped around you. And what's going on out here?"

Sarah's mom said, "Go sit down. Breakfast will be ready soon. You want some coffee?"

He said, "Yes, if it's not too much trouble."

A cup was poured and delivered. Her dad said, "Karl, you look silly wearing that apron."

That was the first time he had said Karl's name. Sarah came out, this time fully dressed. She said, "Is there anything I can do?"

Sarah's mom said, "You can set the table."

Soon they were all seated at the table, eating the breakfast that Karl and Sarah's mom had made.

The kitchen was all cleaned up, and it was time for Sarah and Karl to take Sarah's folks to the care facility. Karl put the little suitcase that had the last of the personal items in the car.

Sarah's dad said, "Where are we going?"

Sarah's mom said, "The kids arranged a special outing for us. We are going to a resort. Just sit back and enjoy the ride."

They drove across town to the care facility. They all walked into the building, down the hall, and to the wing where the folks would be living. Sarah keyed the passcode into the keypad, and the door opened.

"Welcome! Come on in. I'm Mary."

Sarah's dad said, "This sure is a fancy resort."

Mary said, "Let me show you around."

They toured the common area. Mary said, "If there is anything you need, just come up to this desk and ask me or whoever is at this counter, and we will get it for you."

Mary walked them over to their room. Mary opened the door and said, "This is your room for as long as you stay with us."

Her folks walked in, and her dad said, "This is very nice. Look at the size of that TV. Karl, this TV is as big as the ones in the place you took me for lunch."

Mary said, "There is one in the bedroom too, but it's not as big as this one. I hope you enjoy your stay."

Her dad had no idea that he would most likely live here until he passed away. He said, "I could really get used to living in this resort."

Sarah fought back her tears. She said, "We are going now."

She gave her dad and mom each a big hug. Karl, Sarah, and Mary walked out into the common room. Sarah said to Mary, "Thanks."

Mary said, "We will take very good care of your parents."

Sarah and Karl walked down the hallway toward the exit. Sarah said, "That's the hardest thing I have ever done, and that includes burying my husband."

With that, Sarah broke down and started to cry. Karl didn't say anything. He just held Sarah tight to him. A few moments later, they continued to the car and drove back to the folks' house.

CHAPTER 12

Sarah's Folks' House Auction

Once back at the folks' house, Sarah took the lead and said, "My mom insisted that we take what we would like to keep and sell the rest. The first thing we need to do is identify the things we would like to have."

Sarah started in her old bedroom. There were lots of memories there, but she only took a few things she wanted to keep. Sarah said to Karl, "You know my mom wants you to take any and all of the tools from my dad's workshop, and I'm sure my dad would want you to have them too."

Sarah worked her way from room to room, pointing out the items she would like. Karl would carry them to the front room so they could later be packed. Karl said, "I think it's about time we should go get the moving truck."

The two of them drove to pick up the truck they reserved a few days ago. They purchased several packing boxes. After signing the paperwork and paying the deposit, Karl drove the truck and Sarah drove the car back to her folks' house.

They spent the rest of the day packing and loading the truck. The workshop tools, machines, and equipment took up most of the room in the truck. Karl was happy they got the size of the truck that they did. It was important that they got everything they wanted out of the house and loaded into the truck today. Tomorrow, the auction company was coming to group items for the sale on Saturday. The auctioneer said it would take a couple of days to sort through and batch up the items.

Karl and Sarah didn't feel like cooking, so they went out for dinner. After having a big breakfast that morning, they had worked straight through lunch, and both were hungry. They went to a place that Sarah had heard of but had never eaten at before. Karl said, "This place is not bad. Good food and good prices."

After eating, they returned to the house.

They sat in the living room to watch some TV. Karl sat on the couch, and Sarah lay down with her head on Karl's lap. Sarah said, "The house seems so empty to me."

She was emotionally drained. Karl stroked her red hair, and she soon fell asleep. Karl watched TV for about an hour more. He woke Sarah up and said, "Go get your jammies on, and let's go to bed."

Sarah changed into her jammies and got in bed. Karl finished getting ready for bed and got in next to Sarah. Sarah moved close to Karl and said, "Hold me."

This was a side of Sarah that he had never seen before. She had always been so strong, and here she was, very vulnerable. She started to cry. Karl held her a little tighter and said, "I love you so very much. I'm sure everything will turn out all right."

They kissed, and Karl held her some more.

*****

The next morning, Karl got up and made some coffee. He walked in where Sarah was still in bed and said, "How are you feeling?"

She said, "Better. I'm not hungry, but I would like a cup of coffee."

Karl said, "I will bring you a cup, but you are going to have to get up and get dressed. The auction people will be here in about an hour."

Sarah said, "Oh, that's right. It just felt so nice lying here. I will get up right now."

And she got up.

The auctioneer and his people showed up a few minutes late. Sarah had talked to the auctioneer several times over the last few weeks. He knew that everything in the house was to be auctioned off. He said, "As we spoke on the phone, we will bundle items into what we call lots. You added to our standard contract that we will take unsold items that we feel could be sold in our store and deduct the wholesale value from our fee of 12 percent. Any items we don't think we can sell in our store, we will donate in your parents' name to the charities of choice. All other items will be sent to the landfill.

"Sarah, you are the first person in all the years I have been in business that I have ever agreed to do this for. Lady, you drive a hard bargain. Everything I just said is in the contract. Feel free to read it and sign at the bottom."

Sarah read it and signed it. The auctioneer said, "You are welcome to stay, but do not help, and please stay out of the way."

Sarah said to Karl, "Sounds like we need to find something to do."

Then she said to the auctioneer, "You have my cell phone number. We are going to leave now. Call me if you need to."

The auctioneer said, "Will do."

They got in the car. Karl said, "Where to?"

Sarah said, "Let me call Ben and see if he is available. He said there are some papers I need to sign. He also said he wanted us to meet some of the people I will be doing business with."

Sarah gave Ben a call. Ben said, "I just finished with a client, and now would be a good time to come over to the office."

Sarah said, "Good, we are leaving the house and will be there shortly."

*****

At Ben's office, the receptionist called Ben and said, "Karl and Sarah are here to see you."

Ben said, "Thanks. I will be right out."

Ben greeted Sarah and Karl and said, "Come on back to my office."

The three of them walked to Ben's office. Ben said, "Sit down. Can I get you something to drink—coffee or water?"

They both said they were fine and didn't want anything. Ben asked, "How did the folks' move go? And did they like the place? How goes getting ready for the auction?"

Sarah said, "We moved my folks in yesterday. The people over at the care facility are extremely friendly and accommodating."

Ben said, "I've heard nothing but good things about that place. From the outside, it looks immaculate. I have not been inside. How does it look?"

Sarah said, "Just as immaculate." She added, "The auctioneer and his people are at the house right now, getting things together and ready for the auction."

Ben said, "That sounds like everything is falling into place." He went on to say, "Here are the papers you will need to sign to finalize your power of attorney and some other legal matters. I have little stickies where you need to sign."

Sarah quickly read over the documents and then signed at all the indicated places. Ben said, "That takes care of that. Now I want to introduce you two to the people you will most likely be dealing with, Sarah."

After Ben took them around and made the introductions, he said, "I'm sorry I can't spend any more time with you. I'm a little late for my next appointment. Let's plan on having dinner one night before you return back home."

Sarah said, "We would love to do that. Let's see how things go and when we can do it."

With that, they walked out to the car. Karl said, "What's next?"

Sarah said, "Let's just sit here for a minute and give it some thought."

Then she said, "Karl, you have been so supportive through this entire ordeal. I love you so much."

They kissed, and Karl said, "I love you too."

They both sat there in silence, both in deep thought. Karl said, "I think we should get a hotel room."

Sarah said, "Really, Karl? REALLY! I'm not in the mood."

Karl started to laugh and said, "No, silly girl. With all that's going on at your folks' house, it just makes sense that we get a hotel room."

Sarah said, "That does make sense now that you say it that way. Not bad thinking for an unemployed guy."

That cut the tension a bit. Then Karl said, "Too bad we didn't think to bring the camping equipment. We could have camped in your folks' backyard."

They laughed even harder.

They drove back to the freeway, where the hotels were located. There were many to pick from. Sarah said, "Do you have a preference?"

Karl said, "No, you just pick one you think we will like."

They drove up and then back down the freeway's access roads, looking at all the hotels along the way. They all looked okay; they just needed to pick one. Karl pulled into the driveway entrance of the next hotel they came to and went in to register. They took the things they had in the car to their room.

They ate a late fast-food lunch and returned to her folks' house to check on the progress the auctioneer and his people were making. In a few of the rooms of the house, there were little piles of items stacked with a number attached to them. The auctioneer saw Karl and Sarah and came over to where they were standing. He said, "There is a lot of stuff here. We are working on it one room at a time. Looking this stuff over, I think I will be able to auction most of it off and make you a lot of money. I have advertised the auction in lots of places, and I'm expecting a lot of bidders. On Friday afternoon, there will be a pre-auction viewing where people can walk around and see what will be auctioned off. Then, Saturday morning, I will begin the bidding. With the number of things here, it is going to take several hours. Do you have any questions for me?"

Sarah said, "Boy, you and your people have done a tremendous job. We have booked into a hotel and will not be staying in the house."

The auctioneer said, "Staying in a hotel is a good idea. I have arranged for a security guard to be here overnight. I will give you a call if anything comes up. That moving truck is fine right where it is, and I will make sure the security guard keeps an eye on it too."

Sarah said, "Thanks."

Sarah and Karl drove back to the hotel and went to their room. Karl said, "Time to relax. Come lie down next to me."

*****

The time seemed to go by quickly, and it was the day of the auction. They got up early and got ready for the day. There was a restaurant next door to the hotel, and they went for breakfast. They still had a couple of hours before the start of the auction but wanted to get there early. Arriving at the house, it was buzzing with people already. The people from the auction company were making last-minute preparations for the sale to start. The auctioneer was all dressed up in a fancy suit with his company logo all over it. He could tell Sarah and Karl were eyeing him. He came over and said, "Got to look and play the part. What do you think of my getup?"

Karl said, "It suits you fine."

They had a laugh at that. The auctioneer said, "Do you have any last-minute requests or questions? We will be getting started soon. Just want to give the late arrivals a few more minutes to get here."

Sarah said, "No questions here. Just looking to see some bidding wars."

The auction got started. Lots of people had shown up. The bidding was fierce. Lots of bids were being made. The auctioneer was very good at getting the bids up.

Sarah and Karl saw Ben and went over to where he was standing. They had gone out to dinner the other night with Ben and his friend, Andrew, who he had been dating for several months. Andrew was standing next to Ben and said, "Hi, you two. Some event you have going on here. Keep your hands in your pockets. I went to one of these things, waved at someone I knew, and ended up buying something."

That brought a chuckle.

Sarah and Karl said, "Hi. Nice to see you again, Andrew."

They stood around watching the auction and occasionally commenting on how much some things were selling for. There were several bundles that didn't sell. The auctioneer grouped them together and said, "Okay, you flea market professionals, make me a bid on this."

It sold for a very low amount, but it did sell.

Someone in the crowd shouted, "How about the house? There are several of us that want to bid on the house."

The auctioneer said, "Hold on a minute, and I will let you know."

He walked over to Sarah and said, "If you want to auction off the house, I'm prepared and can do it. Here's the deal."

Ben said, "I'm Sarah's attorney, and if there is any on-the-spot deal, I will need to record it. Do you have a problem with that?"

The auctioneer said, "Not at all."

Ben said to Sarah, "This is coming at you quickly, but it can be a done deal today."

Sarah agreed to auction off the house. The auctioneer stated the terms, and Ben recorded them on his iPhone. Holding the phone up to Sarah, he said, "Sarah, do you agree to the terms that the auctioneer has set forth?"

Sarah said, "Yes."

Ben turned off the recording function on his phone and said, "Done deal."

The auctioneer went back to the microphone and said, "The bidding on the house will start in one hour. That should give you bidders time to walk through and around the house to look it over."

Several of the people in the crowd started calling friends, saying that the house was going to be auctioned off and that they had an hour to get there if they were interested.

The hour had passed, and many in the crowd had left. The ones who remained were the bidders and those who wanted to watch. Sarah's heart raced as the excitement built. The auctioneer stepped to the microphone and said, "The bidding will start in just a few minutes, but first you need to know: The sale of the house is as-is. The winning bidder must pay any and all costs associated with buying the property. If the bidding does not meet the minimum price set by the seller, the house is a no-sale. Financial arrangements must be made within ten business days. If you feel like you can agree to these stipulations, feel free to bid and bid often. Okay, let's get started."

The bidding got off to a quick start. As the price climbed higher, the number of bidders dropped out. The bidding exceeded the price Sarah had set. She had talked to a realtor about selling the house and was told what the listing price would be and what to expect the house would sell for. No contract was signed, and Sarah didn't think any problems would come from the house being auctioned off. The bidding was now above what the listing price would have been. There were just two bidders left. One was a known house flipper, and the other had been wanting to buy a house in this neighborhood for quite some time, but houses here rarely came up for sale. The gavel banged, and the auctioneer said, "Going once, going twice, sold!"

Ben turned to Sarah and said, "Well, that's that. I will follow up with the auctioneer and the buyer to make sure the house goes through proper titling and everything is legal."

Sarah said, "How can I ever thank you for all you have done, Ben?"

Ben said, "Oh, you will get my fee statement."

Sarah gave Ben one of the looks that she had given him so often as they grew up together. Then Ben said, "When will I see you two again? At your wedding?"

Sarah smiled and said, "Why don't you come down and bring Andrew with you for a visit? We have a guest bedroom."

Ben said, "You know I'm a very busy attorney. Most of my clients are from the gay and lesbian community, and they rely on my help."

Sarah said, "I'm sure I will be talking with you since you are my attorney. You take care."

And with that, she gave Ben a big hug and kiss, and gave Andrew a hug. Karl shook Ben's hand and then Andrew's hand and said, "Goodbye."

*****

The next morning, they checked out of the hotel. Sarah wanted to see her folks before going back home. On the drive over to the care facility, she was concerned that a visit might confuse or upset her dad. She kicked around in her head whether that was a good idea or not. They arrived at the facility, and the visit went great. Her dad was still thinking they were on vacation at this fancy resort. Her mom said, "Everything is going better than I ever expected. Thank you so much."

Sarah said, "Mom, hearing that makes me happy. Everything went great with the auction. They were even able to auction off the house. It sold for more than it would have if it was sold using a real estate agent. Mom, you guys will never have to worry about running out of money."

Sarah gave her mom and dad a hug and said, "You two enjoy your time here. We have got to go. Bye."

On the way out, Sarah said, "I feel like driving home. At least to our midway café."

Karl said that was okay with him because he would be driving the moving truck.

Sarah said, "What am I thinking? Of course, I will have to drive the car."

They drove to the Midway Café, had lunch, gassed up the truck and car, and were back on the road. Upon getting home, they unloaded the truck's contents into the garage. The garage was completely full. Before leaving the other day to go to Sarah's folks' house, Karl had rearranged things in the garage. He knew they would need the room to put away what they brought back with them. After a short rest, they returned the moving truck, and on the way back home, they stopped for a quick dinner. Back home, Sarah was on the couch, and Karl was in his chair. Karl said, "What a day."

Sarah said, "What a week, and we have to go to work tomorrow."

Karl said, "That's right, I will no longer be unemployed."

Sarah gave him one of her looks and said, "Let's go take a nice hot shower together and go to bed."

Karl said, "You are not going to get an argument from me on that."

CHAPTER 13

The New Jobs

The alarm went off. Sarah and Karl got up and started their normal get-ready-for-work morning routine. Sarah said, "Good morning. How does it feel to no longer be unemployed?"

Karl said, "Good morning. You sure have milked that one for all it's worth," and then gave Sarah a kiss.

The big difference was that they would no longer be working for the same company. No more riding to and from work together. No more lunches together in the company cafeteria. Karl could no longer play on the company's softball team.

It was time for both of them to leave for work. The travel time would be the same for Karl as it was before, but in the other direction. It would be hard for the two of them to have lunch together. Sarah in her car and Karl in his—they set out for work and their new jobs.

Sarah parked her car, walked into the building, and took the elevator. She pressed the button to take her to the executive floor. While at her folks' house, she purchased several business outfits for her new job and position as the executive administrative assistant to Ms. White. Sarah walked from the elevator down the hall to her office, walking tall and smiling at the others as they were getting ready for their day at work.

The door to Ms. White's office was open. Sarah walked to the door and peeked in. Ms. White was by herself and noticed Sarah in the doorway.

Ms. White said, "Just don't stand there, come on in."

Ms. White seemed to be in very good spirits. She said, "Come in and sit down. How did everything go with your parents?"

Sarah knew Ms. White was not known for small talk and was very much a to-the-point person. Sarah kept her answer short and thanked Ms. White for allowing her vacation time to take care of things before coming to work for her.

Ms. White said, "I have an offsite meeting this morning, but I should be back before lunchtime. You will find your business cards in the top drawer of your desk. I suggest, if you have personal items that you want at your desk, you take this time while I'm gone to get your office organized. Remember, you represent me, so I expect your desk to be neat and respectable. My calendar is on your computer. Make arrangements with the IT department to give you a 'how-to' tutorial."

Sarah said, "Will do. Thank you."

She took her seat at her desk, and Ms. White left her office. Sarah adjusted her office chair to fit her petite body and long legs. She opened the top drawer, and there were her new business cards. She looked in each of the other drawers to find them mostly empty. Behind her desk was a credenza. She looked in there and found computer paper and other office supplies. She called the IT department to see when they could send a tech person up to give her the "how-to" tutorial on the calendar and anything else that needed to be done. Bill did not use the company calendar, or if he did, Sarah did not have access to it. The person who answered the phone listened to Sarah's request and said, "It will be about an hour. Will that be okay or would you like a later time?"

Sarah said, "An hour would be just right."

Sarah went down to her old office to get the box of personal items she had left there before going on vacation. Back up to her new office, she started to unpack the items. She carefully looked at each item, doing her own evaluation as to whether it would meet the standards of Ms. White.

A person arrived at Sarah's desk and said, "I'm Carol from IT. I'm here to give you a tutorial on the calendar."

Sarah said, "I'm Sarah."

She stood up to let Carol sit in her seat.

Carol said, "Sit back down. That's not how this is going to go."

Carol pulled the guest chair around Sarah's desk, put it beside Sarah, and sat down. Carol was a good teacher. She set up an example calendar for Sarah to practice on.

Carol said, "When you are done practicing on this calendar, you can delete this stuff and start using it as your personal calendar or just delete it entirely."

Carol went through the common functions first and then moved on to the more complex ones. She showed Sarah how to drop and drag one appointment time to another time or even to another day and time. Carol asked Sarah, "Do you have a smartphone? And would you give it to me?"

Sarah handed her cell phone to Carol. She said, "I'm going to download an app on your phone. You will be able to access the calendar from your cell phone and make changes to it from anywhere you can get cell phone reception."

Carol said, "You are a quick learner. I am your technical support person. If you have any problems with your computer, the app, or the Internet, give me a call."

Since Sarah already worked for the company, her email and Internet access were still good and did not need changing. Carol gave Sarah her phone extension and cell phone number.

Sarah said, "Thanks. You are a very good teacher."

It was just before lunchtime, and Ms. White returned, just as she said she would. Sarah said, "There were no phone calls, and no one stopped by to see you. Carol from IT came by, gave me the 'how-to' tutorial, and trained me on the calendar application."

Ms. White said, "Excellent. It's about time for lunch. Get freshened up for lunch and come back here."

Ms. White had a private bathroom off of her office and freshened up there. Sarah returned as requested.

Ms. White said, "Come with me. Let's get some lunch."

Sarah had heard there was a lunchroom for executives only and wondered if she would be able to eat there or only occasionally be Ms. White's guest.

They walked down the hall in a direction Sarah had not been before. Just before they arrived at the big double doors at the end of this hall, Ms. White said, "Sarah, I don't like this double-class system we have. It's been here forever and probably will be here forever."

She went on to say, "Behind these doors is the executive dining room. It is only open for lunch and special occasions. We executives sit on the near side of the dining room, and staff must sit on the other side. The food is the same on both sides."

She explained that in some ways it was a good thing because it kept the staff from having a working lunch. "You can eat here whether I do or not. You do not have to eat here every day or ever, if you prefer. However, the food here is part of your compensation for working at the executive level. You don't pay or tip for your meals. You will be given a menu to order from. It changes each day, but there are a few items they offer every day."

Ms. White opened the door, and they walked in. Ms. White said, "This is my table. Go ahead to the other side and find a place to eat. When you are done, don't wait on me. Enjoy your lunch. I expect you to be back in your office at the end of lunchtime."

The tables had linen tablecloths and napkins. In the center of each table was a fresh-cut flower arrangement. All of the plates, cups, and saucers were real china and had the company's name and logo on them. The silverware was real silver, and the glasses were made of crystal. Sarah saw a table with an empty place and asked, "Would it be okay if I join you?"

One of the people said, "We are not expecting anyone else. Go ahead and be seated."

Sarah said, "My name is Sarah, and I'm Ms. White's new administrative assistant. Today is my first day working for her. The week before last, I worked for Bill before he retired."

One of the people at the table said she attended Bill's retirement roast and had enjoyed it very much. The others at the table introduced themselves and said who they worked for.

The server handed Sarah a menu and asked, "What would you like to drink?"

Sarah said, "Iced tea, please."

She looked over the menu. This was not your typical company cafeteria food. The items on the menu were ones you would see at an upscale restaurant. The server returned with her iced tea and asked, "Do you require more time? Or would you like to order now?"

Sarah said, "I would like the chef's salad with ranch dressing on the side."

The server asked, "Will there be anything else?"

She said, "No, just the salad."

Sarah and the others around the table had some "get to know you" small talk. It was a nice lunch, and Sarah enjoyed talking with them. Just before the end of lunchtime, they all got up and returned to their offices.

Sarah was in her office when Ms. White returned. She said to Sarah, "Did you enjoy your lunch?"

Sarah said, "Yes. Are you busy? I don't see anything on the calendar right now."

Ms. White said, "Come on in."

Sarah said, "I'm a quick learner, and I don't like to make too many mistakes. It would help me if you could tell me some of the routine things you like. Do you drink coffee? And how do you like it? Black, with cream, and/or sugar? Is there a set time that you like to be reminded of things? I'd just as soon you let me know now instead of me trying to figure them out with trial and error as I go along."

Ms. White told Sarah a lot of these things she liked and would like for Sarah to do. Sarah took notes and wrote them down. She went to her office and checked on the outstanding projects that Bill ran out of time to work on. Sarah could hardly wait to get home and tell Karl about her day and to hear about his.

*****

It was Karl's first day at his new job. He arrived and found his way to George's office.

George said, "How was your week off in between jobs? You know, unemployed?"

Karl said, "Good morning. Not you too. Sarah has been teasing me about being unemployed all week long. Things went really great at her folks' place. We got her folks moved into the care facilities with no problems. The people there are fantastic. Sarah met with her attorney and got up to date on the legal stuff. Had a big auction and ended up auctioning off the house too. The house sold for more than what the real estate agent wanted to list the house for. Yesterday, we drove back home, me in the moving truck and Sarah in the car. I'm a little sore from the unloading. I brought back all of Sarah's father's workshop tools and equipment."

George said, "Are you ready to hit the ground running?"

Karl said, "Just lead the way."

George walked Karl around the office and introduced him to everyone who was not with a client. George stopped in front of an empty office and said, "This is your office."

Karl said, "My office? With a door? I don't have to sit out in the middle with a bunch of other accountants? I don't have to share it with anyone else?"

George said, "That's right, Karl. You are in the big leagues now. Get settled into your new office. You have an appointment with Janet at ten-thirty."

Karl said, "Thank you for everything, George."

Karl went back to his car and got the box filled with his personal office items. He got his desk organized and sat there in disbelief.

It was just before ten-thirty when George stuck his head in Karl's office and said, "You ready to meet with Janet?"

Karl grabbed his notepad and said, "Yes, let's go."

Janet's office was on the other side of the building where all of the firm's partners' offices were located. Janet was sitting at her desk and was on the phone. She held up her finger, indicating just a minute. George and Karl stood outside her office, away from the door. It was just a couple of minutes, and Janet came out and said, "Sorry about that. I just couldn't seem to get off the phone. Come on in and sit down. Good to see you again, Karl."

Karl said, "Good to see you too."

Karl was a little nervous.

George said, "I've got to get back. I have a client appointment in a few minutes. Catch up with you later, Karl. Do you have lunch plans?"

Karl said, "No."

George said, "I will come by your office at noon."

Karl gave George a nod of his head and a thumbs-up.

Janet gave Karl a little background on how the firm worked and how she liked to manage her people. Janet handed Karl a list of clients she had assigned to him. She briefly went over each one and gave Karl a bit of information on each.

She said, "Don't try to memorize what I'm telling you right now about these clients. Just wanted to give you a preview of the clients you will be working with. After six months working here, you become eligible for a bonus. The satisfaction of your clients and how much revenue you bring to the firm will determine your bonus amount. We have a saying around here: 'Happy client, happy accountant.'"

They talked a little more, getting to know one another a little better. Janet said, "Let me take you over to where we keep the files and give you a little office tour."

They walked over to the area where Karl and the other accountants' offices were located. In the middle of the room were your standard cubicle-style offices. Janet said, "This is where the accountants and bookkeepers sit. At this firm, any accountant who is not a CPA is considered a junior accountant. Lower than the junior accountants are the bookkeepers. Some of these people are working toward getting their CPA."

Karl is already a CPA, and he was hired in as a senior accountant. That's why he had his own office. Someday he would have a couple of these people assigned to work just for him. For now, he would share his work with the ones working in the accounting and bookkeeper pool. They were the ones who were not directly assigned to other senior accountants. Janet stopped in front of a half door and said, "You or anyone else are not allowed past this door nor are you allowed to touch any of these file cabinets or the client hard-copy paper files directly. There is a request form that you will fill out, requesting a client's file. One of our file clerks will retrieve the requested client's paper file. When you return the file, you will have a copy of your request form returned to you, noting that you have returned the file.

"I strongly suggest that you keep all of these forms on file in your office. You are responsible for that client's hard-copy file, from the time it leaves the file room to the time it gets returned. If you give the file to one of the accountants or bookkeepers to work on, make a note of it. We treat all of the information we have on a client with the utmost level of confidentiality. Do you understand?"

Karl said, "Yes."

Janet said, "You will find there is a lot of the same client information online, and you can access it from your computer and will not need to request the client's hard-copy file."

Looking at her watch, she said, "Sorry to leave you here, but I need to get back to my office. I have a conference call in a few minutes."

And Janet went off to her office.

Karl wandered around the office. He went past several small conference rooms used for meeting with clients when the accountant's office was too small. They were also used for small group meetings within the firm. There was a very large conference room with the biggest table Karl had ever seen. It must have had twenty chairs around it. Down the hall was the break room. It had a couple of vending machines, two microwaves, a toaster oven, a regular toaster, and a refrigerator. Karl made it back to his office and looked over his list of clients.

A person knocked on Karl's open office door and said, "Hi, I'm Bob from technical support. I stopped by earlier, but you weren't here. Must have been in a meeting. They do that a lot around here. I'm here to get you set up on the firm's computer. You know, help you get your email account and password set up, your Internet access, and show you some of the applications you will be using—that sort of stuff."

Karl said, "Pleased to meet you."

Bob showed Karl how to access the firm's apps and made sure Karl's access was set up correctly. He showed Karl what was needed to access the client information database that was online. He went on to set up and check Karl's email address and finished showing him how to access the Internet.

Bob said, "All of your passwords and accesses seem to be working correctly. My work here is done. If you end up having problems or questions, give me a call. See you around. Oh, by the way, everything you do on your computer is recorded, so no porn. Just kidding."

Karl said, "Thank you. If I have any problems, I surely will give you a call."

As Bob walked out, George was walking in and said, "I see you met Bob. Did he give you the 'no porn' line? Get your coat and let's go to lunch. I'm taking you to this little dive of a place not far from here. It has great food. We have to hurry, lots of people like eating there, and it gets busy quickly."

Karl grabbed his coat, and the two of them were off to the parking lot and into George's car.

George said, "This place is not far away but too far to walk."

George pulled into the parking lot. There were a lot of cars there already, but they found a place to park. Karl thought George was right—it looked like a real dive. They walked in, and the place was almost full, but they were able to get a table.

George said, "This place sure could use a facelift, but the food is fantastic. Everything on the menu is good. Order what you want, I'm buying today."

They looked over the menu.

Karl said, "What are you going to order?"

George said, "I'm going to have the pot roast plate. It comes with mashed potatoes, gravy, and the vegetable of the day—let's see, it's green beans."

Karl said, "That does sound good. I will have the same."

Karl asked, "What's the policy on drinks at lunch?"

George said, "I'm going to have iced tea. That reminds me, you have an appointment to meet with HR at one-thirty. You need to fill out your new employee paperwork, go through the orientation video, and receive your company handbook. You will be asked to read and sign the firm's code of ethics statement. In there, you will read about drinking at lunch and lunch with the client. It will take much of the rest of your afternoon."

They ordered their food. The service was quick, they ate, and as they were leaving, the line to get in was out the door and into the parking lot.

George said, "That's why we needed to get here when we did."

They were back at the office before the end of lunchtime.

Karl said, "That's not a bad place to eat. Thanks for buying."

George said, "No problem. The next one's on you now that you are employed."

The firm did not have a cafeteria. That would be something Karl would miss from his old company, especially not being able to eat lunch with Sarah.

Karl had time before his meeting with HR and decided to send a quick "I love you" text to Sarah.

Sarah sent back, "I love you too. Lots to tell you. Very busy, see you tonight." He had a half-hour before his meeting with HR, so Karl passed the time getting familiar with his computer. He had used a computer most of his life and knew lots about them. The applications he would be using here were very different. He didn't think it would take him long to learn them.

Karl looked at the clock and saw that it was time for his HR meeting. Arriving at HR, he said to the person sitting behind the desk, "My name is Karl Brown. I'm a new employee and here for my one-thirty appointment."

The lady at the desk said, "Take a seat over there, and I will let Susan know you are here."

Karl sat down.

It was a few minutes when he was greeted. "Hello, my name is Susan. Welcome to our accounting firm, please follow me."

Karl stepped into the office. It only had a desk and a couple of chairs.

"I'm the HR director here. We use this office for interviews and new employee orientations. Here is your copy of the employee handbook. I have a packet of the new employee paperwork that I will go over with you. Afterward, you will need to view the video on this laptop."

Susan took a stack of papers out of the envelope. She explained each one and asked Karl to read, sign, and date them. Karl read, filled out the forms, and then signed and dated them. Susan set up the laptop and said, "That does it for my part. When you are ready to view the video, just press this button. When you are finished, you are free to go. Just leave the laptop here. I will get it later, after you leave. It has been a pleasure meeting you, Karl. Good luck in your new position."

Karl said, "Thank you."

Karl viewed the video. It was about the history of the firm, with a welcome message from the firm's president, and included the firm's mission statement, pictures of the partners with a brief bio of each, financial statements, and graphs. The direction the firm's partners wanted to see the firm go. The video ended with a bunch of fun pictures and short clips from the Christmas party, the company picnic, and several other events. When it was over, Karl left the laptop in the room as he was told.

Karl returned to his office. It was about time to go home. Karl turned his office lights out, closed and locked the door, and walked to his car. Traffic was backed up. He hoped it was not going to be an everyday occurrence. Slowly, the traffic moved along, and Karl could see an accident ahead. As he drove by, it didn't look like anyone was hurt. Traffic returned to normal, and Karl made it the rest of the way home without any other problems.

Karl walked in the door and said, "Hi, honey, I'm home."

He had wanted to say that since he saw it on an old black-and-white TV show.

Sarah said, "Hi, I'm in the kitchen making dinner. Go ahead and change your clothes. I just got home myself. It will be a while before dinner is ready."

Karl went to the kitchen. Sarah had on one of his old softball jerseys, and that was just about all she had on.

Karl said, "Not going to change clothes until I get a kiss and a hug."

Sarah gave him a quick kiss and said, "Go change your clothes before you make me burn dinner."

Karl took a beer out of the refrigerator and headed down the hall to change his clothes and took a quick shower.

He returned to the kitchen. Sarah was just about finished cooking, and Karl sat down at the table. As they ate their dinner, Sarah said, "I missed riding to and from work with you today and having lunch with you too."

Then Sarah started to tell Karl about her day. She told him about the experience she had in the executive dining room and how beautifully decorated it is. The tables had linen tablecloths and napkins. The place settings were real china and had the company's name and logo on them, the way they could order from a menu, and it was all free.

Karl said, "I can tell you were impressed with lunch, but how about the job part of your day?"

Sarah said, "Ms. White was out of the office all morning. In the afternoon, we had a meeting. I wanted her to share with me her routines and what she would like for me to do. I think it went well, and I know I will like working for her. Then I spent the rest of the time doing some follow-up work on the projects Bill ran out of time to work on."

Sarah got up from the table and went to her purse. She returned to the table and handed Karl one of her business cards.

Karl said, "How impressive. This looks better than the ones I got from the company when I worked there."

Sarah puffed up and stuck out her chest and said, "You didn't work as an executive administrative assistant to Ms. White."

They both laughed.

Sarah said, "Tell me about your day."

Karl said, "I will tell you as I clean up the kitchen."

Sarah sat at the table and watched Karl clean up the kitchen and listened to his story about his day. Karl went on to tell Sarah about his meeting with Janet, his boss.

He said, "Janet and I went through the client list I would be responsible for and gave me an office tour. George took me to an old hole-in-the-wall place that had really good food. George even paid for it. In the afternoon, I spent time in HR filling out the new employee forms and then watching the new employee orientation video. Toward the end of the video, there were a bunch of photos and video clips of the Christmas party, the company picnic, and other events. It looks like everyone was having a good time. I know I'm going to like working there. I am going to get a variety of things to do."

The kitchen was cleaned up. They went into the living room. Karl sat down in his old, beat-up, comfortable chair, and Sarah sat on the couch. They sat and talked about the last couple of weeks, and they both were surprised at just how much they had done and what they had accomplished.

Sarah said, "And we still have Jill's wedding coming up soon."

Karl looked at Sarah and said, "Do you know how much wearing my jersey turns me on?"

Sarah said, "Yes, I do, and that's why I put it on."

She pulled it up a little, and Karl could see she didn't have any panties on.

Karl said, "Let's go practice making a baby."

Sarah said, "I'm okay with the practice part but not so much on the making part."

With that, they went to the bedroom.

CHAPTER 14

Jill's Wedding

Sarah and Jill had set aside the entire Saturday to get as much of the wedding arrangements done as possible. First on the list was shopping for a dress for Jill to wear for the wedding. Jill thought paying a lot of money for a formal wedding dress was a big waste of money. She had developed a small baby bump and just looked like she had put on a few pounds and really didn't look all that pregnant. Knowing that Jill wanted to hide the fact that she was pregnant, Sarah suggested a loose-fitting, longer dress. Jill looked at several dresses and picked a couple they both agreed would look nice on her.

While Jill was trying on the first dress, Sarah looked for a dress she could wear to the wedding. Jill came out to show Sarah and said, "What do you think?"

Sarah said, "It does look really nice on you and hides your baby bump well. I really like the color."

Jill said, "I think so too, but I think I would like to try the other one on too."

While Jill was trying on the second dress, Sarah tried on the dress she picked to wear at the wedding. Soon Jill came out of the dressing room and said, "Sarah, where are you?"

Sarah said, "I'm in here, trying on a dress. I will be out in a second."

Sarah stepped out, and Jill said, "Sarah, you look so beautiful. Oh, I hate you. I wish I had a body like yours. How do you like this dress?"

Sarah said, "I like this one too, but I like the first one much better."

Jill said, "I think so too."

They each bought their dresses, and it was off to the next stop.

The next stop was the hotel. This was the most important one because it would set the wedding date and time. They had an appointment to meet with the hotel's event coordinator. The hotel Jill picked was the nicest one in town. It had been built in the early 1900s. It has been well maintained. It was very large and was the chosen venue for many upscale events in the area. Jill thought it was the perfect place to have her wedding. She was not planning a large wedding and would not need one of the large ballrooms, but more the size of a smaller convention meeting-type room. Jill had been told the smaller rooms were reasonably priced.

They went up to the hotel's registration desk and said, "We're here to meet with the events coordinator, James."

The person at the desk pointed and said, "Go down that hallway. His office will be the second office on the left."

James was in his office. Jill and Sarah walked in, and Jill said, "Hi, I'm Jill, and this is my friend Sarah."

James said, "Super, you're right on time. Oh, how I like that. Ladies, let us step to the office next door. In there, we have all of our catalogs and facilities information." James started with, "Based on our phone conversations for your wedding, I have preselected some options for your review and approval. The date you asked for your wedding is available in our Ruby Hall. It's just the right size for tables, buffet, bar, and dancing. The doors open out to the courtyard overlooking our little garden pond. The package I've put together for you includes the number of chairs you've estimated for the guests you're expecting, an arch for you and your future husband to stand under with the person performing the ceremony. The arch has a built-in microphone and speaker so your guests can HEAR you saying your vows. Any questions so far?"

Jill looked at Sarah, then turned back to James and said, "No."

James said, "Good. Let's move on to the food. Again, based on the information you provided me in our lovely phone conversations,

I've picked one of our popular wedding packages. You were undecided between the BBQ and Mexican. Have you decided?"

Jill asked Sarah, "What do you think?"

Sarah said, "Mexican."

Jill said, "Mexican."

James said, "Wonderful pick. Mexican is one of our most popular options. The package includes disposable plates, napkins, cups, and plasticware. Any questions here?"

Jill said, "No."

James said, "Then let's move on to the bar package. You said you would like to have a bar at your wedding. You have two choices: you pay or your guests pay for their own alcoholic drinks. As part of the food and beverage package, soft drinks, bottled water, iced tea, and coffee are included."

Sarah said, "I think you should go with the guests paying for their own. Fewer problems with people drinking too much."

Jill said, "Good thinking, Sarah."

James said, "Let's finish with the inside package. The number of tables and chairs for the number of guests you've estimated will be set up with a table covering. A head table will also be provided for you, your new husband, and the wedding party. A congratulations banner will hang on the wall behind the head table. Any additional decorations will be up to you and at your cost, as will any cleanup. Do you have any other questions for me?"

Jill looked to Sarah to see if she had any questions and then said, "I don't think so."

James said, "I will go to my office and draw up the contract for all of these packages for you to sign. There is a deposit you will need to pay today, with the balance due on or before the wedding date. I will return here when I'm finished. It should take more than fifteen to twenty minutes. Would you like anything to drink while you are waiting?"

They both said, "Iced tea."

James said, "I will have some delivered to you."

A few minutes later, a server arrived with their iced tea.

James returned to the office where Jill and Sarah were seated. He said, "I have the contract here. Please read through it to see if everything we agreed upon is in this contract."

As Jill read a page, she would hand it to Sarah to read. After finishing the last page, she said to Sarah, "It looks good to me. What do you think?"

Sarah read the last page and said, "It looks good to me too."

Jill signed the contract and handed her credit card to James.

James said, "I will make a copy of the contract and run your credit card. It should only take a minute or two."

James returned and handed Jill her copy of the contract. Jill signed the credit card slip and handed it to James.

Jill said to Sarah, "I think that went really well."

Sarah said, "I agree."

They said their goodbyes to James and left.

Sarah asked, "What's next on the list?"

Jill said, "The bakery. It's just down the street."

They walked into the bakery. Boy, did it smell good. The owner said, "My name is Nancy. May I help you?"

Jill introduced herself and Sarah and said, "We spoke on the phone about you baking a cake for my wedding."

Nancy said, "Oh, yes, I remember. Come on back. I just finished a cake for a wedding this evening. It's a yellow cake with lemon filling between the four layers."

Jill took one look at the cake and said, "That's it. I want one exactly like this one."

Nancy said, "That was easy. Are you sure you don't want to look through the pictures I have to see if there's one you like better?"

Jill said, "No. I want one just like this one."

Nancy said, "It comes with a groom's cake. It's a red velvet sheet cake with buttercream frosting. It is included in the price of the wedding cake. Full payment is required at the time of the order."

Jill gave Nancy the wedding date and hotel information for the cake to be delivered and handed her the credit card.

Nancy said, "That was easy. Most of the brides come in here and go through the book and can't make up their minds. Sometimes it takes hours."

They walked out, and Sarah said, "I don't know about you, but I could use something to eat."

Jill said, "I could eat. Besides, I'm eating for two."

They both laughed and went off to eat.

After lunch, Sarah asked Jill, "What's next?"

She said, "The florist. I have already arranged for a DJ. He will also be the emcee. He works at the same place as me and does this as a side business."

The flower shop was just down the block from where they had eaten, so they walked. They went into the shop, and Jill said, "Hi. I'm Jill. We talked on the phone the other day."

The manager said, "Hello. Have you decided what you would like?"

Jill said, "I have. I would like two arrangements, one to sit on the ground on each side of the wedding arch. I would like a small table centerpiece for each of the guest tables and a larger one for the head table. I will need a bride's bouquet. Sarah here will need a corsage, as will my mother. My husband-to-be, his best man, and my father will need boutonnieres."

Jill gave the manager her flower and color choices. The manager said, "I will write the order and give you a total price."

The manager handed the order to Jill and said, "If you like the order, you will need to pay the full amount now."

Jill gave the manager the wedding date, the hotel information for the delivery, and her credit card. The manager thanked Jill for her business and said, "It sure is nice working with customers like you who know what they want."

They walked back to the car. Jill said, "Thank you for going with me. I don't think I could have done it alone."

Sarah said, "You did most of the work. All I did was tag along. You have become a good friend. I love you."

Jill said, "I love you too. Let's get you home."

Jill dropped Sarah off at her house and drove home.

*****

It was Saturday morning, the day of the wedding. Sarah was getting ready to leave the house. She said, "I'm leaving now to get my hair and nails done. I promised Jill I would help her get dressed and ready for the wedding later today. The hotel gave them a complimentary room for the night. We will need to be there two hours before the wedding is to start, so you need to be ready to drive us over to the hotel."

Karl said, "Okay. See you later."

Sarah returned several hours later. Karl was sitting in his old beat-up chair watching a game on the TV. Sarah said, "You don't look ready. You said you would be ready."

Karl said, "I'm ready. I've showered, shaved, and all I have to do is put my suit on. Sarah, you look fabulous."

Karl had seen Sarah's red hair in several different styles but never up on the top of her head like it was now.

Sarah said, "Down, boy. I spent a fortune getting my hair done. I know what you're thinking. You're not going to mess it up. Now go get dressed."

Karl said, "How about you? You're not dressed."

She said, "That's because I'm going to get dressed at the hotel with Jill."

Karl said, "Okay, okay."

As Karl was putting his suit on, Sarah was gathering everything she would need to finish getting dressed.

On the way over to the hotel, Karl said, "What am I going to do for two hours?"

Sarah said, "Jack, his brother John, and Jill's father, Mike, should all be together. Go find them and hang out with them. Make sure you keep Jack out of trouble. I heard John might try to get Jack drunk or play a prank on him. Keep Jack out of trouble."

Karl said, "I will see what I can do."

Sarah went to the room that Jill said she would be in and knocked on the door. Jill said, "Is that you, Sarah?"

She said, "Yes."

Jill opened the door, and Sarah walked in. Jill said, "My mother wanted to help me get dressed. I told her I already asked you. Sarah, if she was here and saw my baby bump, well, I would never hear the end of it. I'm just not ready for that right now. You can put your stuff on the bed over there. Oh, Sarah, look at your beautiful red hair. I HATE you."

Sarah said, "So I guess you like it?"

Jill said, "Of course I like it."

Sarah helped Jill, who was just this side of being a basket case. Trying to get her to hold it together long enough to get dressed and put on her makeup was going to be a chore. After helping Jill, Sarah got dressed and put on her makeup.

Sarah said, "We sure do look good all made up like this. What do you say we get you married off?"

It was just about time for them to go downstairs to where the ceremony would be held just outside of the Ruby Hall on the lawn by the garden pond.

Karl had found Jack, his brother John, and Jill's father, Mike, in the hotel's sports bar. They each had a beer and were watching the game, and Karl was watching the clock. It was John's job, being the best man, to see to it that Jack showed up at the right time. Jill had told Sarah to tell Karl that John was unreliable and to keep an eye out. John wanted to order another round, but Karl said, "I don't think we have time to drink one before we are supposed to be back at the Ruby Hall."

Jack's father saw what John was up to and said, "Karl is right. We need to get Jack married off."

It was time to head over to the Ruby Hall. There, they were met by the hotel's wedding coordinator. She told Jack and John to go outside and take their place up by the wedding arch where the JP (justice of the peace) was standing. The guests had already been seated, and the guys walked down the side of the seating area and up to the wedding arch. Karl took a seat with the other guests. Sarah walked down the aisle and took her place at the wedding arch. The wedding march started to play, and Jill and her father walked down the aisle. The JP had the two of them repeat their wedding vows and said, "I now pronounce you husband and wife. You may kiss your bride."

After the kiss, they turned to face the guests, and the JP said, "May I introduce to you Mr. and Mrs. Jack and Jill Hill. You may go inside the hall while the wedding pictures are being taken."

After the pictures were taken, all went inside. Instead of a formal reception line, they chose to circulate among the guests. Jill went to Karl and Sarah and said, "I want to introduce you two to my parents."

All the time Karl was dating Jill, he never went to visit Jill's folks. They all walked over to where her folks were seated, and Jill said, "Mom and Dad, I want you to meet my very best friend Sarah and her friend Karl."

Karl didn't think Jill's parents put two and two together that he had dated Jill. At least they didn't say anything about it.

Karl said, "I met your dad earlier today before the wedding. We were hanging out in the sports bar waiting for the wedding to start."

The DJ, who was also the emcee, said, "To start things off, let's have the father-daughter dance."

Jill and her father started dancing. The DJ said, "Jack and Jill's mother, please join the dance."

They soon exchanged partners; now Jack and Jill were dancing together, as were Jill's mother and father. The DJ said, "Everyone who would like to join in can do so now."

The DJ was good. He played a wide variety of songs—fast ones mixed in with slow ones. He even had a couple of line dance numbers.

The service doors opened, and several servers came in pushing food banquet carts and a cart containing just dinnerware. They lined up the carts, creating a food service line. The DJ announced, "The food has arrived. Let's eat."

People started lining up, and the servers dished out the food. The DJ played background music as the people ate. Later, the DJ said, "If you want seconds, there is plenty. Just get in line again."

After the DJ saw that most people had finished eating, he said, "Okay, folks. It's time for the garter toss. Where are the bride and her husband?"

A chair was brought out and placed in the middle of the dance floor, and Jill took her seat. Jack came out and got down on his hands and knees. He crawled up to Jill and reached his hands up under her dress. You could see he was fumbling around. He pulled out a huge pair of granny panties and twirled them around over his head. Jill's mother just about fainted, and everyone else laughed. He reached up and retrieved the garter. The DJ said, "All of you single guys or want to be single, stand over there."

Sarah said to Karl, "Go ahead and go over there, but don't you dare catch that thing."

Jack pulled back on the garter and let it go. Sure enough, Karl reached out and caught it.

The DJ said, "It's now time for the ladies to have your turn. All of you single girls or want to be single, go stand where the guys were standing."

Jill turned her back to the crowd of ladies that had gathered. Up went her arm, and over her shoulder the bouquet went flying. Sarah stepped right into the flight path, and the bouquet went right into her outstretched hands. There was a big cheer from the crowd.

The DJ said, "The next dance will start with the lucky guy who caught the garter and the lucky lady who caught the bouquet."

Karl and Sarah took to the dance floor, and the music began to play. As they danced, Sarah said, "I told you not to catch that thing."

Then Karl said, "That was a nice catch you made."

They both laughed. The DJ said, "The rest of you can now join the lucky couple on this dance."

It was time for the cake cutting. It was an exact copy of the one Jill and Sarah saw at the bakery. After Jill and Jack did the traditional husband-and-wife cutting of the cake, a couple of the hotel servers came up and served the cake to the guests.

The guests were slowly leaving, and the party was just about over. Karl and Sarah took the elevator up to the floor where Sarah had left her things in Jill's room. Jill had given Sarah an extra card key so she could get in. Sarah gathered her things, and they were soon on their way home.

Karl said, "That was quite a wedding and party."

Sarah said, "It was very nice. The hotel did a good job. I really enjoyed dancing with you. I liked the way you held me in your arms. I love you so much."

They got home, crawled into bed, and kissed several times. Karl said, "You looked so beautiful tonight. I love you."

Sarah snuggled a little closer to Karl and said, "I love you bunches."

They fell asleep in each other's arms.

CHAPTER 15

Three Months After the Start of Their New Jobs

Sarah had been in her job for three months now. She was attending just about every meeting Ms. White held, even the ones offsite. Ms. White did not drive and had a private driver. Charles was his name. He was middle-aged and had been her driver for a very long time. Sarah sat in the back of the limousine with Ms. White. At first, Sarah felt uncomfortable riding in the limo but soon got used to being treated that way. Who wouldn't?

On the ride to the meeting, Sarah had turned the ringer off; the phone was on vibrate, and she received a text message from Jill. It said, "Jack and I are on our way to the doctor's office for my sonogram. The doctor said he should be able to tell the sex of the baby. I'm so excited. I wish you could come with us. We want to know the sex of the baby. We both want a boy."

Sarah texted back, "Good luck, let me know what you find out."

A couple of hours later, Sarah got another text from Jill, complete with a picture of the sonogram. The text said, "It's a boy, check out his tool. HAHAHA."

Sarah returned the text, "Congratulations, you guys got the boy you were hoping for."

Sarah said to Ms. White, "It was from my best friend. She is so excited. They just found out the sex of the baby they are going to have. Since we were not in a meeting, I thought it would be okay to answer it."

Ms. White said, "Only occasionally. Don't make it a habit of texting all day long and never when we are talking or in a meeting."

Sarah said, "I always turn my phone's ringer off during those times."

During the meetings, Sarah would normally be seated in the row behind Ms. White. If there was not a second row of seats, Sarah would sit next to Ms. White, never across from her. Sarah took notes and researched any information that Ms. White requested. By sitting close to Ms. White, she could whisper to Sarah what she wanted her to do, and Sarah could show Ms. White what was displayed on her laptop. Sarah was learning how Ms. White thought and many times had the information ready before Ms. White asked for it. Sarah was becoming a very valuable asset to Ms. White, but she didn't ask for Sarah's opinion. Sarah knew many of the company secrets and also knew how to keep them, something that quickly earned her Ms. White's trust.

Karl was feeling comfortable in his job. He was getting to know the clients on his list, the client online app, and the firm's procedures that needed to be followed. He and George had lunch together a couple of times a week, mostly to talk business away from the office. Karl had met others from the office and occasionally went to lunch with them. He did miss having lunch with Sarah both in the company cafeteria and when going out to eat. He was getting to know the accountants and bookkeepers in the pool and the ones he preferred to work with. He was looking forward to the day when he had his own staff, like several of the other senior accountants.

CHAPTER 16

Sarah's Mother's Passing

Sarah received a call on her cell phone. It was from the hospice nurse taking care of her mother. The nurse said, "I'm sorry to have to tell you, your mother passed away this morning."

Sarah said, "Thank you, and thank you for caring for my mother."

Ever since Karl and Sarah moved her folks to the care facilities, Sarah had talked to her mother on the phone every day. That was until her mother was so heavily sedated that she could no longer hold a conversation. Sarah knew her mother was not in any pain and was being well cared for. She also knew her mother was near the end of her life.

Sarah began to cry. Ms. White's office door was open, and she could hear Sarah crying. Ms. White walked to Sarah's desk and said, "Why are you crying?"

Sarah stood up, went into the arms of Ms. White, and said, "My mom just passed away."

Ms. White had not been married and, of course, had no kids. She had become very fond of Sarah and thought if she did have a daughter, she hoped she would be like Sarah. Ms. White said, "Come into my office and sit down."

Ms. White pulled out one of her cloth handkerchiefs and handed it to Sarah to dry her tears. Ms. White said, "I'm sorry to hear of your loss. Is there anything I can do?"

Sarah explained, "My folks had purchased side-by-side burial plots a number of years ago. While I was up there, just before starting work for you, my mom and I made and prepaid all of the funeral arrangements for both her and my dad. My mom also requested not to have a service. So I don't have a need to go up there."

Sarah burst into tears again.

Ms. White said, "Sarah, I would like for you to take the rest of the day off."

Sarah said, "Thank you, Ms. White, you have been so very kind to me. In the state I'm in, I guess I wouldn't be any good to you today after all."

Sarah went to her car. She texted Karl, "Sorry to give you this bad news via a text message, but I just can't talk on the phone right now. My mom passed away earlier this morning. Ms. White gave me the rest of the day off. I'm going home and want to be left alone. I don't want you to come home early. Stay at work and come home at your regular time. Don't worry, I just need this time to myself. I love you."

Karl texted back, "I'm sorry that your mom has passed. I hear you and understand your wishes. I will come home at my regular time. I want you to call me if you change your mind, and I will come home right away. I will pick up something for us to eat on my way home. I love you. Are you okay to drive? If not, see if Charles could give you a ride home."

She texted back, "I will send you a text when I get home so you don't worry."

*****

Sarah made it home and sent a text to Karl: "I'm home."

She fixed herself a cup of hot tea and sat on the couch. She cried and sipped her tea. Memories of her mother flowed down her face. She had wanted to visit her mom before she passed, but her mom would have none of that. Her mom told Sarah, "I want you to remember me not as how I am now, waiting to die, but as I was when we baked, played games, and had our special times together.

The times we went to the park. The times I helped you with your homework and school projects. I enjoyed watching you play on your high school softball team. Seeing you graduate at the top of your class. Oh how I enjoyed watching you grow up. Sarah, I don't want you to see me now."

Sarah remembered her words as if they had been said just a minute ago. Sarah sent a quick text to Jill, and she replied, "If there is anything I can do, please let me."

Sarah texted back and said, "Thanks."

She sent another text to Ben. Ben texted back, "Sarah, I know you are hurting right now. You have been preparing yourself for this day for a while, but I know it doesn't lessen the pain you are feeling. I will follow up on the legal things and make sure you get a copy of the death certificate and the notice of burial. Please take care of yourself, my dearest friend. I know you said your mother didn't want a service. Let me know if you need anything. I love you."

By the time Karl got home, Sarah's tears were gone, but her eyes and nose were very red. Sarah had made peace with herself. She heard his car pull up. She went to the bathroom, quickly ran a comb through her hair, put a cold washcloth on her face, and straightened herself up. Karl put the dinner he brought home on the kitchen table and went to hold Sarah. He held her tight, and Sarah said, "I'm okay now. Thanks for giving me my space today. That's what I needed, and thank you for that. I love you."

Karl said, "All I could do today was think of you. I'm happy to hear you are feeling better now. You think you could eat a little something?"

Sarah said, "All I have had today is a couple of cups of tea, and I think I could eat. What did you end up bringing home?"

Karl said, "Your favorite Chinese takeout."

CHAPTER 17

Mr. White's Retirement

The next day at work, the announcement was made that Mr. White, Ms. White's father, was retiring, and Ms. White would become the president and CEO of the company. That would also mean that Sarah would get a title change to administrative assistant to the president and CEO. She was hoping that title change came with a raise and, of course, new business cards. Sarah knew that Ms. White was basically running the company and didn't think her duties would change all that much. It still would be nice to get a raise.

There was a company retirement party held in the cafeteria for the employees who wanted to attend. All employees were given the afternoon off to attend the party. The next week, the big retirement party was by invitation only. It was to be held in the same hotel where Jill had her wedding. The affair was formal. The biggest hall of the hotel was to be decorated with all sorts of congratulatory and happy retirement banners. Ms. White had everything contracted out.

Sarah received an engraved invitation, and it said, "Sarah and Guest."

Sarah wondered if the dress she wore to Jill's wedding would be formal enough or if she should go out and buy a new special dress. She took the dress out of the closet and took a look at it. Sarah told Karl, "You are going to need to rent a tuxedo. I am going to buy a formal dress. That dress I wore for Jill's wedding is not going to do, especially since now I'm the administrative assistant to the president of the company."

The morning of the party, Sarah had an appointment to have her hair and nails done. She was happy with the way her hair was fixed for Jill's wedding and had it done the same way again. Karl went over to try on the tuxedo to make sure it fit.

When they said formal, they were not kidding. Both the male and female servers were dressed in vests with matching pants, white shirts, and black shoes. They walked around carrying trays of hors d'oeuvres and trays of champagne. There was also an open bar. The people attending were dressed to the nines. They were all friends of the family or business associates. Even the local TV news station had a crew there. Mr. White was introduced, and he gave a speech. In his speech, he made the official announcement that his daughter would become the president and CEO of the company and conduct all the duties of the company.

There was a live band, and many people were dancing. Karl asked Sarah, "Would you like to dance?"

Sarah took Karl's arm, and they walked to the dance floor. They danced several dances, had several glasses of champagne, and Karl had lots of hors d'oeuvres. They had a good time, but it was getting late, so they decided to go home.

As they were getting undressed and ready for bed, Karl said, "I sure did have a good time. I think I got a sample of how the other half lives."

Sarah said, "Yes, it was some party."

They got into bed. Karl kissed Sarah, and Sarah kissed him back, soon enjoying each other and ending up practicing, *not* making.

CHAPTER 18

Good News about Karl's Job

It had been six months since Karl started his job at the accounting firm. This marked the beginning of when Karl could start accumulating points toward his bonus. Every one of the clients on the list given to him by his boss Janet had been contacted at least once, and his top clients several times. Some he met with in one of the small meeting rooms at the accounting firm's office. But most of the meetings, Karl had at the client's office. Karl turned out to be quite the salesman and was bringing a lot of accounting business to the firm. His clients were beginning to outsource many, if not all, of their accounting to the firm. This way, they could reduce staff and save money.

Karl now had several accountants and bookkeepers so busy they were working only for his clients. Some were only doing payroll, while others were handling other accounting needs like accounts payable, accounts receivable, and general ledger. Karl was sure he would also be doing his clients' tax accounting and reporting when tax time rolled around. Now that Karl was eligible for a bonus, that would be the real telltale as to who was the best senior accountant. George had been telling Karl he was looking forward to some competition for who was the top accountant. George had been the top performer for the last couple of years.

Karl was called into Janet's office. Janet said, "Karl, you have been doing an outstanding job. I have been getting excellent reviews from your clients, and you have been bringing a lot of new business to the firm. You have a good chance of beating George this next quarter. A couple of the clients on your list were mostly inactive, but you were able to get them to hand over more of their accounting needs to us."

Karl said, "I really like working here, and I really like my job duties. At my old job, I didn't have the scope of what I have now."

Janet said, "Do you think you are ready to take on some more clients? The firm's sales staff has been busy bringing more clients to the firm. Most of what you currently have on your client list are mom-and-pop places and a few medium-sized businesses. I have some very large corporations that I would like to assign to you. How would you like to take more on?"

Karl said, "I would like that very much. I'm concerned about the support staff that I have been using. They mostly have been doing my clients' accounting, but they also are doing work for other senior accountants. If I'm going to take on more clients, I sure would like a dedicated staff."

Janet said, "Give me a list of the ones you would like on your team, and I will see what I can do. I will get back to you next week with your new clients. I might have to hire more people if we keep growing like this."

Karl went back to his office and started working on who he would like on his team. With larger corporations, the accounting tasks would be the same, but the volume would be much bigger. Not knowing just how many new clients he would be getting, he just had to come up with the best estimates he could. He created a few different models.

That night at dinner, Karl said, "I had a meeting with Janet today. You know today is the first day after my six months, and I can now start accumulating points toward my bonus. Janet said I was doing a good job and wanted to give me more clients if I thought I could handle the extra workload. We are to get back together next week to work out the details. George has been the top accountant and telling me he was looking forward to some competition. George has been the top performer for the last couple of years. I intend on giving him a run for his money."

Sarah said, "That's great news. That will be something to watch—two old friends battling it out for top dog."

CHAPTER 19

Sarah's Company Picnic

Since Karl was no longer working for his old company, he could not play on that softball team. Karl tried to get a team together at the accounting firm, but there were not enough people wanting to play. Karl found a team to play on that was in a different league. The team needed a pitcher, and Karl fit right in. He really wanted to play in the coed league with Sarah, but she was really busy, working a lot of late nights now that Ms. White was running the entire company. Ms. White had visions far beyond those of her father and wanted to grow the business. She was even looking at buying other companies. Sarah went to as many of Karl's games as she could. She really liked watching him play; she said it turned her on.

The date of the company picnic had been set a year ago, but no information had been posted. The picnic was just two weeks away. When Sarah got to work, there was a notice in her inbox announcing details of the annual company picnic. Included in the notice, there was a section about this year's company softball tournament. It would be coed and open to a company employee and the employee's guest. Team signup sheets could be found in the company's cafeteria. Sarah went down and signed her and Karl up.

That evening, during dinner, Sarah told Karl, "The annual company picnic is coming up in two weeks."

Karl said, "It won't be the same watching the softball tournament as it was when playing in it."

Sarah got a big smile on her face and said, "They have changed the softball tournament up this year. It's going to be coed, and a company employee and the employee's guest can play. I signed us up. There are a lot of husband/wife and boyfriend/girlfriend pairs already signed up. The only rule is there must be four girls on the field and four girls in the batting lineup at all times."

Karl's eyes lit up, and he said, "That's great. We will finally get to play on the same team."

Karl said, "You think your body will be up for it?"

Sarah said, "I can whip your ass right now, buddy."

Karl thought to himself that just might be true. Sarah was not only good-looking but very strong too.

Karl and Sarah practiced throwing the ball, and Karl pitched batting practice to Sarah. Sarah said, "This is supposed to be for fun, you know."

Karl said, "I know, I just want you to be ready. It would be nice to bring home another trophy."

Sarah said, "I'm ready enough."

It was time for the tournament to start. There were four teams. The two teams played on one field, and the team Sarah and Karl were on played the other team on the other field. After the first games were over, the losers played the losers, and the winners played the winners. The team Karl and Sarah were on won their first game. The second round of games started. The two winning teams would play against each other while the two losing teams played against each other.

It was Sarah's turn to bat. She hit a long fly ball out to center field, and the outfielder missed catching the ball. Sarah ran all the way to third base. Karl was the next batter. He hit one over the fence. They easily won their second game. The team they were about to play had won one and lost one. This would be the final game and determine the tournament winner and second-place team.

It was a hard-fought game. One team was in the lead, then the other. They were evenly matched, and everyone was getting tired. In the end, the team Sarah and Karl were on lost in the bottom of the last inning. They both got a second-place trophy. Everyone had a good time. Karl would have liked to have won but enjoyed playing on the same team with Sarah. Karl did renew several friendships with guys he used to play softball with and several he used to work with.

On the way home, they stopped at a fast-food restaurant. Several others had the same idea as they recognized others from the company picnic. Sarah said to Karl, "After the company picnic last year, you took me out to dinner. That was a nicer, better place than this."

Karl said, "Yes, in a couple of weeks it will be our one-year anniversary. I was going to surprise you and take you out for dinner and have a repeat of that night a year ago."

Sarah said, "That would be nice. Are you getting romantic on me?"

Karl just smiled, and they both chuckled. After they ate their dinner, Sarah and Karl went all home *sweaty and dirty*. When they got home, Sarah said, "Let's take a shower together."

Karl said jokingly, "Oh, all right, if you insist."

They made sure each other was clean from head to toe.

CHAPTER 20

Karl's New Clients

After stopping by his office to check for any emails or phone messages that needed immediate attention, Karl went on to Janet's office. Karl knocked on her open door. Janet said, "Come on in. I was just about to call your office."

Karl went in and sat down. He said, "Here is the list of people I would like on my team."

She said, "Most of these names are the ones you have been working with already?"

Karl said, "Yes, I had developed a good working relationship with them and know their strengths and weaknesses. The problem I'm having now is they are not always available because they are also doing work for other senior accountants. It has put me behind in getting my work done for my clients."

Janet said, "If I assign these people to only work on your clients, it will take these people out of the pool. I will need to hire people to replace the ones you are requesting. Karl, the people you are requesting will be reporting directly to you. You will become their manager, and you will be responsible for their reviews and raises."

Karl said, "I had several people working for me at my old company. I don't see that as being a problem."

Janet said, "I will make the announcement later this week, and it will become effective after the three-day weekend. There will be a slight salary increase. You are not up for review or a raise for another few months. This raise will not change your review date. I don't want to reassign any of your current clients. You have only had them for a short time, and it's not fair to have them switched to another senior accountant right now."

Karl said, "I would hate to lose any of them. I have worked hard to gain their trust and business."

Janet said, "Now on the new clients to be added to your list."

Karl and Janet went over the new clients the accounting firm would start doing business with. Janet explained, "Not all of these are going to be assigned to you. Some will be assigned to other senior accountants."

Karl was relieved to hear that because there was no way he could handle that many new clients. Janet said, "Go ahead and read through the list and put a check mark next to the companies you would like added to your client list."

She added, "In all fairness, the most senior of the senior accountants will get to pick first and then the next ones down the line. Since you're the last one to join the firm, you get to pick last. That doesn't mean you will get the bottom of the barrel. What is left over might have been your first pick even if you were the most senior. I want to see the picks from all the senior accountants, but I will be the one who assigns them. The ones that nobody picks, I will assign them to whomever I choose. Bring your picks back to me by the end of the day. By the end of the week, we will have a meeting, and I will hand out the new client lists. Have a good day."

Karl said, "Thanks, I will have my picks back to you by the end of the day."

Karl returned to his office.

Janet called each of her senior accountants, one by one, into her office. She gave each an unmarked list and asked that they place a check mark next to each new client they would like added to their client list and return it to her by the end of the day. She told them the same thing she told Karl about selecting additional clients, and she would be the one to do the final assignments, which would be announced in a meeting on Friday.

CHAPTER 21

Planning a Trip to See Sarah's Dad

It was a sunny Monday morning. Karl and Sarah were getting ready to go to work. Sarah said, "There is a three-day weekend this weekend, and I would like to go see my dad. I will give the care facility a call to see if there is a problem with us having a visit. I will also call Ben to let him know we will be in town."

Karl said, "That would be nice for you to visit with your dad. It will give you a chance to see how he is doing, check on the care facility, and see if there is anything they need. When you talk to Ben, see if he and Andrew can have dinner with us on Saturday or Sunday evening."

Sarah said, "Okay, I will text you later and let you know."

Karl said, "Remember I have a softball game on Thursday night."

Sarah said, "I have it on my calendar. I hope I don't have to work late that day."

They both left for work.

On Friday last week, Sarah and Ms. White had moved their offices to the ones her father had used while president and CEO. Sarah's office was bigger, as was Ms. White's. Sarah made it into work and said, "Good morning, Ms. White."

Sarah thought Ms. White had a secret bedroom there at the company to get to work so early.

After checking Ms. White's calendar to see if there was anything that needed immediate attention, Sarah called the care facility. Holly, the head caregiver, answered the phone.

"Hello, this is Holly. How may I help you?"

She said, "This is Sarah."

Holly said, "Sarah, how nice to hear your voice. Your dad is adjusting to the loss of your mother. He has started to interact with the other residents living here. I think he is going to do alright. He is in good health."

Sarah said, "That's such good news. Karl and I are planning to come up this weekend to visit my dad. Do you think that's a good idea?"

Holly said, "No problem. I think he would enjoy that. When do you think you will visit?"

Sarah said, "We will drive up on Saturday, visit sometime mid-morning Sunday, and drive home on Monday."

Holly said, "Great, it's my turn to work the weekend, so I will get to see you. I will make a note on the calendar."

Sarah then called Ben. Ben answered his cell phone and said, "Hi, Sarah, I have just a few minutes before I have to be in court. What's up?"

Sarah said, "I will make this quick. Karl and I are coming up to see my dad this weekend. We would like to see you and Andrew if you are going to be home. We would like to go out to dinner with you guys either Saturday or Sunday evening."

Ben said, "I want you two to stay the weekend at my house. Andrew is a fantastic cook and would love to cook dinner for all of us Saturday night. We can go out for dinner Sunday night. Now, Sarah, I will not take no for an answer. Got to go."

Ben hung up. Sarah didn't have a chance to say anything, let alone goodbye. She looked at her phone and said, "I guess that's that."

Sarah texted Karl, "Everything is set for the weekend. Ben said we are staying at his house and said HE WILL NOT TAKE NO for an answer."

Karl texted back, "I guess we will be staying at Ben's house."

CHAPTER 22

Karl's Softball Game

The days of the week seemed to pass quickly, and the softball season was just about over. It was Thursday night, the night of Karl's softball game. Sarah beat Karl home, had changed clothes, and was in the kitchen when Karl came walking through the door.

"Go put your uniform on, and by the time you're done, I will have dinner ready," Sarah said. She knew that Karl didn't like to eat a big meal before a game and made sandwiches. They ate dinner, then it was off to the softball park.

Karl went out on the field and started warming up with the rest of the team. They did some exercises, stretching, threw the ball around, and did a little running. Karl practiced his pitching. Tonight's game should be an easy win for the team. The other team had not won a game yet.

Sarah sat in the stands with the other girlfriends and wives. There was one that she really liked, and they sat together most every game. Karl's team was up to bat first. The first batter hit a long, easy pop fly, and the outfielder had no problem catching it.

"You're still swinging for the fence," one of the guys on the team said.

The next batter hit an easy standup double. It was now Karl's turn to bat. As always, Karl let the first pitch go by. On the next pitch, Karl hit a line drive between the shortstop and the third baseman. The ball rolled all the way out to the outfielder. Karl rounded first base on his way to second as his teammate scored. The outfielder had a super good arm and threw the ball to the second baseman. It was going to be close. Karl slid into second base. He was safe. When Karl tried to stand up, he went straight back down. He was hurt. Several guys rushed out and helped Karl off the field and to the bench. A pinch runner was put in the game for Karl. Sarah rushed to the dugout.

"We better go to the hospital," Karl said.

The guys helped Karl to the car, and another got a bag of ice for Karl to put on his ankle. Sarah drove to the hospital. Karl was in a lot of pain.

They arrived at the ER, and luckily, the ER was not busy and took Karl right in. Karl had already taken his shoe off and kept the ice on his ankle that the guys gave him before leaving the softball field. Shortly, the doctor came in and said, "What do we have here?"

"I was playing softball, slid into second base, and hurt my ankle," Karl said.

"Let's take a look at it," the doctor said. Karl's ankle was already swelling up. The doctor said to the nurse, "Wheel him down to X-ray and have them take a couple of pictures of his ankle."

X-rays were taken, and Karl was wheeled back to the ER room.

"Keep ice on your ankle, and I will be back in with the doctor as soon as the X-rays come back," the nurse said.

Karl asked if he could have something for the pain.

"I will ask and let you know," the nurse said.

It seemed like hours to Karl, but it was more like minutes. The doctor and nurse came back in, and the doctor said, "The X-ray shows you did not break anything, and it doesn't look like you tore anything either, but you have one hell of a sprained ankle. I am going to prescribe some pain pills for you to take. I want you to keep up with the ice—twenty minutes every hour for the next couple of hours, and keep your foot elevated until the swelling goes down. No pressure on that ankle for two weeks, and after that, only as much as you can tolerate. We will get you some crutches before you leave here. You may want to buy one of those knee scooters. Crutches can really hurt the underarms. You will see a lot of bruising—black and blue will be normal. All of the swelling should be gone in a couple of days, but I don't want you to put any weight on it for two weeks.

"Young man, you really hurt yourself. You are very lucky you didn't break or tear anything. If you did, you would have needed surgery to repair it. If you try putting weight on the ankle before the two weeks, you could cause permanent damage and would probably have a limp the rest of your life. You are too young to let that happen, so follow my instructions. The nurse will wrap your foot and ankle. Check your toes to make sure the bandage does not get too tight due to swelling. The bandage is to immobilize your ankle. Have someone rewrap it every day for the next three or four days. Do you have any questions for me?"

"No," Karl said. He thanked the doctor and nurse. They filled out the paperwork, and Sarah drove to a drive-through pharmacy to get Karl's prescription filled.

Sarah helped Karl into the house and sat him in his chair. She got him a glass of water and handed him one of the pain pills. She got a pillow and propped his foot up to elevate it.

"I will be right back with some ice," Sarah said.

She put the ice on Karl's ankle and sat down on the couch. She just looked at Karl. She knew he was hurting. There was nothing else she could do for him right now. It didn't take long for the pain pill to kick in. Sarah got her pajamas on, got out two blankets—one for Karl and one for her—and she curled up on the couch. Later, she put more ice on Karl's ankle and checked his toes. Karl had fallen asleep in his chair. The pain pill did its job. The medicine was working. Karl was feeling no pain. Sarah decided to sleep on the couch in case Karl needed anything in the middle of the night.

The next morning, Sarah called Karl's work and talked to Janet.

"Karl hurt himself in last night's softball game. He messed up his ankle really bad but didn't break it. Karl is taking pain medicine. He is in no shape to go to work today. Being a three-day weekend, he should be able to be back to work on Tuesday," Sarah said.

"That's too bad. Tell Karl to take it easy, and we will see him on Tuesday," Janet said.

Karl was left at home to care for himself as Sarah needed to go to work. Sarah called and texted Karl several times during the day.

"The pain pills are helping a lot, and I'm getting around on the crutches okay. Don't worry, and I will see you tonight. Let's still plan on going to see your dad tomorrow," Karl texted.

"Are you sure?" Sarah texted back.

"Yes, sitting around is sitting around, and I can do that anywhere," Karl texted.

CHAPTER 23

Back Home to Visit Sarah's Dad

The next day, Sarah put their suitcase in the car. She went back in the house to help Karl get into the car. After Karl got in, Sarah put the crutches in the back seat. Before they left the house, Karl had taken two pain pills, thinking he might need them for the long drive ahead. The bottle said to take one or two pills as needed for pain, every four to six hours, so two would not be an overdose. It was not long before the pills kicked in, and Karl was in his own little world. He was looking around, but it was questionable if he was seeing much of anything. Karl laid the seat back down. The pain pills were doing a number on him, and he was out like a light. Sarah flipped through the radio channels between listening to news talk radio and music. She dared not sing along, thinking that would surely wake Karl up.

For it being a three-day weekend, traffic on the freeway was moving along nicely. There were lots of cops out, and they seemed only to be going after the real speeders. Sarah watched her speed, knowing she would never hear the end of it from Karl if she got a speeding ticket.

Time went quickly as they approached the Midway Café. Sarah pulled into the parking lot, parked the car, and said, "Time for lunch, sleepyhead. Wake up."

Karl sat up and said, "We are here already?"

"Not at Ben's house. We are at our Midway Café. Time to have some lunch," Sarah said.

"I'm hungry," Karl said.

Sarah got the crutches out of the back seat and helped Karl out of the car. He was a bit wobbly and needed Sarah's help.

They went inside and were greeted.

"Say, I haven't seen you two in a while. Sit anywhere you like, and I will bring you some iced tea and a menu," the waitress said.

They sat down, and the iced tea and menu were delivered.

"What happened to your foot?" she asked.

"I got hurt playing softball," Karl said.

"That's too bad. Hope you get better soon," she said.

"Thanks," Karl replied.

They ordered their lunch. After they finished, Sarah helped Karl back into the car and drove over to fill the car's tank up with gas.

Before getting back on the freeway, Sarah checked the GPS. It indicated the arrival time at Ben's house. Sarah sent a text message to Ben: "We should be arriving around four-fifteen."

Ben sent a text back: "Andrew is cooking something up special and will not tell me what it is. Better bring your hunger with you. See you when you get here. Be safe."

Sarah got back on the freeway, and Karl turned into a real chatterbox. Sarah didn't want to tell him to be quiet, but she did turn the volume up on the radio. Karl must have gotten the message because he stopped talking and was listening to the music.

"Do you think you need another pain pill?" Sarah asked.

"I took one at lunch," Karl replied.

When they got to the neighborhood, Sarah drove by the old house. She wanted to see if anything had been done to it. The new owners had painted the outside of the house. They also had removed all of the old landscaping and had replaced it with an assortment of flowers and shrubs.

"They really made that house look nice," Sarah said to Karl.

"They sure did put some money into the place. They did keep the porch swing," Karl said.

Soon they were pulling up in front of Ben's house. Sarah was helping Karl out of the car. Ben was coming out of the house to greet them.

"What happened to Karl?" Ben asked.

"He got hurt playing softball Thursday night," Sarah said.

Sarah got the crutches out of the back seat and handed them to Karl, then opened the trunk to get the suitcase out.

"I'll take this. You make sure Karl can get up the steps and into the house okay. All we need is for him to fall and hurt himself more," Ben said.

They walked in, and Sarah said, "Something smells good."

"Hi, guys! Busy at the moment. Be in to visit in a few," Andrew said from the kitchen.

"Hi, Andrew," Sarah and Karl said.

"Sit down. Can I get you anything? Beer, wine, water, or iced tea?" Ben asked.

"I'll take a beer," Karl said.

"Karl, you're taking that pain medicine. No beer," Sarah said.

"I'll have water," Karl said.

Ben got two beers and a water. Just a few minutes later, Andrew came in and said, "How is everybody?"

Then he noticed Karl's bandaged-up foot.

"Oh, you poor thing! What happened to you?" Andrew asked.

"I got hurt playing softball Thursday night," Karl said.

"You must be more careful. Dinner will be ready in about an hour," Andrew said.

"Do you need some ice for your ankle?" Sarah asked Karl.

"That would be helpful. I think the car ride caused me to swell up some," Karl said.

"I will bring you some ice right away," Andrew said. He brought a bunch of ice wrapped in a towel.

"Will this do?" Andrew asked.

"Yes, that is perfect. Thank you, Andrew," Karl said.

"All of the legal matters in association with your folks have been completed, and I don't think there is anything more to be done," Ben told Sarah.

Sarah thanked Ben. They all talked about what was going on in their jobs. Sarah talked about the retirement of Mr. White and that Mrs. White was now the head of the company.

"I got an automatic promotion out of the deal," Sarah said.

"My new job is going well, and I really enjoy working there. I will be getting my own staff soon and some additional clients," Karl said.

Ben talked about a major court battle he had won.

It was dinnertime, and Andrew called everyone to come and eat. Talk about a formal affair—the table was set like one would see in a fancy food magazine. The plates and silverware were placed just so.

"Please, everyone, sit down," Andrew said.

The three of them sat down, and Andrew brought over the bowls and platters of food, set them on the table, and then sat down.

"I would like to say grace," Andrew said.

They all held hands around the table, and Andrew said a heart-felt grace that included a quick recovery for Karl's ankle. They passed the serving bowls and platters around and served themselves.

"I hope you all have saved some room for dessert?" Andrew asked as they were finishing eating.

"What a wonderfully delicious dinner. Can't eat another thing at the moment. Dessert later, okay?" they all said.

"Let me help you clean up the kitchen," Sarah said to Andrew.

"That's sweet of you to offer. You have to understand this is MY kitchen. Ben is not even allowed in here," Andrew said.

Ben, Sarah, and Karl went into the living room. Ben pulled out a board game, and they waited for Andrew to finish cleaning up the kitchen so he could join them. Soon they were all playing and having a good time. Andrew served up the dessert, and they continued playing until it was getting late.

"Andrew and I have some places we want to go to in the morning. You said you were going to visit your dad, so that works out best for all of us. Here is a key to the house in case you get back before we do," Ben said.

Sarah took the key, and she and Karl went off to bed.

*****

The next morning, Karl and Sarah got up, dressed, and walked to the kitchen.

"Good morning! Would you two like some breakfast?" Andrew, who was in *his* kitchen, asked.

"Just some coffee and toast," they said.

"Are you sure you don't want some eggs or pancakes or waffles? I have some cereal or maybe some oatmeal? I would be happy to cook for you," Andrew offered.

"Thanks, but no thanks. Where's Ben? Is he still sleeping?" Sarah asked.

"Oh, for heaven's sake, no. That man is up early every day. He said he was going out to run a quick errand and would be back soon," Andrew said.

It was only a few minutes later that Ben came bounding through the door carrying a knee scooter for Karl.

"I was going to get one of those things as soon as we got back home. Thanks, how much do I owe you?" Karl asked.

"It's a gift," Ben said.

"Thank you very much, Ben," Karl said.

"Give it a try," Ben said.

Karl put his knee to the cushion and pushed himself down the hall.

"I need to adjust it a bit to fit my body," Karl said.

A couple of quick adjustments, and Karl was off again.

"This is going to work out fine. I will need this to get around the office when I get back to work on Tuesday," Karl said.

"Yes, if you don't kill yourself first. Better stick with the crutches until we get home," Sarah said.

Ben and Andrew left the house. It was a little too early for Sarah and Karl to go to the care facility. They turned on the TV to get the latest news and weather reports. When it was time to go, they put the knee scooter in the trunk of the car so they would not forget it. Sarah

114

watched Karl go down the steps. She was ready in case he needed help. Karl did well and had been off the pain medicine since the one he took at lunchtime yesterday. Sarah opened the door, and Karl was able to get in without any help. Sarah put the crutches in the back seat and got in the car.

They drove to the care facility. Karl was able to get out of the car without any help. Sarah got the crutches out and handed them to Karl.

"Remember what the doctor said about putting any weight on that foot. I don't want to see you limping the rest of our life together," Sarah said.

They walked down the hall to the wing where her dad was living. Sarah tried the key code, but it didn't work.

"They must have changed the code since the last time we were here," Sarah said.

She rang the doorbell; the door buzzed, and she pushed the door open. She walked in and held it open while Karl made his way in.

"Hi, Sarah. Hi, Karl. Good to see you two. Karl, what happened to you?" Holly greeted them at the door.

"I got hurt playing softball the other night," Karl said.

"I hope it's not that bad," Holly said.

"Nothing broken, just a severe sprain," Karl said.

"Sarah, your dad is having a good day and is in good spirits. We didn't tell him that you were coming, so it should be a surprise. He is over there playing checkers," Holly said.

Sarah and Karl walked over to where her dad was playing. The two of them were arguing.

"It's your move," one said.

"No, it's your move," the other said.

Sarah placed her hand on her dad's shoulder. He looked up and said, "Sarah, what a pleasant surprise."

He stood up, and they hugged, and he gave Sarah a kiss on her cheek as he always did when he saw her.

"You remember Karl?" Sarah asked.

"Why, yes. Hi, Karl. What happened to your foot?" her dad asked.

"Hi, sir. I hurt my ankle playing softball," Karl said.

"This is my friend," her dad said, turning to the gentleman he was playing checkers with. There was a pause; her dad couldn't remember his name right away.

"My name is Robert. Your dad and I play checkers every day. He talks about you all the time. Pleased to finally meet you," the gentleman said.

"Let's go over here and sit down. I want to hear all about what you two have been doing," Sarah's dad said.

The three of them had a nice, long visit. Her dad asked the same questions several times and repeated a few of his stories. Sarah knew that was all part of dementia and could tell he was getting worse. He looked at the clock and said, "It's getting on to lunchtime. Can you two stay and have lunch with me?"

"I don't know," Sarah said.

"I was hoping you could stay to have lunch, and I took the liberty of ordering lunch for you two," Holly said, overhearing their conversation.

"Holly, you are so thoughtful," Sarah said, giving Holly a big hug. "Thank you so much."

"Lunch should be delivered shortly if you would like to come sit at this table," Holly said, leading the three of them to a table.

"I don't sit here. I sit over there. I have my meals at that table over there," Sarah's dad said.

"It's a special day. Sarah and Karl are going to eat lunch with you at this table," Holly said.

Her dad calmed down, and the trays of food were delivered. The food was good. Everyone had the same meal except those on a special diet. They finished eating, and the trays were collected. They felt they had been there long enough and saw that her dad was getting tired.

"He usually takes a nap shortly after his lunch," Holly said.

Sarah and Karl thanked Holly.

"Come visit whenever you can," Holly said.

They said their goodbyes and walked out.

"I'm happy to see they are taking such good care of my dad," Sarah said to Karl.

They got into the car and drove back to Ben's house. Ben and Andrew had returned and were just finishing up eating their lunch.

"Can I fix you guys some lunch?" Andrew asked.

"Thanks, we ate with my dad at the care facility," Sarah said.

"How did the visit go?" Ben asked.

"I can tell Dad's dementia is getting worse. He is in excellent health for his age. I don't know what is worse—having a good body and a bad head or having a good head and a bad body," Sarah said.

"Neither is good. Just let me die quickly when the time comes," Ben said.

"Not too soon. Besides, I get to go first. I don't want to be around after you go. I love you," Andrew said.

Everyone chuckled except Andrew, who said, "It's true."

Seeing Andrew's feelings were hurt, Ben said, "I love you too, Andrew."

"I have made reservations for dinner at six-forty-five. We have several hours to kill. Is there something you guys would like to do? There is a new movie house that just opened up here in town. It's one of those ones that has ten movie screens, an arcade room, a bowling alley, a mini golf course, and laser tag. The place is gigantic," Ben said.

"We haven't been to a movie in a long time," Karl said.

They all decided to go to the movies. They got there just before one of the movies was about to start. They heard it was a good one and purchased their tickets and went right in.

After the movie was over, they had a few minutes to walk around before needing to go back to Ben's house and get ready to go to dinner. They all took turns playing the same video game to see who could get the highest score, and that was Andrew.

It was time to head back to Ben's house and get ready for dinner.

Ben had made reservations at Ben and Andrew's favorite restaurant. It's a good thing that he did. For a Sunday night on a three-day weekend, the place was packed. Lots of people decided they wanted to eat out. Ben was well known in the city and had eaten at this restaurant many times. The owner saw Ben and came right on over to greet Ben and Andrew.

"These are my dear friends, Sarah and Karl," Ben said.

"Welcome to my restaurant," the owner said, showing them to their table. "Your server will be right with you."

"You always treat me and my guests so well. Thank you," Ben said.

"It's my pleasure. Enjoy your dinner," the owner said.

"Good evening, Mr. Ben and Mr. Andrew. Pleasure to see you again. I see you have brought along guests. May I get you anything from the bar?" the server asked.

"Nice to see you too, Trevor," Ben said.

They all ordered drinks, looked over the menus, and each picked what they wanted to eat. After dinner, Karl took the dinner bill and said, "This is on me. You have been so good to Sarah and me. Let me do this."

They got back to Ben's house. It was too early to go to bed.

"Ben, get out the board game we played last night. I want a rematch. Tonight, I'm going to be the winner," Karl said.

Ben got out the game, and the four of them played. Karl still did not win but had a good time. It was getting late, and they all went off to bed.

The next morning, Andrew was in the kitchen and was frying up some bacon. The kitchen was smelling so good.

"Andrew is at it again and insists that he make breakfast for all of us before your drive back home," Ben said.

Andrew had made biscuits from scratch, and they were just about to come out of the oven.

"Are scrambled eggs okay with everyone?" Andrew asked.

They all agreed that would be great.

After breakfast, Sarah packed up all of their things and was taking the suitcase to the front door.

"Let me take it to your car for you," Andrew said.

They all walked to the car. Karl got in, and Sarah put Karl's crutches in the back seat. She gave both Andrew and Ben a big hug and said, "Thanks for everything. We had a wonderful time. It's your turn to come our way for a visit."

They all said their goodbyes.

Sarah got in the car, and as she drove off, she said, "Next stop, Midway Café, a fill-up, and then on to home."

"Lead on, my dear," Karl said.

They arrived home early in the evening. When it became dinnertime, neither one of them felt like cooking, so they ordered some food to be delivered. They were sitting around relaxing when Sarah's cell phone rang. The caller ID said Jill.

"Hello, Jill," Sarah said.

"No, it's Jack. I'm using Jill's phone, it has all of her phone numbers in it. We just had our baby. Both Jill and the baby are doing great. Jill wanted me to call you and let you know. She said she would call you later with all of the details. Got to go, I have more calls to make," Jack said.

"Congratulations! Bye," Sarah said.

Sarah told Karl the news.

"I'm happy for them," Karl said.

"We should go see her tomorrow," Sarah said.

CHAPTER 24

The Surprise Birthday Party

Soon it would be Karl's birthday. Sarah wanted to give him a surprise birthday party and knew it would be hard to surprise him. Sarah came up with the idea of a morning party. The invitations read: "Come to the party wearing your pajamas, nightie, nightgown, or jammies—whatever you call what you sleep in. No underwear or naked bodies. Please bring breakfast potluck food instead of gifts. There will be a prize for the best-dressed person."

The invitations went out. The few people she talked to thought it was a fantastic idea.

The night before the party, Sarah fixed a late-night snack for her and Karl but put a sleeping pill in Karl's snack. They watched a late-night show, and the pill was starting to kick in.

"I'm getting really sleepy. I'm going to go to bed," Karl said.

They went to the bedroom, and Sarah said, "I have a little birthday something for you."

Karl slept in his underwear, and that wouldn't do for the party. She pulled out matching satin pajamas.

"See, they are matching," Sarah said.

"You know I don't sleep in pajamas," Karl said.

"Come on, Karl. I bought these special for your birthday. Please wear them, if just for this one night," Sarah said.

"Okay, for tonight," Karl said.

Karl put them on and crawled into bed. He was asleep almost as soon as his head hit the pillow.

The next morning, Sarah slid out of bed so as not to wake Karl. She went into the living room. Jack, Jill, and baby Jack had already arrived and had brought the decorations. Baby Jack was asleep in his car seat. The three of them decorated the house. Sarah had put a sign on the door: "Do not ring the doorbell or knock. Just come on in." They had just finished decorating when the guests started to arrive. They brought breakfast burritos, donuts, orange juice. One brought a pan of what must have been three dozen scrambled eggs, another brought a Crock-Pot full of oatmeal. There were homemade biscuits and gravy, another brought a platter of sausage links, sausage patties, bacon, and ham, and one guy even brought a box of cereal. A real potluck to pick from. Sarah had purchased a bunch of hot beverage cups, plates, bowls, and plasticware. She made several pots of coffee.

Karl thought he was hearing voices and was thinking he might still be asleep having a dream. No, he was hearing voices. Then he smelled the coffee and food. He looked over and saw that Sarah was not in bed. Karl walked into the living room, and all of the people started saying, "Surprise! Happy birthday."

One person started singing the Happy Birthday song, and everyone joined in.

"I need a cup of coffee," Karl said.

Everyone laughed.

A line was formed, and people began to serve themselves. Everyone was having a good time.

"Everyone, look around, and we will take a vote on who is the best dressed," Sarah said.

In the room was a lady with face cream smeared all over her face, wearing a bathrobe and bunny rabbit slippers. Everyone voted for her. As it turned out, it was Sarah's next-door neighbor. She saw all of the people going into Sarah's house wearing pajamas. Being a nosy neighbor, she wanted to know what was going on. Sarah gave her the prize—a potted flowering cactus plant. She stayed and had something to eat, thanked Sarah and everybody, and left with her new plant.

As people were leaving, they wished Karl a happy birthday and said to Sarah that it was a brilliant idea for a party. Karl seemed really surprised, and that made Sarah happy that she could pull it off.

It was now down to Sarah, Karl, Jack, Jill, and baby Jack. The girls started cleaning up what food was left. Sarah said, "Let's leave the decorations up. I'll take them down tomorrow."

The guys were on the other side of the room talking sports. Jill handed baby Jack to Sarah for her to hold. Sarah asked Jill, "Are you planning on having more?"

Jill said, "I would like to have another. Jack wants to have two more. I told him he wasn't the one baking them, and we'll take it one baby at a time."

Sarah said, "I guess that's where the expression 'got one in the oven' came from."

They both chuckled.

Sarah, looking at baby Jack, said, "You two sure made a beautiful baby."

Jill then asked Sarah, "When are you two going to get married? If you're planning on having kids, you better get started. You're not getting any younger, you know."

Sarah said, "We've been talking about it."

Jill gave Sarah a big smile.

Karl said, "That was some surprise birthday party. You really did surprise me. Thank you so much."

Sarah just smiled, picked up a big bow, held it up against her, and said to Karl, "Hey, birthday boy."

Karl walked over to Sarah, picked her up, and said, "I think I'll unwrap this birthday gift in the bedroom."

Off Karl went down the hall, carrying Sarah in his arms.

CHAPTER 25

Their Wedding

Several of Sarah and Karl's friends had asked, "When are you two going to get married?"

Karl and Sarah had talked about it, but it was just talk—well, until now.

Sarah said, "We've been together for over a year now. Do you think we should be getting married?"

Karl said, "I know we've talked about this before, and I felt that you didn't want to ever get married again. The pain you suffered after losing your husband was so much, and you didn't want to go through that again. I love you and would very much like for us to be husband and wife."

Sarah said, "I did feel that way for a while, but not anymore. I love you too and want to be your wife and live our lives together forever."

They held each other and kissed.

Sarah said, "I had a big wedding when I married my husband. I don't really care to have another one like that. You've never been married, and I don't want to rob you of that experience if that's something you wanted."

Karl said, "I would just as soon have a small wedding here at our house or we could go to the courthouse and get married there."

Sarah said, "If we were to get married at the courthouse, a bunch of our friends would never speak to us again."

He said, "Probably so. Look at how many have said, 'Invite me to your wedding.'"

She said, "I guess we better work up a guest list." Sarah said, "Karl, you've never talked about your family."

Karl said, "I know. Not that I don't want to talk about it. It's just that there's not much to talk about. I was adopted as a baby. I never knew my real parents and didn't ever pursue trying to find out who they might be. My adopted parents had two kids prior to adopting me, a boy and a girl. They are thirteen and fifteen years older than me. Growing up, probably because of the age difference, they didn't have too much to do with me.

"My folks were very supportive of me. They encouraged me to join the Boy Scouts, and I worked my way up to Eagle Scout. They went to most of my high school baseball games. I got a baseball scholarship to college and worked to help pay for it. The folks paid as much as they could afford, but that wasn't much. I had taken a bookkeeping class in high school and fell in love with accounting. That was my major in college. I did play baseball on the college team, but I was never good enough to be picked up by any pro team. That didn't matter; accounting was my passion.

"That's where I met George. We were in most of our classes together. George didn't play any sports. His love was women. In my junior year of college, my folks were killed in a small airplane crash while touring in Alaska on what they thought was a dream trip of a lifetime. They had worked hard and saved up a long time for that trip.

"They had a will, and the estate was split evenly among the three of us kids. I used my money to pay for the rest of my college tuition, books, and student loan. There was a little left to get me started after graduation. That's when I applied for a job with the company where we are both now working. After the estate settlement, I never saw my brother or sister again. I tried to stay in touch with them, but they didn't seem to want to stay in touch with me. I don't even know where they might be living."

Sarah said, "That's a sad story. I'm sorry."

Karl said, "That's all right. It was a long time ago. What do you say we work on that guest list?"

Sarah and Karl made a list of people they would like to invite to their wedding, in keeping with the small wedding they both wanted. They were satisfied that they had the guest list they wanted.

Sarah said, "Now that's been taken care of, we need to pick when."

They pulled out a calendar and started to look at the functions, activities, and commitments they had. They finally picked a date, and invitations were sent out.

Sarah made arrangements to have the wedding catered and ordered a few flowers. Andrew was a little upset that Sarah was having it catered when he could have done it himself. He got over it after thinking out the details of how he would do it. She had asked Jill to be her matron of honor, and Karl asked George to be the best man.

The day of the wedding, Jill and Jack came over to the house to help decorate. Sarah bought a new dress, and Karl bought a new suit for the occasion. As planned, the wedding was small. Sarah and Karl had custom matching wedding bands made. After the wedding ceremony was over, they ate, drank, and visited with the guests. Just about all had gone home except Jack and Jill, George and his wife, and Ben and Andrew. They all talked about how each couple had met. Sarah and Karl said, "We love the close friendships we have with you."

George and Andrew spent the night and went home the next day.

CHAPTER 26

The Honeymoon

Ever since they checked out the camping gear in Sarah's backyard, they talked about going camping but never did. The week after the wedding, neither could get that week off. For now, they planned a camping trip for their honeymoon. For their one-year anniversary, they would go on a cruise or to one of those fancy island resorts when they could get more time off together. They finally arranged to have the same week off together. Karl had researched places to camp and had picked a place not too far from home. The campground was located beside a lake. They both loved the water.

The car was loaded with everything they thought they would need. After checking in at the campground office, they went to their assigned campsite. They picked a place to pitch the tent. Since they had pitched the tent before, they had it up and ready to occupy in a short period of time. The air mattress was inflated, and the sleeping bags were unrolled. Karl got the little BBQ out of the car along with the camp stove, cooler chest, and lounge chairs. Earlier in the week, Sarah had prepared meals, vacuum-packed and froze them, figuring it would make meals a lot easier. After all, she was on her honeymoon.

Karl said, "I'm going up to the campground store and recreation center to check it out. Do you want to come along?"

Sarah said, "I'd like to just sit in this lounge chair, relax, and read this book I brought. Take your time. I'll be here when you get back."

Karl walked up to the camp store. He went into the men's room. It was very clean and had nice showers. He found the recreation hall. Inside, there was a small room with two pool tables and a couple of video games. The hall itself was big. It had lots of tables. A person in the hall asked Karl, "You coming to Bingo tonight? We just finished setting the hall up for Bingo and card night. After Bingo is finished, there will be a lot of people playing all sorts of card games. You should come and join us."

Karl said, "I'll check with my wife and see if she would like to play."

Karl went into the camp store. It had an assortment of camping supplies and a small variety of food items. The lady asked, "Are you looking for something in particular?"

Karl said, "No, just looking. Wanted to see what all you have."

"Well, if you need any help, I'm here."

Karl said, "Is there a place you can recommend to eat close by here?"

The store clerk said, "The restaurant over at the marina is one of the best places to eat in this county."

Karl said, "Good to know, thanks," and walked out of the store.

The campground was divided. On the smaller side was the tenting area, and on the other side was where the RVs were parked. There was a mix of trailers and motorhomes, big and small. Karl walked over to one of the big rigs. There was a guy sitting outside of his motorhome bus.

Karl said, "Hi there."

The guy said, "Hi."

Karl said, "My name is Karl, that is some rig you have."

The guy said, "If you have a moment, come sit a spell. You want a beer?"

Karl said, "How nice of you to offer. Yes, I'll have a beer."

The guy handed Karl a beer and said, "My name is Bud. Are you from around here?"

Karl said, "No, I'm here with my wife, and we live about an hour and a half away from here. We're tent camping on the other side of the campground."

Bud said, "My wife and I started out tent camping. That was a long time ago. We stepped up to a trailer and then to our first motorhome. This one here is our third one."

Karl asked Bud, "Do you get to camp much with this thing?"

Bud said, "My wife and I are both retired, and we get out as much as we can. I would like to sell the house, live in just the motorhome, and travel all the time. The wife wants a place to call home and the kids and grandkids living near us."

Karl said, "If you don't mind, how much does something like this cost?"

Bud said, "We got a real deal on this. We bought it used. The couple only had it out a couple of times before her husband had a heart attack and died. You don't want to buy one of these things new. Their value drops like a stone in water as soon as you drive it off the RV dealership's lot. We got this baby for $325,000."

Karl thought to himself, *That's more than the house he and Sarah are living in.*

Bud said, "You want the tour?"

Karl said, "Sure."

Bud opened the door and said to his wife, "We have company, okay if we come in?"

She said, "Sure, come on in."

Bud said to Karl, "Step on up and in."

Karl climbed up the stairs and stepped into the motorhome. Bud said, "Karl, take a seat in the driver's seat."

Karl sat down. It was like sitting in a living room recliner. Bud said, "The driver's seat has air ride shocks, and the bus has airbag suspension. You just float down the road. Never feel a bump while driving, even on a bumpy road. Come on, I'll show you the rest of the place.

"This bus has three slide-outs. Gives you more than twice the space of if you didn't have the slides."

Karl saw the size of the living area. It had a big-screen TV and another TV in the bedroom. The kitchen had everything a real house kitchen had—a big refrigerator and freezer, microwave/convection oven, and a three-burner stovetop. Lots of granite countertops and a nice dining table. The bathroom was small but very functional, with a shower almost big enough for two. The bedroom had a queen-size bed and lots of closet space.

Karl said, "What a place you have here, Bud. Thanks for the tour and the beer. I better get back before my wife starts to wonder if I got lost."

Karl returned to their tent site. Sarah was sipping on a glass of wine and reading her book. Karl thought she probably didn't even miss him. Sarah looked up from reading and put her book aside. She said, "Did you enjoy your fact-finding mission?"

Karl told her about the rec hall and that they were going to have bingo later tonight, followed by card games. He said, "The bathroom shower house is very clean. I got a tour of one of those big motor-homes. It sure was decked out. The lady in the camp store highly recommended the restaurant over at the marina. She said it's the best place to eat in the county. I'd like to try it out come dinner time."

Sarah said, "Okay, for tonight, but I packed a lot of food to eat while we're here camping."

Karl refilled Sarah's glass with more wine, grabbed a beer out of the cooler chest, and sat down on the lounge chair.

Come dinnertime, the two of them walked to the marina restaurant. Karl gave their name to the hostess. They were told it would be a forty-five-minute wait.

Karl said to Sarah, "Let's see what they have over at the marina."

They had Jet Skis, paddle boats, kayaks, fishing boats, and all kinds of floats that one could rent. The guy said, "Is there something I can help you with?"

Karl said, "Yes, we're looking at the Jet Skis."

The guy said, "They go quickly on the weekend. I have a pair I can rent to you in the morning for just a half day. All of the others have already been reserved. The only reason I have these two available is the people called and canceled about ten minutes ago."

Karl said, "We'd like to reserve them."

They filled out the paperwork and paid the deposit. They arrived back at the restaurant just as their name was called.

They ate dinner, and it was every bit as good as the camp store lady said it would be. Walking back to camp, Karl asked Sarah, "Do you want to go up to the rec hall and play bingo and maybe some cards?"

Sarah said, "I'd rather prefer that you build a campfire, and let's watch the stars come out."

Karl built the fire, and they relaxed, looking up at the stars until it was time to go to bed. They got ready for bed and kissed each other good night. One thing led to another, and they ended up having sex. After all, they were on their honeymoon.

*****

The next morning, they put their swimsuits on and hurried over to the marina. There was a coffee bar next to the rental place, and they figured they could get a cup of coffee and something quick to eat. The guy at the rental place gave them life jackets to wear and said, "You must wear them at all times."

He gave them instructions on how to start and ride the Jet Skis, and Karl and Sarah were off.

They putt-putted around in the marina area to get the hang of riding them and then headed out to open water. The lake was huge, and not a lot of people were out on the lake this morning, just a few fishermen and a couple of water skiers. They found an empty spot, and Sarah said, "I'll race you to that place over there," pointing to a big tree on shore.

Karl said, "You're on," and off they went. Karl beat Sarah, but not by much.

Sarah said, "I want a rematch."

Karl pointed to a spot and said, "Okay, to there."

Sarah got a bit of a head start. Karl was quick to catch up. This time Sarah won, but just barely.

Sarah said, "Tied, you won one, and I won one. Now let's go for the best two out of three races."

Just as they were ready to start the third race, the lake's safety patrol boat pulled up and said, "Sorry, folks, there is no racing allowed on this lake. This is the only warning we give. If we see you racing again, you will be given a ticket, a $150 fine."

Karl said, "We're sorry, we didn't know. Thanks for the warning."

They decided to go ride down to the dam where the power plant was located. The dam was constructed to create the lake for recreation, flood control, and to provide water for the surrounding area. The dam was not built as a hydroelectric dam. That's why the power plant was built. The power plant pumped water from the lake, heating it to create steam to drive the turbines. It was a closed system. After the steam passes through the turbines, it was returned to the lake and not released into the air. The place where the water returns was nice and warm, but it was in a no-swimming area. It was about time to return the Jet Skis, so it was back to the marina.

Once back at the marina, Sarah and Karl talked about renting a fishing boat. Sarah said, "The last time I went fishing was when I was a little girl and went fishing with my dad."

They checked with the guy at the marina about renting a fishing boat.

The guy said, "There is a fishing package deal that includes the boat, life jackets, rods, reels, lures, some live bait, a map of the lake, a foldout guide to identify the fish with size and number of the fish you can catch. Also included are two two-day temporary fishing licenses. However, it does not guarantee that you will catch anything."

With that, they all laughed.

Karl said, "I bet you say that line a lot. That is an all-inclusive package. When would one be available?"

They were told tomorrow morning.

Karl turned to Sarah and said, "You want to go fishing?"

Sarah said, "Yes, but if we do catch any, I would like to release them."

Karl said, "That is if we catch any. Besides, I didn't want to clean them."

The guy said, "If you do decide to keep what you catch, the marina restaurant will clean and cook them for you."

They signed up for the boat and paid the deposit.

Walking back to camp, Karl asked Sarah, "What do you want to do for the rest of the day?"

She said, "Mostly relax. It has been forever since the last time I had a real vacation. I want to relax as much as I can. Let's go swimming later this afternoon."

Karl said, "I like the way you think."

Later, they did go swimming, but not before Sarah put on a thick layer of sunscreen. With her fair skin, she easily sunburns. Karl was happy to put a bunch on her back—and all over, as a matter of fact. The water was nice and warm. They did a little swimming, but mostly just stood in the water.

Come dinnertime, Karl filled the little BBQ with charcoal. Steaks on the grill for dinner. After they ate, Karl dumped the charcoal into the fire pit and added some firewood. In no time, they had a nice cozy fire going. Karl and Sarah sat in their lounge chairs. The sun had not fully gone down yet. Sarah read her book with a little additional light from the lantern. Karl had access to the campground's free Wi-Fi and logged on to the internet. He watched a movie on his laptop that he knew Sarah would not like or want to watch. When it got dark, they just sat and watched the stars come out by the warmth of the fire.

The weekend was over, and the weekenders had all left. It was time to get the fishing boat and go fishing. The guy took Sarah and Karl to the boat and gave them a quick safety rundown. He said all of the gear was in the boat. He handed them the map of the lake and said, "On the map, I marked the likely places you'll catch fish. You must wear the life jackets at all times. Be safe and have fun. I hope you catch some fish."

Karl started the boat's motor and drove the boat out of the marina. Sarah had the map and was giving Karl directions to one of the places the guy had marked. Karl stopped the boat, and they got the rods out and picked the fishing lure they thought would catch the fish.

Sarah said, "Let's make this interesting."

Karl said, "A little competition, why am I not surprised?"

She said, "First one to catch a fish, the biggest fish, and the most fish caught."

Karl said, "Okay, you're on."

After about a half-hour and several lure changes, Karl caught a fish. It was a sunfish, all of about two and a half to three inches long.

Sarah said, "You call that a fish? It looks more like bait."

Karl said as he unhooked the little guy and put it back in the water, "It's still the first one caught, and right now, it's the most caught AND the biggest one TOO."

Of course, this made Sarah's blood come to a boil, and she said, "The day's not over yet."

They moved to some of the other spots marked on the map and fished until it was time to return the boat. Sarah said, "You may have caught the first one, if you can even call that little thing a fish, and you did catch the most, but I caught the biggest one, and that one, I bet, weighed as much as all of yours combined."

Karl said, "You sure are a competitor."

They returned the boat and walked back to camp.

Karl said, "Let's go play some pool."

Sarah said, "That sounds like fun."

They went to the rec hall. No one was playing pool. It was a coin-operated pool table. Karl put the fifty cents in, and out came the balls. He racked them up and said to Sarah, "Go ahead and break."

Sarah drew back the cue stick and struck the cue ball. The balls scattered around the table, but none fell into any of the pockets. It was Karl's turn. He missed his shot. It looked like it was going to be a long game. They both were lousy pool players.

As they were playing, Karl said, "How about we go home tomorrow?"

Sarah said, "I was just thinking the same thing."

The next morning, they packed up the car and drove home. When they got home, they unpacked the car and put everything away.

Karl said, "I'm going to mow the lawn."

Sarah said, "Okay. I'm going to do some laundry and clean the house while you're out here working."

Sarah fixed dinner with some of the food she had prepared for the camping trip that had not been eaten. The rest of the evening, they relaxed—Karl in his favorite chair and Sarah on the couch. Sarah read more of her book, and Karl watched some shows on the TV until it was time to go to bed.

They got into bed. Sarah snuggled up next to Karl and said, "Tomorrow, I'm going to get my driver's license changed to my new married name. What do you think you'll do?"

Karl said, "I need to get my car inspected and pay the registration fee for the next year. I also need to get the oil changed."

Sarah said, "I'd like for us to go to the bank and open joint bank accounts."

Karl said, "I think that's a good idea. Now that we're married, do you want any kids?"

Sarah began to cry. She said, "When I was married before, my husband and I wanted kids. I got pregnant, and six weeks later, I had a miscarriage. I was devastated. I even went into grief counseling. On my follow-up visit to the doctor, he said that my body was healthy, and there was no permanent damage and that miscarriages just sometimes happen. I tried to get pregnant again but was terrified that I might have another miscarriage. I really didn't want to go through that again. The other day, when I held baby Jack in my arms, I thought how nice it would be to have a baby of my own. Karl, I love you and want us to have a baby. I want to have your baby."

Karl held Sarah tight in his arms and said, "I love you with all of my heart and soul. Let's stop practicing and start making."

Sarah said, "That sounds good, but not tonight. Sorry, but I'm really tired and would not enjoy it. Let's start trying tomorrow night or, better yet, in the morning."

Soon Sarah fell asleep in Karl's arms. He kissed her on the forehead and fell asleep.

CHAPTER 27

Pregnant?

Sarah had just gotten to work and sat down at her desk when her cell phone rang. It was Jill.

Sarah said, "Good morning, Jill. How are you?"

Jill said, "I have some news for you. I'm pregnant again."

Sarah said, "Me too."

Jill said, "Are you kidding me? We must have gotten pregnant at the same time. Hey, do you remember you and Karl came over and we played cards? Jack and I had sex after you two left."

Sarah said, "I remember. When we got home, Karl and I did the same thing."

Jill said, "I have a doctor's appointment tomorrow at two at the Baby Doctors' office."

Sarah said, "That's the place my Dr. Ford has his practice, and my appointment is at two also."

Jill said, "Come on, Sarah, that's just too weird. I guess I'll see you there. Got to get some work done. Got to go. Bye."

Sarah said, "See you tomorrow. Bye."

It was a few minutes later when Ms. White buzzed Sarah on the intercom and said, "Sarah, can you come into my office?"

Sarah grabbed her iPad and said, "On my way."

Ms. White, looking at the calendar, said, "I see you have an appointment at two o'clock tomorrow with Dr. Ford. Is he an

OB-GYN doctor? Are you having female problems? I know it's not my place to ask, but I am concerned."

Sarah said, "I took a home pregnancy test, and I'm pregnant. I have my first prenatal appointment with him."

Ms. White said, "That's wonderful news! What are your long-term plans? Are you planning to be a stay-at-home mother?"

Sarah said, "Oh no. I love my job and love working for you. I was hoping that after I have my baby and maternity leave is over, I could come back and continue working for you."

Ms. White said, "Sarah, of course, you'll have a job here working for me. You have been the best administrative assistant I've ever had. You, with that iPad of yours, have provided me with the information I have needed to make very important business decisions. You are my right-hand person, and you seem to know what I'm thinking and have what I need before I even ask for it. You have a review and raise coming up next month. I will make sure there is a little extra in there for your baby."

Sarah said, "Thanks for your kind words, Ms. White. I have never worked for anyone like you. I better get back to work. I want to review my notes and check to see if I have everything covered in that report you're wanting. I just need to proofread it one more time and print it out. It should not take more than fifteen to twenty minutes."

Sarah finished the report and gave it to Ms. White. She read it and said, "This is excellent work. Thank you, Sarah."

*****

That night, Sarah told Karl that Jill was pregnant again and had the same appointment time as she did at the Baby Doctors' place. Sarah also told Karl what Ms. White said.

Karl said, "Ms. White does like you."

When Sarah got to the Baby Doctors' office—she loved what they named the place—Jill was already in the waiting room. Sarah walked up to the receptionist and said, "My name is Sarah, and I have an appointment with Dr. Ford at two."

The receptionist said, "I will let Dr. Ford's nurse know you are here. Please take a seat."

Sarah sat down in the chair next to Jill and said, "Good afternoon. How have you been?"

Jill said, "This pregnancy is a piece of cake compared to the first one. How about you?"

Sarah asked, "How long does this morning sickness go on?"

Jill said, "Not long."

Jill's doctor's nurse called Jill's name, and Jill followed the nurse. A moment later, Sarah's name was called. She followed the nurse down the hallway. They stopped at the scale, and the nurse said, "Step on the scale, and let's get your weight."

The nurse pointed and said, "Go ahead into that room."

The nurse took Sarah's temperature and blood pressure and said, "Temperature is normal, and your BP looks good. Take all of your clothes off and put this gown on. I will be back in with Dr. Ford in a few minutes."

Sarah took off all of her clothes, put the paper gown on, and sat on the exam table. There was a knock on the door, and in came Dr. Ford, followed by the nurse. Dr. Ford said, "Let's take a look at you."

The doctor listened to Sarah's heart and lungs and said, "Everything sounds good. I'm going to examine your breasts."

The doctor checked Sarah's breasts for any abnormalities and found none. Dr. Ford said, "Lie down and slide down to the end of the table for me."

Sarah did as the doctor requested. This was not the first time she had had a pelvic examination. She did regular checkups and knew what to expect. The doctor performed the examination and said, "You look very healthy, and I see no problems. I saw on your chart that you had a miscarriage. I don't think you will have any problems this time around. It appears you are about eight weeks along. I want you to take vitamins and supplements and follow the instructions I have on this paper. It's important that you not drink alcoholic beverages and that you drink plenty of water during your pregnancy. I see that you are not a smoker, which is good. Do you have any questions for me?"

Sarah said, "No. When do you want to see me again?"

The doctor said, "The nurse will let the receptionist know, and she can schedule you an appointment."

Sarah said, "Thank you," and got dressed.

Jill had finished before Sarah. Sarah asked Jill, "When is your next appointment?"

Jill said, "I was waiting for you to see when yours was going to be."

They both went up to the receptionist and made appointments for the same day and time.

*****

That night, Sarah told Karl, "The doctor said I looked healthy down there and I should not have to worry about having another miscarriage."

Karl said, "That's great news." He continued, "I've been thinking, with the baby coming, this house is just too small for us. Now that I'm on bonus and making more money, and you are making very good money, and Ms. White said you are going to get a raise next month, I think we should look for a new place to live."

Sarah said, "I do love this little place, but you are right. It will be too small for us after the baby is born. It's time to get a new place to live."

CHAPTER 28

House Hunting

Karl told Sarah, "George said he read about a new subdivision development just outside of town. Some rancher has set aside some of his ranch for this subdivision development. I would like to take a look at it this Saturday."

Sarah said, "Okay, it's a date."

Saturday midmorning, they drove out to the new subdivision. It was called Pony Express Estates. It had a beautiful entrance. All the streets were paved, complete with streetlights and Western street names.

Karl said, "I like what I see already."

Sarah said, "It sure is impressive. Do you think we can afford anything in here?"

Karl said, "We won't know until we look. I didn't see any price signs as we came in."

Karl followed the signs to the office and parked in front of a temporary building with a big welcome sign. Inside, they were met with a big smile and a guy saying, "Hello, folks. My name is Ted. I'm the builder and head salesperson here at Pony Express Estates. Over there is Billy. She is my home decorator and my assistant."

Karl said, "My name is Karl, and this is my wife, Sarah."

Ted said, "Sit yourselves right down. Can I get you all something to drink? We have coffee, water, sodas, iced tea, and I think there is some juice in there too."

139

Karl and Sarah said, "No, but thanks anyway, we are fine for now."

Ted asked, "What do you folks have in mind?"

Karl explained that they were living in a small house in town. They were expecting a baby and wanted a bigger place to live. Ted told them how this place came about. He said how the rancher had 5,000 acres of land and wanted to subdivide about 200 acres into single residency homes on two- and three-acre lots. He wanted the houses to be no smaller than a certain number of square feet. They worked together to get the subdivision zoned and put in the streets and utilities. All of the lots had water, electricity, sewer, natural gas, and cable TV. There were several homes where people were already living, some under construction, and some waiting to be built. "After you pick your lot, you can bring me your house plans, or you can pick from the plans I have. It takes about a year from start to finish to have a house built."

Karl said, "That long?"

Ted said, "And that's if we don't have a bunch of weather and material delays. I do have something you two might be interested in. We had a couple, the Jordans. We started building their house, and they had to default on their contract. I won't go into the details of what happened. The construction on that house has been halted. Billy, could you pull the Jordans' file for me?"

Billy handed the file to Ted. Ted pulled out the plans of the house and unfolded them on the table. He said, "The house foundation is finished, and it is already framed. You can't make any structural changes. The Jordans had worked with Billy to pick the brick and stone for the outside, as well as all of the lighting fixtures, ceiling fans, carpet, laminate, and tile. All of the countertops, kitchen cabinets, stove/oven, microwave, dishwasher, and the like. None of this has been ordered or purchased before the contract default. You can work with Billy to change any and all of those choices. The plans call for a workshop and a barn with four horse stalls. It has not been started yet. There are riding trails on the rancher's land that you can ride on if you do get some horses. If you don't want the workshop/barn, the cost will be deducted from the contract.

"If you are interested in this place, this is how this deal would work. You would take over the contract. One big advantage is all that you see has already been paid for. You would be paying from this point forward. That's going to be a big savings to you right away— better than half the cost of the home. The Jordans' loss would be your gain. On all of the items for the house that were chosen by them, you can change it to your liking. If what you choose is more or less than the contract, the amount will be adjusted. Just work with Billy. Do you have any questions so far?"

Karl said, "I'm sure we do. That is a lot to process."

Ted said, "Let me take you down to the place and show you what has been done so far. You can take a look around. Then if you like what you see, you can come back to go through this file, and we can talk some more. Now I don't want you to think that I'm trying to pressure you into this deal. You can pick any unsold lot and have the house you choose to be built. This just came up earlier this week, and I felt it could be a good match for you two folks."

They all got on Ted's golf cart, and he drove off. Ted said, "This is just phase 1. After it's 90 percent completed, we will start phase 2. As I said, all of the utilities are in, including natural gas lines. The Jordans contracted for gas for the stove/oven, hot water heater, fireplace, and house heating system. All of the gas lines have been put in place there in the house. If you choose to go all electric, we will just cap off the gas lines and not connect the house gas line to the main line. This house is on a three-acre lot. As you can see, there are a lot of old, mature trees. We try to save as many trees as we can when we build.

"Go ahead and walk around. I have a couple of phone calls I need to make. Take your time, and when you are ready, I will give you a ride back to the office."

Sarah and Karl got out of the golf cart and walked up to what looked like the front door to the house. The walkway had not been done and probably was one of the last things to be done. They walked through each room, imagining what the rooms would look like when finished. The kitchen was of nice size and had an island with a place for a sink. There was a separate laundry room. The house had a total of five bedrooms. Each of the four bedrooms had a nice-sized closet, plus the master bedroom had a sizable walk-in closet. The master bathroom, from the looks of the plumbing, had both a tub and a large shower stall and a double-sink vanity. There were three other bathrooms. There were lots of windows throughout the house. Sarah liked that because she loved a house full of sunshine. Off the back of the house, the roofline extended to form a built-in covered patio.

Karl said, "This would be a nice place to entertain and have BBQs."

Later, if we wanted to enclose it, it would be a simple thing to do. The house was nicely located on the three acres, surrounded by lots of old shade trees."

Sarah said, "I like this layout, and we can pick the flooring, cabinetry, countertops, the color schemes, and just about everything to our liking."

Karl said, "We can even pick the outside brick and stone colors. What do you say? You like it enough to take it to the next level?"

Sarah said, "Yes, let's go and talk to Ted some more. Having so much paid for already, it has to be too good to pass up."

They walked back to where Ted had parked the golf cart. Ted was still talking on the phone, so Sarah and Karl took a little walk down the street to see what else was down there. Ted finished his phone call and drove down to pick Sarah and Karl up.

Ted said, "What do you guys think so far?"

Karl said, "We think we would like to talk to you more."

Ted drove the long way back to the office, showing Karl and Sarah some of the completed houses where people had already moved in. Ted said, "All of the houses I build in this subdivision have solar panels. They are included in the building cost."

Karl said, "I noticed that and was wondering if they were an add-on option."

Ted said, "No, included. The Jordans chose to have a balanced power home using gas and electric. During the hot summers we have, the solar will cut that air conditioning cost way back, and you can't beat gas to heat a house in the winter."

Sarah said, "I like cooking on a gas stove."

Ted said, "There you go."

They returned to the office, and Ted said, "If you two are really interested in the Jordans' house, I know you will want to talk it over, but I will need to know your answer soon. If you give me a check for $1,000, I will hold the house for you until the end of the week. That way, no others could buy the house between now and then."

Karl looked at Sarah, and she gave him a nod of her head. Karl wrote the check and handed it to Ted.

Ted said, "Take the details of the contract and the financing. Here is my card. Just give me a call if you decide you want the deal. We will set up another meeting and get the papers signed and things rolling. It's been a pleasure meeting you two. Looking forward to doing business with you."

They said thank you and left.

As they were driving home, Sarah said, "I'm going to call Ben and see if he could pass the contract information by his real estate attorney."

Karl said, "That's an excellent idea."

She called Ben as they were driving home. Ben answered his cell phone and said, "What a pleasant surprise."

Sarah said, "I have some news to tell you and a question to ask."

Ben said, "Okay, let's hear it."

Sarah said, "I'm pregnant. We are expecting a baby. I'm eight weeks along."

Ben said, "That's wonderful news!" Sarah could hear Ben shouting to Andrew, "Sarah and Karl are going to have a baby!"

Sarah said, "Ben, we just looked at a house. It's under construction."

Sarah went on to explain the details of the house and the contract. She said, "I will write up the details and email them to you along with a copy of the current contract. Could you pass it by one of your real estate attorneys to see what they think of the deal?"

Ben said, "Sure, but I will have to charge you a fee for this one. It will be around $200 for the services."

Sarah said, "That could be a cheap price to pay if it's a bad deal. They are holding the deal for us until the end of the week, so there is a bit of urgency."

Ben said, "I will make sure my guy reviews it first thing Monday morning and give you a call when he is finished."

Sarah said, "Great, I will type it up and email it to you today."

They said their goodbyes.

As soon as they got home, Sarah typed the details in a letter, scanned the contract, and sent it to Ben.

*****

The rest of the weekend, Karl and Sarah talked about the house deal and dreamed about how things would be living there.

Karl said, "I like the idea of having a barn out back. I could have a nice space for a workshop, and you could have that craft room you have always wanted. Also, there would be plenty of room to store all that other stuff we have in the garage now. The new house is built with a three-car garage. We could park the cars inside. I don't think I want any horses, do you?"

Sarah said, "Not right off. Maybe after the kid gets older."

*****

Midday Monday, Ben called Sarah and said, "My real estate attorney looked over the letter and the contract. He said it was a fantastic deal, and if you didn't take it, he would. Sorry I don't have more time to talk to you now. I have to go."

Sarah said, "That's great news. Tell your real estate attorney thanks, and don't forget to invoice me. Thanks, goodbye. Talk to you later."

Sarah then sent a text message to Karl. "Good news. Ben said the deal looks good. Give Ted a call and set up a meeting."

Karl sent a message back: "Okay, on it."

He called Ted, and a meeting was set up for that evening.

Ted said, "I was planning on working late tonight. Come on over whenever you can. Just let me know when you are on your way."

*****

On their way over, Sarah and Karl stopped by a fast-food place and had a quick bite to eat. Ted was in the office.

Ted said, "So what have you two decided on?"

Karl said, "We want to take over the contract."

Ted said, "I will give David at the bank a call in the morning and fill him in on the fact that you guys want to take over the Jordans' contract. He will call you and set up an appointment for you to fill out the loan application papers and explain how a construction loan works and how that flows into the mortgage loan."

Karl said, "That sounds great."

Ted pulled out some paperwork for them to sign to lock in the house deal.

Ted said, "I normally ask for some up-front money, but that would be if you were starting from scratch. Since you are taking the contract over, I have already collected some of the construction money. Before the next phase of construction begins, a payment will need to be made. David will tell you when the next construction payment needs to be made, and it will come out of your bank loan."

*****

The next day, the banker David called Karl, and the appointment was made. Sarah and Karl went to the bank. It just so happened that it was the same bank where they had their accounts. David gave them the loan application papers. While they were filling out the loan papers, David did a credit check on both Sarah and Karl. Each month, Sarah and Karl paid off their credit cards in full. Both cars were paid for. The only debt they had was the mortgage on their house, and it was just about paid off. They listed their employment information and how much they were making and the bank account numbers. When they were finished, they handed the paperwork back to David.

David said, "This is very impressive."

Karl asked, "Since I have been only working at the firm for a short period of time, will that cause any problems in getting the loan?"

David said, "I don't think so. Your prior job history shows that you are a sound employee. Besides, that change you made gave you a sizable salary increase. You should have no problem qualifying for the loan. I already did a credit check on both of you, and you both are above 800."

David went on to explain, "The loan application would be sent to the bank's loan approval board. They will review all of the paperwork and let me know their decision. As soon as I know, I will call and let you know."

Sarah asked, "How long will that take?"

David said, "They meet again tomorrow morning, and I will see to it that your loan is reviewed then. I should be able to let you know in the afternoon. With what I have seen on your paperwork, I see no reason that you will not be approved, but it's not up to me—I'm not on the review board."

They thanked David and left.

That afternoon, David called Karl and said, "Congratulations! You've been approved. I will call Ted and let him know."

Karl said, "That's good news, and thank you."

Karl made a quick call to Sarah and said, "We are on the way to getting a new home."

Sarah said, "I can't tell you how happy I am right now."

CHAPTER 29

Baby Checkups and New House Progress

It was time for Jill's and Sarah's next prenatal checkups. During their examination, a baby monitor was hooked up, and Sarah could hear her baby's heartbeat. The doctor said, "On your next visit, we will do the sonogram, and if you want to know the sex of your baby, I can tell you then."

Sarah and Jill met back in the waiting room, and they both went up to the receptionist to make their next appointment.

The receptionist said, "Are you somehow related?"

Sarah said, "Not by blood, but we are sisters in spirit. We have a special connection to one another."

The receptionist set up matching day and time appointments for the two of them.

Jill asked Sarah, "How have you been feeling?"

She said, "Much better. I'm always hungry but have this full feeling, like there is no room down there."

Jill said, "Wait until the baby gets bigger and decides to do a dance on your bladder. My doctor told me on my next visit, he would try to tell the baby's sex."

Sarah said, "That's what Dr. Ford said to me too. I want to know before the baby is born."

Jill said, "I want to know too but don't want to be disappointed if it's another boy."

The house was moving right along. Well, that is, as construction goes. You go for a look, and it looks like nothing has been done. The next time you go for a look, you think, *How did they get that much work done that quickly?*

Sarah and Billy worked together on the details for the flooring, kitchen cabinets, countertops, and everything else. Billy said, "We need to stay ahead of the builders. It takes time to get the material and items ordered and delivered. The last thing you want is to have a delay on your house because the stuff is not there."

Karl was happy that he didn't have to get involved with those details. He was okay with whatever Sarah picked. Karl did work with Ted on the barn. Ted would build the barn's shell and wire the electricity. Karl would finish the inside. The barn would be big enough for all of his equipment and tools, a place for Sarah to do her crafts, and room for all of the things they wanted to store. It was big enough for a couple of horse stalls if they wanted to add some later.

The workers have finished the brick and stone work, and the roofers finished doing the roof. Ted had several crews working in different areas of the house so they would not be getting in each other's way. Workers were installing the drywall. The rooms were starting to look like rooms. The stonework on the fireplace was outstanding and would dominate the look in the living room. The open concept was used between the living room area and the kitchen. Sarah really liked that she could cook and still feel close to the living room. She thought this would really be nice when they were entertaining. She was happy with how things were progressing.

Both Sarah and Jill had developed sizable baby bumps. Sarah had to buy new outfits from time to time because she was outgrowing them. She still had to have that professional look for the office. They were looking forward to the next doctor's appointment. They wanted to know the sex of their babies. Jill, already having baby Jack, really wanted a girl. Sarah didn't care as long as her baby was healthy. She and Karl had talked about whether they preferred to have a boy or girl. It didn't make a difference to either of them. Karl said, "I am just looking forward to being a dad."

They had started to buy some baby items but didn't want to get too far ahead of themselves, especially since they didn't know the sex of the baby. They did buy a crib, changing table, car seat, bassinet, diapers, a rocking chair, and a few other items.

Today was the day for the doctor checkup and sonogram. The husbands wanted to be there for the revealing. The appointment was in the middle of the day. They all had to take time off from their jobs. Karl still laughed at the name the doctors had picked for their practice, the Baby Doctors. The girls had already arrived and were inside. When Karl pulled into the parking lot, Jack was just getting out of his car.

Karl said, "Hi, Jack, today is the big day."

Jack said, "I've been through this before, but it is all new to you. I sure hope it's a girl for me this time. Jill is so wanting a girl."

Karl said, "Yes, Jill has said many a time to Sarah how she wants her girl. We have talked about it, and all we really want is a healthy baby."

They walked into the waiting room and joined the girls. The receptionist let both doctors' nurses know their patients were here.

Soon, the nurse was taking Jill and Jack to their room, and the other nurse took Sarah and Karl to their room. The nurse said to Sarah, "Get undressed and put on the gown," and said to Karl, "You might want to step out."

Sarah said, "It's okay, he has seen me naked before."

The nurse just smiled, and you could tell she chuckled under her breath as she stepped out of the room and said, "I will give you a chance to put on the gown and be back shortly with the doctor."

A few minutes later, there was a knock on the door, and in walked the doctor, followed by the nurse. The nurse took Sarah's temperature and blood pressure and said to Dr. Ford, "Everything is normal."

Dr. Ford said, "How have you been feeling? Are you ready to see your baby's image and find out the sex?"

Sarah said, "The baby is very active, always moving around. Actually, I have been feeling great since I got over my morning sickness, but I do get tired easily. I'm having weird food cravings and am hungry most of the time."

Dr. Ford said, "That is normal. Let me say, if you think you are tired now, just wait until after the baby is born and the fun begins." The doctor listened to Sarah's heart and lungs and said, "Sounds great." He turned to Karl and said, "How are you doing, future father?"

Karl said, "Hanging in there and looking forward to being a dad."

Dr. Ford squeezed some gel on the wand and pressed it on Sarah's baby bump. He said, "Let's see what we can see."

Sarah was lying on the examination table, Dr. Ford was on one side of the table, and Karl was on the other, with the nurse working the monitor. All were looking at the monitor.

Dr. Ford started moving the wand around on Sarah's baby bump and said, "Would you take a look at that. I see two heads."

Moving the wand around some more, he said, "There are four arms and four legs. You two are going to have twins."

Karl sat down and said, "TWINS.* He stood up again and said, "TWINS. Sarah, we are going to have TWINS!"

Sarah said, "Yes, that's what the doctor just said." She asked Dr. Ford, "Why didn't the heartbeat monitor detect the two babies' heartbeats?"

The doctor said, "Many times, the two babies' heartbeats are in sync with one another, and it sounds as one. With twins in there, that's why you thought your baby was so active and you are full. The two are in there moving around, trying to get comfortable. Now let's see if we can see the sex."

Moving the wand around, the doctor was searching to see if he could center on the sex. He said, "Look here"—pointing to the image on the screen—"you can see this one is a boy." He moved the wand around and said, "The other one is being shy."

The baby moved just a little, and the doctor said, "I didn't get a clear look, but I'm 85 percent sure it's a girl. Looks like you are going to have one of each sex." The doctor moved the wand around some more and took pictures of the baby images. He then said, "Yes, the other one is definitely a girl." He said, "The nurse will give you copies of the images. I guess you both would like your own copies. It takes a few minutes for the images to print. Do you have any questions?"

Sarah looked at Karl and said, "I don't think so."

Dr. Ford said, "One more prenatal visit, and then the next time I will be seeing you is in the delivery room. Have a nice day."

Sarah got dressed, and Karl, still in shock, was saying, "TWINS, we are going to have TWINS." There was a knock on the door, and the nurse opened the door and handed the images to Karl. He looked at them and said, "TWINS. Look, Sarah, TWINS." Sarah said, "I know, Karl, we are going to have TWINS."

Karl said, "We are going to need to buy a lot more stuff for our second baby."

They walked out into the waiting room. It was just a minute later that Jack and Jill walked into the waiting room.

Jill said, "It's another boy. I guess we will have to try again to get my girl. How did it go with you two?"

Sarah said, "TWINS."

Karl held up one of the images.

Jill said, "Get out of here. TWINS!" Jill and Jack took a look at the picture and asked, "What sex?"

Sarah said, "The doctor could clearly see that one is a boy. The other one was shy, but he thought he saw the baby was a girl."

Jill said, "Lucky you, a girl. I hate you both."

With that, they had a laugh. The girls made their next appointments, and it was back to work for all.

*****

When Sarah got back to her desk, a bunch of the ones working on the executive floor gathered around to get the news and see the images. Sarah said, "I'm going to have twins."

She showed the sonogram image with the two heads. One of the ladies said, "We need to have a baby shower for Sarah."

They agreed, and one said, "I will take on all of the planning."

*****

When Karl got back to the firm's office, George saw Karl and followed him to his office and said, "Well, Dad, a boy or girl?"

Karl said, "One each. Sarah's going to have twins."

Karl showed George the images.

George said, "Well done, old boy, well done."

*****

Late in the next week, they had Sarah's baby shower in the executive dining room. It was well attended. Even some of the ones that Sarah worked with when she was working for Bill came. Ms. White was there. After the party was over, Ms. White said, "Just leave the gifts here. Come quitting time, I will have someone help you get all of those gifts down to your car."

Sarah and Ms. White walked back to Ms. White's office. She said, "I have a gift for your babies I want to give you."

Ms. White wanted to expand and grow the company. The best way to do it was to go public and issue stock. Ms. White kept controlling interest in the company. She gave stock options to the senior executives and offered stock purchases to all employees. Sarah and Karl even had purchased 500 shares.

When they got to Ms. White's office, she handed Sarah two stock certificates and said, "These are for your babies."

Each certificate was for a hundred shares.

Sarah's mouth fell open, and she said, "Ms. White, you are so generous. Thank you so much. I know the way you are growing the company, these stocks will be worth a lot."

Ms. White said, "You are welcome."

Sarah and Ms. White had a meeting they had to attend. Sarah took notes, researched the questions that were asked, and later wrote up the recap report and put it in Ms. White's inbox. She drove home with a carload of baby gifts.

That evening, she waited for Karl to get home. She said, "Help me unload the car. Today was the baby shower at work. You have to see all of the great gifts the babies got. Look at what Ms. White gave the babies."

Sarah held up the stock certificates for Karl to see.

Karl said, "Ms. White sure has been very generous to you."

Sarah said, "She sure has. Now help me unload the car."

They unloaded the car, and she and Karl looked at all the gifts the babies received.

One of Jill's friends organized a baby shower for her, and Sarah was invited. Baby Jack was crawling around, playing with the wrapping paper. Jill, with her baby bump getting bigger, found it hard to carry baby Jack around. After the party, Sarah stayed to visit. Sarah asked Jill, "Have you picked out a name for the new one yet?"

Jill said, "We have been kicking around a few names but have not settled on one. We think maybe Steven. How about you and Karl?"

Sarah said, "Same here. We have picked a few names. We are trying to decide. We don't want to have rhyming boy and girl names. We want them to have completely different ones. Karl definitely does not want a baby Karl."

They laughed at that. Jill said, "I wasn't crazy about Jack Jr., but Jack wanted it so much."

Jill said, "My mom is coming to help me after my baby is born. I know I'm going to need the help, especially with baby Jack. Do you have somebody coming to help you?"

Sarah said, "We are looking into hiring a nanny."

CHAPTER 30

Moving into the New House

The house was just about finished. Everything was looking so nice. It was like a dream come true. The landscape was about the only thing left to do. Karl and Sarah divided calling to get the utilities in their names and turned on. The final walk-through was scheduled. They found a few minor problems, but all in all, Ted's crew did a fantastic job. David handled all of the loan paperwork. Sarah and Karl did the closing at the title company, and the house was theirs.

Next was the move-in. Sarah and Karl had been boxing things up to get ready for the move. There was only so much that Sarah could do with her baby bump getting in the way. They wanted to hire a moving company to move them. When word got out, they were going to do that, their friends said, "Don't be foolish. You are moving from a small house, and there is not all that much."

Even Ben and Andrew were planning on coming down to help. Karl knew the hardest part would be all of the equipment, tools, and all that stuff they had stored in the garage.

On moving day, everyone that said they would help showed up. George and his wife, Jack and Jill, a few of the coworkers, and a couple of guys Karl used to play softball with. After Karl's injury, the doctor said he would have to sit the rest of this season out. That didn't stop Karl and Sarah from going to several of the games to cheer the team on.

Karl had rented a moving truck. The biggest part of the move was the garage, and the unloading would be quick because everything would go into the barn. With so many helping, and several had pickup trucks, it took no time to get things moved. Sarah had ordered a bunch of pizzas to be delivered, and Karl had gotten a keg of beer and some bottles of wine.

The other thing that made the move easy was that they had bought a lot of new furniture for the new house and had it delivered. George's wife, Sarah, and Jill unpacked the kitchen boxes and put things away. Sarah's new kitchen had way more cabinet space than her small kitchen in the old house.

Everything was unloaded and moved in. Now it was party time. They all sat around on the covered patio and on the grass in the backyard. Everyone was having a good time and was saying how much they liked the house and area. Karl said, "I have George to thank for putting me on to this area."

Ted came walking around the side of the house. Karl saw him and said, "Hey, everyone, I want to introduce you to Ted. He is our builder."

Karl said to Ted, "Grab yourself a beer and some pizza and come join us."

As evening came, people started to leave. Ben and Andrew were going to spend the night and go back home tomorrow. Ben asked, "What are you going to do with the little house?"

Sarah said, "We have decided to turn it into a rental property. It is in good repair and in a nice neighborhood. We should be able to rent it quickly. It's almost paid for, so soon all of the rent income will be profit."

Ben said, "We have some standard rental agreement forms back at the office. When I get back, I will send copies of them to you."

Sarah said, "That would be wonderful, thanks. You do take good care of me."

Karl and Sarah were getting settled in their new house. Karl worked in the barn, setting up his workshop. He had plenty of room for all of the machines and equipment that he had gotten from Sarah's dad's workshop. Karl built a nice big workbench and was working at building a place to hang all of the tools. Karl fixed up a place for Sarah to have a garden. Her mom had a garden as long as Sarah could remember, and she wanted one too.

In the evening, he and Sarah would walk around the neighborhood, saying hi and getting to know their new neighbors. There was a lot of new construction going on, and Pony Express Estates was growing. Karl said, "Ted is doing a terrific job filling this phase 1 up. It won't be long before they will be starting phase 2."

CHAPTER 31

Having the Twins

Sarah was sitting at her desk working on a report for Ms. White. She felt a pain. Maybe the babies were just jockeying for position. She thought, *It's another week before my due date. I surely couldn't be going into labor.*

Sarah thought maybe if she stood up, the babies would rearrange themselves, and the pain would go away. She had another sharp pain, and that's when her water broke, soaking her pants all the way to her knees.

Ms. White heard Sarah making noises and walked out of her office to see what was going on. Sarah said, "My water just broke. I'm in labor!"

Ms. White picked up the phone and called Charles to bring the limo around to the front door. She said, "Charles, you will need to drive Sarah to the hospital. Her water broke, and she is in labor."

Sarah said, "Look at me. I will mess up your limo!"

Ms. White said, "Don't be silly, that old limo can be cleaned up. It's important that we get you to the hospital."

Charles had put a blanket down on the seat for Sarah to sit on. She got into the limo, and Charles drove off to the hospital. On the way, Sarah called Karl and said, "My water broke, and I'm on my way to the hospital. Call Dr. Ford's office and tell them I'm on my way to the hospital."

Sarah sent a text message to Jill: "Water broke, on way to hospital."

*****

Charles drove the limo right up to the emergency room door and helped Sarah out. One of the attendants saw Sarah and brought out a wheelchair and took Sarah straight up to the maternity floor. Sarah told the receptionist her name and the name of her doctor.

The receptionist said, "Your doctor has been notified, and he is already here in the hospital. He just finished delivering a baby. Looks like it's going to be a busy day for him."

Sarah wondered, *Is it Jill?* She knew the doctors at the Baby Doctors did deliver each other's patients' babies if they were on call. Sarah thought how great it would be if she and Jill delivered on the same day.

Sarah was wheeled into one of the labor delivery rooms. The nurse said, "Here is a gown. Let me help you get undressed and out of those wet pants."

Sarah got in the bed just as she was having another contraction. The nurse hooked Sarah up to all of the monitors. The nurse said, "Let me take a look. Yes, you are going to have a baby real soon."

Sarah said, "There are two of them in there."

The nurse said, "So you are going to have twins. I have always wanted twins. I have three kids but no twins."

Sarah could hear Karl's voice asking, "Where is my wife?"

Sarah said, "I'm in here, Karl."

Early on, it was arranged for Karl to be present during the delivery. The nurse said to Karl, "You need to put this on over your clothes."

She handed Karl a surgical gown. The nurse said, "I'm going to get Dr. Ford. It's getting close to delivery time. You are a lucky one. You are going to have a short labor. I guess those twins of yours are anxious to see their mom and dad. Don't go pushing until the doctor says to."

A few minutes and several contractions later, Dr. Ford appeared. He said, "Let's take a look. Yes, the nurse was right. It won't be long now."

The girl twin was the first to be delivered. Soon after, out came the boy twin. The nurses took the babies and cleaned them up. Dr. Ford examined them both and said, "You have yourselves two very healthy babies. They are both big enough that neither will need to be placed in an incubator. You should be able to take them home the day after tomorrow."

The doctor turned to Karl and said, "You did turn a little pale there for a minute. We do get a few husbands that can't handle it. Karl, you did okay. Congratulations, you are a father. How does it feel?"

Karl said, "Great. You did a super job delivering the twins."

Dr. Ford said, "Sarah did all of the work. All I did was catch the babies as they came out."

The nurses finished cleaning the babies up, wrapped them in their baby blankets, and placed both babies on Sarah's chest. Sarah said to the twins, "I'm your mom, and that's your dad."

A few minutes later, another nurse came into the room and said, "Your room is ready. Someone will be here shortly to take you to your room."

Sarah, Karl, and the twins were taken to her room just down the hall. The twins were in their own hospital bassinet. Sarah was lying in the bed, and Karl was pacing around the room. He was looking at one baby, then the other, then Sarah—a proud father and husband for sure. He gave Sarah a kiss and said, "You did a wonderful job. I love you so much. You are going to be the best mom ever."

A nurse stepped into the room and said, "We need to take your twins to the nursery. We will bring them back for you to breastfeed them later. It's best you take a rest while you have a chance."

The nurses wheeled the twins out just as Jill was arriving. The nurses stopped just long enough for Jill to take a quick peek. The nurse said, "The twins will be in the nursery. You can view them through the nursery window. Don't stay long as visiting time is over."

Sarah said, "I was told that Dr. Ford had delivered a baby before the twins. Seeing you tells me it wasn't you. I was thinking how cool it would be if our kids were born on the same day."

Jill said, "It sure wasn't me. I can tell you I'm ready to get this kid out of here."

She patted her baby bump.

Jill said, "I got here as quickly as I could. You sure had a short labor."

Sarah said, "I guess the twins wanted out."

Jill said, "It will probably be another week or so before I have mine."

"You heard the nurse telling me visiting time was over. I better go. I will come back tomorrow during visiting hours. You need to get some rest. Love you, Sarah. Bye."

Sarah said, "Thanks for coming. Love you too."

Karl said, "You do look tired. Are you okay?"

Sarah said, "Yes, I'm okay, just really tired and sore."

Karl said, "I'm going back to work and will see you after I get off work. I love you."

Sarah said, "Could you call Ms. White and let her know I'm okay and so are the twins? Thank her for having Charles drive me to the hospital."

Karl said, "Charles brought you here in the limo?"

Sarah said jokingly, "Oh yes, only the best for me and the twins. Now get back to work. They will take good care of me and the twins."

Sarah called Ben with the news and took a nap.

That evening, Karl went straight to the hospital from work. The hospital policy for the maternity ward allowed fathers to visit anytime, but family and friends could only visit during visiting hours. Karl stepped into Sarah's room and said, "How's it going?"

Sarah said, "I'm doing fine, and so are the twins. I love them so much, and I love you. They brought the twins in for a couple of feedings. We did great."

Sarah opened her hospital gown, exposing her milk-engorged breast, and said, "Take a look at these."

Karl had always liked the look of Sarah's breasts. They were of a nice size and shape and very firm, but now! Sarah could see Karl's eyes bulging and said, "Down, boy, these belong to the twins for now. Just before you arrived, the nurse said she was going to bring the babies in for another feeding."

Karl said, "I brought you some clothes to wear home. I will put them in that little closet over there. I talked to the nanny. She said, 'I'm ready whenever you bring Sarah home.'"

Sarah said, "They told me because I had twins, they are going to keep me until the day after tomorrow."

The twins were wheeled in. Sarah set the bed up to accommodate feeding the twins. The nurse gave one of the twins to Sarah, and she positioned the baby to start suckling. Then the nurse gave Sarah the other twin. They were both going to town. The nurse said, "You won't be able to feed them like that very long. They will be getting bigger, and you will have to feed them one at a time. Depending on how much milk you produce, you may need to supplement their feeding with formula. Some mothers produce lots of milk and don't need to supplement. Others can't produce enough milk for just one baby. I have been watching, you are doing fine. You seem to be producing a good amount. Try to make sure that both babies get the same amount. You will need to keep your fluid intake level up."

Karl said, "Are you still wanting to name them what we had talked about before?"

Sarah said, "I still want to name the girl Emily."

Karl said, "I have liked that name ever since we first came up with it. What about the boy's name?"

Sarah said, "I have been kicking that one around. We both agreed that we didn't want rhyming names, and that's good because I don't know any boy names that rhyme with Emily. You also said you don't want a Karl Jr. Take a look at him and see if a name comes to you. If not, we will just stick with the one we picked, Todd."

Karl said, "I've been thinking about Todd. How about Kevin?"

Sarah said, "I like that name even better."

She tilted her head down and said, "You two have names. You are Kevin, and you are Emily."

161

Karl said, "How can you tell them apart?"

Sarah said, "A mother knows, and you will, too, after you are around them more."

Feeding was over, and Sarah buzzed the nurse to take Emily and Kevin back to the nursery.

Visiting hours were now open to family and friends. Jill had been in the waiting room to see Sarah. She walked in and said, "There's that new mom. Hi, Karl. How are you feeling? I stopped by the nursery to see the twins, and they were not there."

Sarah said, "I thought you said you would come by tomorrow."

Jill said, "I just had to come see my best friend and the twins."

Sarah said, "Happy to see you. I'm feeling good. I just finished feeding them. The nurse just took them back to the nursery. You must have just missed them. How are you coming along? Are you going to have your baby soon?"

Jill said, "I just came from a doctor's visit. He said any day now. Oh, Sarah, I am so ready to have this baby. I'm afraid he is going to be as big as a house. I hope I don't have to have a cesarean delivery."

With that, Karl said, "I'm going to leave you two to visit. I'm going down to the nursery and look at the twins, get something to eat, and go home."

Sarah said, "Can I have a kiss before you leave?"

Karl said, "Sure thing."

He gave Sarah a kiss and said, "I love you. Give me a call before you go to sleep tonight."

Jill and Sarah visited for a while longer. Jill asked, "Have you named the twins yet?"

Sarah said, "Karl and I just finalized the names just before you came: Kevin and Emily."

Jill said, "I love those names."

Sarah said, "Have you and Jack come up with a name for yours?"

Jill said, "We settled on Steven."

Sarah said, "You said you might name him that. I'm so excited that your twins and my baby will be so close in age. I hope they grow up to be as good friends as we have become."

They talked and talked until visiting hours were just about over. Jill said, "Goodbye. I will see you when you get home."

Sarah said, "That is if you are not having your baby. Goodbye."

CHAPTER 32

Bringing the Twins Home

Karl went up to Sarah's room. He said, "Are you ready to go home?"

Sarah said, "Just about. The nurses need to finish getting the twins ready to go. I have everything I need. Thanks for bringing me something to wear home. I am really missing you and can't wait to be home."

Karl said, "Margo has moved into the guest bedroom and is ready to help you. We had a nice talk, and she has been a nanny off and on for over twelve years. You sure did a good job picking her. I gave her a tour around the kitchen."

She said, "She would just look until she found what she was looking for. She is very down-to-earth. I asked her to make a list of things she needed, and I said I would go shopping."

The nurse brought a wheelchair in for Sarah to ride down to the hospital exit door. Another two nurses came in with the twins. One nurse said to Karl, "Go pull your car around to the exit door. By the time you do that, we will have finished Sarah's discharge and meet you there."

Karl said, "See you in just a few," and left. Karl had purchased another baby car seat. He had them strapped in the back seat. Just as he pulled up, Sarah, the nurses, and the twins were coming out of the door. Before the nurse would put the twins in the baby seats, one of the nurses said, "Let me see if the seats are installed correctly.

You would not believe how many I see that are not right. These look good."

One by one, the twins were securely placed in their seats. Karl was a bit apprehensive about putting the twins in the car. He was happy to let the nurses do it. He did help Sarah out of the wheelchair, but Sarah said, "I think I can manage, thanks anyway."

Karl said, "You sound like me when I injured my ankle."

Karl put the things the hospital gave Sarah in the trunk. With everyone in the car, they were off. At first, the babies were very quiet. Kevin started to make some noise, and Emily joined right in. Sarah said, "It is about their feeding time."

She said to the twins, "Hang in there, kids. Dad will get us home soon, and I will feed you."

Karl pulled the car into the garage. Sarah said, "How did you get my car home? I left it in the company parking lot, and Charles took me to the hospital."

Karl said, "George helped me. Let's get you and the twins inside so you can feed them."

Margo, hearing the garage door open, came out to help. Karl helped Sarah out of the car, even after she said she didn't need any help.

Sarah said, "Hi, Margo, so happy that you agreed to come help us out."

She said, "Thanks for picking me."

Margo took one of the twins, and Sarah took the other. Karl said, "I will get the things out of the trunk."

Once inside, Margo and Sarah took the twins into the nursery. Sarah and Karl bought all of the extra furniture after learning she would be having twins. They thought they had everything they needed for now. There was one changing table, two rocking chairs, and two of most everything else. They figured the twins could be in the same room for a while. It sure would be a lot easier than running back and forth between two rooms. Their new house was designed and built with five bedrooms. They thought, *What will we do with so many bedrooms, especially after having lived in a small two-bedroom house?*

Sarah said to Margo, "I know you are going to be a big help to me. I hope things work out that you can watch the twins during the day after I go back to work."

Margo said, "We can talk about that later. Right now, we need to get these kids fed. They must be starving."

Margo picked up one of the twins and handed it to Sarah. Sarah got him to start suckling, and Margo handed the other twin to Sarah, and they both were feeding.

Sarah said, "They sure are hungry."

Margo said, "What did you end up naming the kids?"

Sarah said, "Kevin and Emily."

Margo said, "Those are nice names. As they get a bit bigger, you will have to start feeding them one at a time. You will not be able to handle two at a time for very long."

Sarah said, "The nurse said the same thing. I can see that will be happening soon. They are already squirming around a lot."

Margo said, "I'm going to see what kind of trouble that husband of yours is getting into and will start dinner. When you are finished, I will help you put Kevin and Emily in their bassinets. Now don't you try doing it all alone. After all, you hired me to help you out. Let me earn my wage."

Karl was in the living room sitting in his favorite chair. He had gotten himself a beer. Wondering about holding the twins. Karl had not held a baby before, not even baby Jack. He didn't know how.

Margo said, "Boy, you look deep in thought. This new baby thing is a bit overwhelming for you?"

Karl said, "Let me tell you, Margo, I have never held a baby before. To tell you the truth, I'm afraid I might drop it or not hold it right."

Margo said, "Never you mind. I will teach you. You will be a pro in no time. Let's go into the kitchen. You can peel the potatoes. You need something to ease your mind."

Karl said, "Now that's something I know how to do."

Karl felt very comfortable with Margo and knew that Sarah had picked the right person.

Sarah called out, "The twins are done feeding. I could use a little help."

Margo said to Sarah, "Be right in. Don't try to do anything on your own just yet."

Sarah said, "Okay."

Margo turned to Karl and said, "Come on, you're on. Just watch what I do and do exactly what I do."

Karl followed Margo into the nursery. He watched every move Margo did and did the same.

Sarah said to Karl, "You did that just like a pro. I'm impressed."

Karl turned to Margo with his back to Sarah and mouthed "Thank you." Margo winked at Karl and said, "Karl, we best get back to the kitchen and finish making dinner. Sarah, why don't you lie down on your bed and rest? I will give you a call when dinner is ready. It should take about an hour longer."

Karl helped Margo finish cooking the meal. He went down to their bedroom, where Sarah was sound asleep. He pondered whether to wake her or let her sleep. He gently touched her and said, "Dinner is ready. It's best that you eat something, even if it's just a little."

Sarah was still sore from having the twins, and Karl helped her sit up on the side of the bed. Sarah stood up, and the two of them walked down to the kitchen to eat. While they were eating, Sarah said to Margo, "I don't expect you to do everything around here."

Margo said, "Just you wait a doggone minute. You haven't been home for two hours yet. You just got out of the hospital after having twins. This is something we will work out over time. As time goes on and we get into our routines, you will be able to do more and more. Let's not push it just yet."

What could Sarah say? Everything Margo just said was so true.

For the first couple of weeks, Margo was going to stay twenty-four hours a day. She said, "For tonight, when I hear the twins crying, I will check on them. If it's only a diaper change, I will take care of it. If it's feeding they are wanting, I will wake you, and you can feed them. You may want to use a breast pump and fill a couple of bottles with your breast milk over the next few days as your milk production allows. It will come in handy."

Sarah jokingly said, "Moo."

They all laughed at Sarah's humor. "We will work on getting the twins on some kind of schedule. It will help us all."

Sarah said, "It sounds like a good plan. If it's okay with everybody, I'm tired and want to go back to bed."

It was still early. Karl said, "I'm going to watch TV for a while."

Margo said, "I have a book that I've been trying to read but never seem to have the time. I'm going to my bedroom and read. Good night."

Karl said, "There is a TV in there too. Good night. See you in the morning."

CHAPTER 33

Living Life at Home with the Twins

The next morning, Margo and Sarah worked out some schedules for their daily lives. As Sarah was able to do more things, naturally, the routine changed. Mostly, Sarah took care of the twins while Margo did the chores around the house, like cleaning and cooking. Occasionally, Margo helped with the twins when Sarah needed assistance, especially at bath time.

The doorbell rang. Sarah said, "I'll get it. My best friend Jill asked if she could stop by this morning. It's probably her."

Sarah went to the front door, and sure enough, it was Jill.

Sarah said, "Come on in. Boy, you sure are looking big. Are you ever going to have that baby?"

Jill replied, "I sure hope so, and soon. I'm already overdue. The doctor said if I don't have the baby by the weekend, he's going to induce labor."

"Keep me posted," Sarah said. "I want to introduce you to Margo. She is our nanny. I can't tell you how helpful she is. She has taught me so much already about caring for the twins. She's becoming a real part of the family."

Jill said, "Pleased to meet you."

Margo responded, "You too."

She continued, "I have some things I need to do. Enjoy your visit."

Sarah asked Jill, "By the way, I thought you were going to work up until your baby was born."

Jill said, "That was the plan. My company put me on maternity leave as of today."

"You look fabulous for just having twins," Jill said.

"Thanks," Sarah replied. She pulled up her shirt and said, "Look, no stretch marks."

Jill looked at Sarah's bare stomach and said, "Not only no stretch marks, but look at how flat it is already. Sarah, I hate you, and I'm going home to never talk to you again."

Sarah knew Jill was just kidding. Jill had always admired how Sarah looked.

Sarah said, "Come take a look at the twins."

Jill followed her down the hall to the nursery. The twins were in their bassinets, sound asleep. Sarah picked up Kevin and handed him to Jill. Jill sat down in one of the rocking chairs in the nursery. Sarah picked up Emily and sat in the other rocker.

Jill said, "The twins have your beautiful red hair."

Sarah responded, "And they have my blue eyes too."

Jill said, "Don't give me more reasons to hate you even more."

Emily was getting a little fussy. Sarah said, "It's getting on to feeding time."

She unbuttoned her blouse and bra and started nursing Emily. Jill continued to rock Kevin.

"They are so peaceful when they're sleeping," Jill said.

"And both have a nice pair of lungs when they're not," Sarah said.

Emily finished feeding, and they switched babies so Kevin could feed while Jill held and rocked Emily.

Sarah asked, "What are your plans for the day? Why I'm asking: if you're free, the twins have a doctor's appointment for their first checkup. Margo was going to go with me. I'm sure she would enjoy a little peace and quiet for a change if you could go in her place."

Jill said, "I really don't have anything pressing to do. I was mostly going to go home and sit around waiting for Steven to pop out. Let me call the babysitter to see if she can stay longer. I didn't want to bring baby Jack over. He's getting into everything and wouldn't give us a chance to visit."

Jill called, and the babysitter said, "That's okay. I could use the extra money. How much longer do you think it will be? I don't have any plans—just wanted to know so I could tell my boyfriend when he had to go home. Just kidding. Baby Jack is playing right now, and I'm working on my term paper."

Jill said, "I'll call or text you when I'm headed that way. If something comes up, give me a call, and I'll come straight home."

The four of them loaded up into Sarah's car. The twins' doctor was in the same office as Dr. Ford, the Baby Doctors.

Soon they were all in the waiting room.

The receptionist said, "You two are still together, I see. Jill, I don't see that you have an appointment. I only see an appointment for Sarah and the twins."

Jill said, "I'm here to help Sarah with the twins. A bit much for her to handle right now."

The receptionist said, "I'll let the nurse know you're here."

Several minutes later, Jill said, "They must be busy today. It's been a while, and we're still waiting. The twins sure are being good."

Sarah asked Jill, "Is your mother going to come and help you like she did last time?"

Jill said, "Yes. She's on her way. I told her that I didn't know when the baby would be here and that the doctor would induce me if I didn't have the baby by the weekend. She said that was enough of a reason to come."

Sarah asked, "How did it go the last time?"

Jill said, "It really went better than expected. My mother did the math and said the baby was too big to be two months premature. We had a talk about her being controlling and smothering me. We came to an understanding and worked things out. Actually, I'm looking forward to her coming. I've sent her videos of baby Jack. I think she's really looking forward to seeing her only grandkid. Well, that's until I have this one; then it will be grandkids."

Sarah said, "I'm happy that things got all worked out. I miss my mom. She would have been a wonderful grandmother."

Jill asked, "What about your dad? Does he know he's a grandfather?"

She said, "I called the care facility and told him I had twins and he was a grandfather. I'm not sure he understood. After the twins get older, we're going up for a visit. His memory is getting really bad. I was calling him every week, but he kept asking, 'Who are you?' So I stopped. I talk to Holly about every other week to check on him. He's still in good health, it's just his memory."

The door opened, and the nurse called Sarah's name. Jill and Sarah followed the nurse to the baby exam room. It was nicely decorated with baby-style wallpaper.

Jill said, "This is the same room they put me in for baby Jack's visit."

There was a knock on the door, and Dr. Simons walked in.

The doctor said, "Hello, Sarah. Remember me? I was the doctor who examined your twins while you were in the hospital."

Sarah said, "I do, and that's why I picked you as the doctor for the twins. Besides, you are part of the Baby Doctor group."

Dr. Simons said to Jill, "Good to see you too. It looks like you are about to have your number two child."

Jill said, "I'm overdue, so yes, any day now."

He asked, "Where is that baby Jack of yours?"

Jill said, "Oh, he's home with the babysitter. I'm here helping my friend Sarah with the twins. I hope to see you in the hospital very soon. I'm past ready for Steven to join the outside world."

The doctor said, "Which twin is going to be first?"

Sarah handed Kevin to the doctor and said, "This is Kevin."

The doctor said, "Let's take a look at you, young man."

The doctor checked his heart and lungs and checked all over his body. He handed Kevin to the nurse to get his weight. Then came the hard part—it was time for Kevin to get his first baby shots. He did not like it one bit and started to cry.

Dr. Simons said, "The kid has a set of lungs."

He handed Kevin back to Sarah.

Sarah said, "You should hear them do a duet."

It was then that Emily heard her brother crying, and she joined in.

Sarah said, "There's the duet."

She put a pacifier in Kevin's mouth.

Jill handed Emily to the doctor and said, "This is Emily."

Dr. Simons did his exam, handed Emily to the nurse so she could be weighed, and then gave Emily her shots. Dr. Simons handed Emily back to Jill, and Sarah put the pacifier in Emily's mouth, and she stopped crying.

Dr. Simons said, "Your twins are doing great. The nurse will have the receptionist set up your next appointment. Jill, I hope to see you soon."

Sarah stopped by the front desk, paid for the visit, and got the appointment card for the next visit.

They drove back to Sarah's house. Jill helped Sarah get the twins back into the nursery and said, "I better get home. I'm not sure the babysitter was joking about her boyfriend."

They both laughed.

Sarah said, "Thanks for the visit and helping me with the twins on their first doctor's visit. The next time, bring baby Jack with you. I sure would like to see him again."

Jill said, "The main reason I didn't bring him is that he's beginning to crawl. Well, it's more of a scoot. I thought I had babyproofed my house. He sure has proven me wrong. That kid is into everything."

Sarah had to laugh at that. They said their goodbyes, and Sarah said, "Let me know when you go into labor."

Margo asked, "How did the doctor's visit go?"

Sarah said, "The doctor said they looked very healthy and to keep up the good work. They got their first round of baby shots. They probably will be sore for a short time."

Margo said, "I will be careful. Jill, are you leaving?"

Jill said, "Yes, I really need to get home. Nice to meet you. Goodbye, all."

CHAPTER 34

Staying in Touch with the Office

Sarah still had access to Ms. White's calendar on her phone app and kept up with Ms. White's appointments. Sarah wanted to be able to hit the ground running once her maternity leave was over and she returned to work. Sarah called Tammy, the temp who was filling in for her, at least once a week to get the inside story of what was going on. Ms. White even emailed Sarah a few times to have her do some research work and write up some reports while Sarah was on leave. Sarah didn't mind. It gave her something to do, and she felt that she was still needed.

Tammy answered the phone. "Ms. White's office, Tammy speaking."

Sarah said, "Hi, Tammy, it's Sarah."

Tammy said, "Hi, Sarah. How are you and the twins?"

Sarah said, "They're growing and getting bigger every day. I'm beginning to think the two of them are having a competition to see who can grow up the quickest. I see on the calendar that Ms. White doesn't have an appointment right now. Is she busy?"

Tammy said, "Just a minute."

Tammy pressed the intercom and said, "Ms. White, Sarah is on line one."

Ms. White picked up the phone and said, "Sarah, how are you and the twins? I sure am missing you around here."

Sarah said, "That's nice of you to ask. We're all doing good, and my maternity leave is just about up. I miss you and working."

Sarah's company email account was still receiving all the company notices. She also got emails from Ms. White, letting her know what was going on. Most of these were confidential in nature and only for Sarah to see. Ms. White had been busy growing the company. On the open land next to the company building, construction had started on what would be the new company headquarters building. Included with the new headquarters building would be a childcare center, exercise facilities, and a healthcare center with a full-time nurse.

Ms. White said, "I'm guessing you have been keeping up with the emails."

Sarah said, "I have, and you sure have been busy while I've been away."

Ms. White said, "All of the research and reports you did for me have made this come about. I'm by no means finished and need you back here for my next phase."

Sarah said, "I have two more weeks left on my leave. Before I return to work, I'd like to come by and bring the twins over so you and others can meet them. Can you tell I'm a proud mother? Do you think that would be all right?"

Ms. White said, "That would be nice. You still have access to my calendar. Book yourself an appointment."

Sarah said, "I will do just that. Thanks, and goodbye."

No sooner than Sarah hung up the phone, she received a text message from Jill saying, "In labor on my way to the hospital."

Sarah sent a text message saying, "After Karl gets home and it's visiting hours, I will come to the hospital to see you."

Karl got home, and Sarah told him the news about Jill going into labor. She said, "I have fed the twins, and after we eat dinner, I'm going over to the hospital."

She also told him about the conversation with Ms. White and her plans to visit the company with the twins.

Margo was still living there with Karl and Sarah. Sarah was getting around really well and was mostly taking care of the twins by herself. It was nice that Margo was doing the cleaning, laundry, and helping with dinners. Many times, Karl or Sarah would help her with the cooking or cleanup. After all, Margo had become part of the family, and that's what families do. The plan was for Margo to nanny the twins when Sarah went back to work. She would be doing day care as Sarah and Karl would be home after work. Margo had been such a big help.

Sarah said, "I just got a text from Jack. Jill just had the baby. I'm leaving now. I won't be late."

Karl said, "You didn't finish your dinner."

Sarah said, "Got to go."

*****

Sarah drove to the hospital and went up to the maternity ward's waiting room.

Jill's mother and baby Jack were in the waiting room. Jill's mother said, "Hi, Sarah. Jill and the baby are doing great. The delivery was natural. They thought they might have to do a cesarean because the baby was so big. Jack is back there with her now. He sent me a text message saying it would be a while before I could come back for a quick visit. They were cleaning the baby and Jill up. That was a while ago."

The door opened, and the nurse said, "Jill's mother?"

Jill's mother said, "I am."

She turned to Sarah and said, "Would it be okay with you if you watch baby Jack while I'm in with Jill?"

Sarah said, "I would be happy to do so. Go visit."

Jill's mother followed the nurse down the hall to the room Jill was in.

She asked, "Where is the baby? Is the baby all right?"

Jill said, "Take it easy, Grandma. They took Steven to the nursery. He's just fine. You can see him through the nursery viewing window. You can hold him tomorrow when you come for a visit. Where is baby Jack?"

Her mother said, "I left him with Sarah out in the waiting room."

Jill said, "Sarah is here?"

While waiting for her turn to see Jill, Sarah took baby Jack down to the nursery viewing window. She showed baby Jack all the babies in the nursery.

Sarah said, "See that one over there? That's your baby brother."

Of course, baby Jack was too young to understand. Sarah returned to the waiting room just as both Jack and his mother-in-law came through the door.

Jack said, "We're going down to the viewing window to see if Steven has made it there yet."

Sarah said, "We were just down there. Your new son is there, Papa Jack."

Jack took baby Jack from Sarah and said, "Jill is in the second room on the left."

Sarah walked down to Jill's room and stepped in. Jill really looked beat.

Sarah asked, "Rough labor?"

Jill said, "That's only half of it. Steven was so big, the doctor was talking about taking me up to the OR and doing a C-section. I said, 'Let me push some more.' Steven decided he better come on out after all. Oh, I am sore. The pain medicine is starting to wear off."

Sarah had to laugh, and that caused Jill to laugh too.

Jill said, "Stop, it hurts to laugh."

Sarah said, "I was told I couldn't stay long because you had just delivered. I will wait a couple of days and come visit you after you get home. I am going back to work the week after next. My leave is up."

Jill said, "Time sure does pass quickly. How is everything? And how are the twins?"

Sarah said, "Things are going great. Margo will be doing day care for us when I go back to work. Karl and I have talked about me being a stay-at-home mom. Karl knows how much I love working and how much I love my job. He is okay with that. I better get out of here before I get a security guard escort out to the parking lot. Call me if you get bored."

Sarah returned home and gave Margo and Karl an update. The twins were asleep for the night.

Margo went to her room, and Karl and Sarah sat up for a while before going to bed.

CHAPTER 35

Returning to Work

As always, Ms. White was in her office when Sarah arrived at her desk.

Sarah said, "Good morning, Ms. White. I looked at your calendar, and you are going to have a busy day."

Ms. White said, "Good morning, Sarah. Welcome back. We sure are going to be busy today. Get that laptop of yours. Charles is waiting for us."

Sarah got her laptop and purse and followed Ms. White down to where the limo was parked. Charles was there with the limo door open.

Sarah said, "You purchased a new limo. It sure looks nice."

Ms. White said, "It was about time. The old one was beginning to cost too much to upkeep."

Charles said, "Good morning, Ms. White, good morning, Ms. Sarah. Thank you for letting me see those twins of yours last week."

Sarah said, "Good morning, Charles. It was my pleasure. After all, it was you that got us to the hospital."

Ms. White told Charles where the first stop of the day was, and Charles drove on.

When they arrived, Ms. White and Sarah were escorted to the conference room where the meeting would be held. There were several people already seated when they stepped into the room. They were asked if they would like any coffee. There was bottled water and glasses on the table.

Ms. White said, "Nothing for me, thanks."

Sarah said, "I'll just have one of the waters."

Sarah usually sat behind Ms. White, but there were no chairs making a second row.

Ms. White said to Sarah, "Take that seat next to me. I want you close in case I need you to do some research."

A few more joined the meeting, and introductions were made. Sarah still had no idea of the reason for the meeting. The building sign indicated it was a manufacturing company.

The meeting seemed to move along smoothly. Sarah took lots of notes on her laptop. Sarah thought to herself, *I'm sure glad I fully charged my laptop before going to work today.* Ms. White made a presentation to the people. The presentation was mostly about what her company could do for them. Sarah had heard this presentation before, but Ms. White hit this one out of the park. After the meeting, they all shook hands and said they thought it was a very productive meeting and looked forward to doing business with Ms. White's company.

Ms. White and Sarah walked out and got into the limo.

Sarah said to Ms. White, "I have heard you give that presentation before, but this time was really outstanding."

Ms. White said, "Thank you. If this company follows through and decides to do business with us, it will put us on track to having the most profitable year since my father retired and I took over the company. It was important that I did a good job."

She told Charles the next stop, and Charles drove off.

Ms. White said, "This next stop should be a quick one. Sarah, I would like for you to sit this one out. You can wait here with Charles."

Sarah said, "Yes, ma'am. Is there anything you would like for me to do while you're gone? If not, I'll go over the notes I took during the last meeting and start writing up the recap report."

Ms. White said, "No," and walked off to her appointment.

Sarah looked over her notes and made some additions. She started writing up the recap report of the meeting. After completing the report, Sarah took time to call Karl.

Karl answered and said, "How goes your first day back?"

Sarah said, "Talk about hitting the ground running. I had no sooner said good morning than Ms. White said for me to get my laptop and let's go. We have places we need to go. I know I'll be tired tonight. Ms. White had another appointment and asked that I wait in the limo. Karl, she bought a new limo. It is so much nicer than the one she had before. I hope it wasn't because Charles took me to the hospital after my water broke. I did sit on a blanket. I will give Margo a call later today to see how she and the twins are doing. I love you."

Karl said, "Happy to hear you're earning that raise you got. New limo? You'll have to tell me all about it tonight. I called Margo just a little while ago. She said everything was going fine and not to worry."

It was taking more time than Ms. White had said. Sarah had finished writing the report, and she and Charles had a nice visit. Charles was interested in hearing about the twins. Charles was married, but they didn't have any kids.

Soon Ms. White returned and said, "Sorry, that took longer than I expected."

Sarah said, "No problem. It gave me time to review my notes and write the recap report from the last meeting."

Ms. White said, "That's my Sarah, always keeping that one step ahead."

Ms. White said to Charles, "It's getting on to lunchtime. Do you know of any restaurants in this area? If so, take us to one."

When they were away from the office and not around clients, the atmosphere was less formal. Charles dressed nicely but did not generally wear a chauffeur uniform.

Charles said, "I know of a place not far from here. How does Mexican food sound?"

Ms. White said, "That would be fine."

Sarah thought, *Great, spicy food. The twins are going to love that.* Sarah was trying to wean the twins off breast milk and onto formula.

She was using the breast pump, and the kids were still getting a bottle of her milk a day. She was trying to cut down her milk production gradually. She had heard that going cold turkey to stop breastfeeding was painful for the mother. Sarah looked over the menu and ordered something that she felt would be less spicy and didn't eat any of the hot sauce or peppers.

After lunch, Charles asked, "Where to next?"

Ms. White said to Charles, "To Harlow's, the construction builder's main office."

Ms. White said to Sarah, "This is the last stop for today, but I expect it to be a long one. This one is with the builder who is constructing the company's new headquarters building."

The construction company's office building was as modern as one could be. There were lots of live plants and pictures on the walls of buildings this company had built. On the wall behind the receptionist's desk was a large hand-painted mural. It showed a construction crane lifting steel beams up to a building under construction. There were lots of workers wearing hard hats, people running equipment and machinery, and welders welding beams into place.

The receptionist said, "Hello, Ms. White. We've been expecting you. Please follow me."

They walked down a long hall. On both sides of the hall were offices. The receptionist said, "Go on in; there is coffee and refreshments on the back table. Please help yourselves. I'll let Mr. Harlow and his team know you're here."

Sarah asked Ms. White, "Is there anything you would like to drink?"

Ms. White said, "No, but get yourself whatever you want."

Sarah got herself a glass and a bottle of water.

She asked Ms. White, "Where would you like me to sit?"

Ms. White said, "Why don't you sit across the table from me this time."

Sarah walked around to the other side of the table, put her glass, the bottle of water, and her laptop down. This seemed strange to Sarah because Ms. White always wanted Sarah to sit behind her or next to her.

The Harlow team marched in. There were over a half-dozen men and women. They sat down and introduced themselves. Blueprints were laid out on the table. Various people on the team explained where they were on the project. They projected images of the project on the screen and showed various pictures of the building. Several members of the team gave updates in the areas they were responsible for.

When the team got to the inside decorations update, Ms. White said, "You will be working with Sarah, who will be representing me for the building's interior decorations, including my new office and the rest of the offices. That also includes the cafeteria kitchen and executive kitchen and dining room."

Ms. White could see Sarah's reaction to this news.

Ms. White said, "You will find Sarah is easy to work with. She and her team will be working closely with your team in these areas instead of me. I will still be involved in all other aspects of the project and expect regular updates. I will get the interior decorations update directly from Sarah. Let's continue with the rest of the construction progress and your presentation."

The meeting went on, and Sarah took notes. An appointment was set for Sarah to meet with their interior design manager, Judy, and her team. A couple of hours later, the meeting ended.

Ms. White said, "A very informative meeting."

She thanked everyone, and she and Sarah left.

Sarah and Ms. White walked out to the limo. Charles opened the door and let the two of them in.

Ms. White said, "Charles, take us back to my company."

Ms. White closed the window between the driver's seat and where they were seated and said to Sarah, "I have been thinking about who I could trust to do the best job, and you came up in my thoughts over and over again. I was going to talk to you about the position, but I felt pressured to announce you at the meeting. I didn't want to give them any excuse to fall behind on the construction because of us."

Sarah said, "I am so flattered that you think so highly of me. I only have one year of college. I had finished my first year and started the next when my husband was killed in an accident. I was so devastated and depressed that I quit school and never went back."

Ms. White said, "Sarah, don't sell yourself short. The time you have worked for me, you have proven yourself over and over again. I have dealt with book-smart people that you could run circles around. I believe in you and know you will do a tremendous job."

Sarah said, "I'm not sure about this yet, but I'm willing to give it my all. What about my job as your administrative assistant?"

Ms. White said, "Oh, you will still be my right-hand person. We will work around your extra duties while working with Harlow's people. When you think you need extra help, we can get Tammy back in here for a day or two. You can hire people to help you when you think you need help. You will see, everything will work out. You have already had experience in doing it with what you did on that new house of yours."

Sarah said, "I believe the new building will be a much bigger job."

Ms. White said, "That's true—on a bigger scale than your house—but you know how to work with people and get things done. Besides, you will have a hand in finishing the design of the new day care facility that your twins will be staying in."

Sarah said, "I'm just a little overwhelmed right now. I can't do everything by myself. Do you think I could bring my old boss, Bill, out of retirement to come and work for me?"

Ms. White said, "I think that is an excellent idea, and I was just going to suggest that to you. Feel free to contact him when you think you will need his help."

*****

When they returned to their offices, Sarah checked for messages and emails. She passed them on to Ms. White, saying, "Nothing pressing."

Ms. White said, "What a first day back. You must be exhausted. Go home. I will see you in the morning."

Sarah got her things and said, "Thank you. I'm not going to say no. I will see you in the morning—you didn't scare me off."

That put a big smile on Ms. White's face, something that Sarah did not see often. She just waved at Sarah and said, "See you tomorrow."

Sarah couldn't wait to get home and see the twins and hear what Margo had to say about how their day went. Since Ms. White let her go home early, she sent a text message to Margo: "I'm on my way. Got off work early. Be home soon." With Sarah getting home early, she would be home way before Karl, and she could have some one-on-one time with Margo.

Sarah got out of the car and rushed into the house.

Margo said, "Where's the fire?"

Sarah said, "Hi, Margo. I had such a day today. I hardly had the chance to think about the twins and really wanted to see them."

Margo said, "They have been good all day."

Sarah went to the nursery, picked up Emily, sat down in the rocker, and started to rock and love on her. After a few minutes, she traded babies, and it was Kevin's turn. After rocking and loving on Kevin for several minutes, Sarah went out to the kitchen where Margo was emptying the dishwasher.

Sarah asked Margo, "Is there anything I need to know? Is there anything you need?"

Margo said, "Calm down, Sarah. Sit down and take a deep breath. Here is a glass of iced tea. The twins did great. They got a little fussy around feeding time. Those two can put the milk down, and oh, how they can fill their diapers! Next week, I will start them on some baby food. That will make their poop smell bad. No hurry, but we will need more diapers soon."

Sarah said, "I can finish emptying the dishwasher. Why don't you go home early? I'm going to get dinner started. Karl should be home before long."

Margo said, "Are you sure?"

Sarah said, "Go."

Margo left, and about an hour later Karl got home.

Karl came in and said, "You must have gotten home early."

185

He gave Sarah a kiss.

Sarah had changed into one of Karl's softball jerseys and said, "Ms. White sent me home early. Boy, what a day we had. Here is a beer. Take it and go change your clothes."

Karl took the beer, stopped in the nursery for a peek at the twins before going to change his clothes. He came back out, and Sarah said, "Dinner will be ready in just a few. Can you set the table for me, please?"

During dinner, Sarah told Karl all about her day.

Karl said, "Wow, you are going to be in charge of the inside of the entire new building?"

Sarah said, "Yes, I am. Not the size of the offices. That has already been done but everything else—desks, chairs, filing cabinets, and conference room tables, plus both kitchens and all of the kitchen equipment. That's not all. The day care and exercise facilities too."

Karl said, "You are going to get help, right?"

Sarah said, "Of course. That's a lot of work."

They finished dinner, and together they cleaned up the kitchen. The twins started crying.

Sarah said, "They must be hungry. We better go feed them."

She mixed up two bottles of baby formula. She handed one to Karl and said, "Pick a twin to feed and a rocker, and I will feed and rock the other one."

Sarah, with one twin and Karl with the other, fed their babies. After a diaper change, they put the twins in their bassinets.

Sarah said, "It won't be long before we will be putting them in their cribs."

Karl said, "They are growing up fast."

They went into the living room. Karl sat in his chair.

Sarah said, "Don't you think it's about time we get you a new chair?"

Karl said, "I like my chair. It is broken in, fits good, and is very comfortable."

Sarah gave Karl one of her looks. Sarah said, "I'm tired but not too tired. Do you want to mess around? I'm not back on the pill. I want to wait until the twins are weaned off of my milk before going

186

back on it. You will need to use a condom and be gentle. It's been a while."

Karl said, "Well, I don't know."

Sarah said, "You ass. Come on."

They went down to the bedroom. Karl was gentle, and they made each other very happy.

CHAPTER 36

Ms. White's Vision

Sarah said, "Ms. White, good morning. Looking at your calendar, I see you have blocked out your morning and have scheduled a group meeting at four-thirty today."

Ms. White said, "Good morning, Sarah. Come on in and sit down."

Sarah grabbed her trusty laptop and took a seat.

Ms. White said, "I know you got a big surprise dropped on you yesterday at the meeting we had over at Harlow Construction. I'm sorry for doing that to you. I have been waiting for you to return from your maternity leave to do some planning with you. Things just started happening quickly, and I had to respond."

Sarah said, "I understand. Not everything is always under your control."

Ms. White said, "Harlow scheduled that meeting. I had to attend to keep on schedule. You were presented as our inside decorator. Sarah, that was just the tip of the iceberg. I have more planned for you. You are wise well beyond your years. I see a lot of me in you. Yes, my father taught me a lot, and I grew, as did the company. I worked hard to get where I am today. You, too, have worked hard, and it shows. You have watched and studied me. I want to be your mentor, watch you grow, and help me grow this company. Here are your new business cards."

Taped on the end of the box was one of the business cards inside. It had Sarah's name and the title of Director of New Facilities and Planning.

Ms. White said, "Sarah, just listen to me for a few minutes. I know you are trying to process thousands of thoughts in your head right now. I hope what I am about to tell you will answer many of your questions. While you have been on leave, I have been working on my vision, and you are going to be a major part of helping me make that vision become a reality. Before you went on leave, you were with me in lots of business meetings and could see what I was planning. Several of those deals are just about to be finalized. You know I bought that company downstate about a hundred miles from here. That is just the beginning, along with attracting more manufacturing contracts here."

"Sarah, I know you have Tammy's cell phone number. I want you to call her, find out how much she is making, double it, and offer her your old job as Executive Administrative Assistant to me. She will take over your day-to-day responsibilities, but you will still accompany me on all of the business meetings as you previously have been doing, but under your new job responsibilities. Taking notes, doing research, and providing me with reports. You need to see first-hand what is going on to do the planning for our new ventures. Not only will you be planning the rest of the new headquarters facilities and the move to the new one, but also the merger of new companies with ours as they are purchased.

"Remember that meeting where I made that presentation that you said I hit it out of the park? Well, I just signed a contract with them that will increase our current production by 50 percent. I know this sounds like a lot, and it is. Remember you can't eat an entire cow in one dinner. Along with your new title and responsibilities, I have increased your salary by 33 percent on top of the raise you got just before going on leave. You will need an administrative assistant, so hire one. That person will be the first of many who will be working for you. Let's go down to my old office. I have something I want to show you."

Sarah and Ms. White walked down the hall to Ms. White's old office. She unlocked the door, and they walked in.

Ms. White said, "Many have asked to move in here, but you will need the extra room to do your job."

Ms. White handed Sarah the key and said, "This is your new office."

On the conference table were a bunch of blueprints of our new headquarters facility. On the wall were architectural drawings of what the building will look like, and of all things, a picture of a cow with all of the different cuts of meat drawn on it.

Ms. White pointed to that picture and said, "This is to remind you that you can't eat that entire cow in one dinner. One meal at a time. I know you will look at it often as I did when I was working my way up in the company. My father did not give me anything. I had to earn everything. He was tough, but he was also fair. Here is the updated company organization chart. You report directly to me. This will come in handy as you talk to the department heads, directors, and vice presidents. If you have any problems, and I don't think you will, let me know and they will be taken care of. You are very likable, and you know how to deal with people. Your new title, duties, and position are the subject of the four-thirty meeting today."

Ms. White started pointing out the major areas of the building. "This is where the childcare facility will be, with an outside playground. There is going to be an exercise room with all sorts of exercise machines and equipment. A place to take showers. Two inside handball/racquetball courts with hardwood floors. Outside there will be a half-court basketball court and two pickleball/tennis courts. Over here is a covered area with tables. People can eat out here or just sit and enjoy the small park and fountain. The plans include a health care facility with a full-time nurse. Here is where the new employee cafeteria is located. Over here is the conference facility. We will no longer have to rent a place to hold our big shareholders' meetings. It will be large enough to hold all of our employees, and we will have the annual company employee meetings there and other special events too. The center will have movable walls that can divide the large room into several smaller ones."

The area set aside for the offices was enormous. Ms. White said, "This might look like overkill, but with the additional people I envision coming from the purchases of companies, we will need that space. I want to be the leading company to work for in this area. I want to have a backlog of people who want to come and work here. Okay, Sarah, it's your turn to talk and ask your questions."

Sarah said, "You sure have done a lot of work while I was on leave. That is a lot to process. Thank you for all of the confidence you have in me. The new title and raise are something I could never have imagined. The job duties—well, I am surely overwhelmed at the moment. I will be looking at the cow picture a lot."

Ms. White laughed at that, and Sarah joined in, and they laughed together. That seemed to break the tension.

Ms. White said, "In the meeting scheduled for this afternoon, I will announce your new position. I'm sure there will be a lot of questions that people will have. I hope many of those questions will be answered when we lay out some of the new facility plans. Expect to say a few words. They will want to hear directly from you. You know they will base their first impressions on how confident you are in saying what you have to say. Keep it short, and don't commit to anything. Just explain that over the next several months, you and your team will be meeting with the department heads, directors, and vice presidents to coordinate with them on their new facilities and the move to the headquarters building.

"Sarah, don't say anything about future company expansion. Keep everything you say focused on the new facility only. I guess you have figured out you will have a long-term job ahead of you. Go ahead and work in here to get more familiar with the new facilities and process this morning's information. I will be in my office the rest of the day if you need me. See you at the four-thirty meeting. And Sarah, I know you will do great—no worries."

Sarah sat down at her new desk, thinking to herself, "What do I do first?" She started a list. She didn't want to get overwhelmed and stressed out just yet. The first thing she did was move the cow picture to where she could see it from her desk just by looking up. She picked up her cell phone and called Karl.

Karl answered and said, "Hey honey, what's up?"

Sarah said, "Where do I start? Are you in the middle of something? I really need to talk to you."

Karl said, "Sounds serious. What I'm working on can keep."

Sarah said, "Remember what I told you last night about me being the inside decorator for the new building?"

He said, "Yes."

"Well, to put it in the words of Ms. White, that was just the tip of the iceberg. I got a promotion. My new job title is director of new facilities and planning. I got a 33 percent raise on top of the raise I just got before going on leave. I'm moving into her old office. I'm supposed to hire an administrative assistant."

Karl interrupted her and said, "Whoa, slow down, take a deep breath. That's a lot that has happened. New job, new title, more money. Maybe we should wait until we get home to finish this conversation?"

Sarah said, "That's probably best. I have a lot to do. I love you, bye."

Karl said, "Congratulations, Director Sarah. Bye."

Sarah called Jill. She answered and said, "Hey, girlfriend. What's up?"

Sarah said, "I'm coming over for lunch. We need to talk. I have a lot to tell you."

Jill said, "Okay, I will tell my mom, one more for lunch."

Next, Sarah called Tammy on her cell phone.

"Tammy, can you talk?"

Tammy said, "I can. I'm home. I don't have a job assignment today. Sure, what's on your mind?"

Sarah said, "How would you like to come work here full-time with all of the company benefits? You will replace me for Ms. White's day-to-day activities like you did while I was on leave. Your title will be Executive Administrative Assistant. How much are you making now?"

Tammy told her.

Sarah said, "I am offering you a starting salary doubling that. Sorry, that was a lot, all at once, for me to say. Maybe you need time to think it over?"

Tammy said, "Sarah, you are starting to sound just like Ms. White—right to the point, without any buildup. It sounds all too good to be true. I have been looking for a new job. I'm tired of bouncing around from company to company doing this temporary fill-in work, not knowing if I would be working the next day or week. I like Ms. White and her company. You said you are going to double what I'm making now—what is there to think about? Yes, I will come to work. When do I start?"

Sarah said, "That's fantastic! When would you like to start? Is tomorrow okay?"

Tammy said jokingly, "Let me check my calendar. Yes, I have an opening. Tomorrow will be fine."

They both laughed.

Tammy asked Sarah, "What are you going to be doing? Did you quit to become a full-time mom?"

Sarah said, "No, I got a promotion. I will still accompany Ms. White on her business meetings. My new title is Director of New Facilities and Planning. The new company headquarters building being built—well, that's my new baby. I'm moving into Ms. White's old office. I started my new position this morning. There is a meeting at four-thirty to make the announcement."

Tammy said, "Congratulations, Director Sarah. I guess I'll see you in the morning."

Sarah said, "Yes, I will see you in the morning."

It was time to go over to Jill's place. Jill answered the door with Steven in her arms and said, "Come on in. My mom has lunch ready for us."

Sarah said, "How's everything going?"

Jill said, "Come on, Sarah. You didn't invite yourself over for lunch to ask me how everything is going. That's not like you—what gives?"

Sarah said, "A lot has happened to me. I got a promotion. My new title is Director of New Facilities and Planning, and I got a raise too."

Jill said, "You're not going to be working for Ms. White anymore?"

Sarah said, "Not in my old capacity. The day-to-day stuff will be done by her new executive administrative assistant. She starts tomorrow. I will be moving into Ms. White's old office. I will need the extra room for what I will be doing. Ms. White told me to hire myself an administrative assistant. That's why I'm here. I want to hire you as my administrative assistant. I'm sure I can offer you more than you are making now.

"It will be hard at first because we both will have to develop split personalities. One of friends, and one of boss/employee. There will be times when you will have to do what I tell you to do and just do it. I hope you will not think I will be a terrible boss. So what are you thinking?"

Jill said, "I'm thinking I'm hungry. Let's eat."

Sarah smiled and gave Jill one of her looks that she gave Karl all the time. They ate and talked about what Sarah will be doing in her new job position. Jill said, "Can you wait long enough for me to get the okay from the doctor to go back to work? I have an appointment in just over an hour from now. I will call you as soon as he is done with the examination and tell you what he said."

Sarah said, "Are you saying you want the job?"

Jill said, "I was waiting for you to ask. Of course, boss lady—or should I call you Director Sarah?"

Sarah gave Jill another one of her looks.

*****

Sarah returned to work. She didn't want to move her personal belongings into her new office until the announcement meeting was over. She didn't want a bunch of rumors to start. It was bad enough that people saw her in that office. She hoped they just thought she was in there cleaning it out for someone else to move into. She closed the door and studied the building plans, making notes for what she would say at the meeting. She tried to think of questions she might get and the answers to those questions. She wanted to come across as being knowledgeable and the right person for this job, just as Ms. White had suggested.

Sarah knocked on Ms. White's open door and said, "Are you busy?"

Ms. White said, "Come on in."

Sarah said, "I just wanted to bring you up to date on what I have done. Tammy will be here tomorrow to start her new job working for you. She said she liked working here and for you. She said she was already looking for a steady, permanent job. I checked with HR—doubling her salary will give her plenty of room in her pay grade."

Ms. White said, "Those temp agencies pay their people nothing, and they charge us plenty. Go on."

Sarah continued, "I have a person I want to hire as my administrative assistant. I have already talked with her. She had a baby not too long ago and wants to check with her doctor to see if it's okay to return to work. She said she will let me know by the end of the day. If she does not get released for a couple more weeks, I may need to get a temp person."

Ms. White said, "Sarah, you do what you need to do to do your job. Only come to me with the big stuff. Things like getting a temp are not one of those big things. Do what you need to do. Remember, you are now a director. You need to think at that level. You make good decisions and don't have to ask my permission on the small things. Do you have more?"

Sarah said, "I understand. I'm a director and need to act as one. It's so new to me. I have been working on my speech for our meeting. I have included a lot of information in hopes I won't get too many questions. I have tried to think of questions that I might be asked and have answers to those questions."

Ms. White said, "That's my Sarah, always staying ahead of the curve. We will take questions together. I will answer the ones you may not know the answer to or feel uncomfortable answering. Being prepared can't be bad. Remember to stick to the matters associated with the new facility and not future business dealings."

"Sarah, you have done a lot in such a short period of time. That only adds to the fact that picking you for this job was the correct decision."

Sarah said, "After the meeting, I will move my belongings over to my new office. I didn't want to do it now and start any rumors."

Ms. White said, "Yes, we have enough of them floating around right now. That's another reason why I wanted to have this meeting."

Sarah returned to her new office to go over her notes and calm down. She walked over to Ms. White's office and said, "It's four-twenty, Ms. White. We best go on down to the cafeteria for the meeting."

Sarah carried some notes she wrote on some index cards. Ms. White had a notebook.

Ms. White picked the cafeteria because of the number of people she was expecting to attend. The meeting was supposed to be for department heads, directors, and vice presidents only, but she knew some of them would bring their key people with them or to represent them. This was not Ms. White's first rodeo, as they say.

Ms. White started by saying, "Thank you, all, for coming. As the memo stated, this meeting is to give you an update on the new facility and our plans to move out of this building and into the new one. I have not decided on what we will do with this building once we vacate. I want to introduce you to Sarah. Many of you already know her from the time she worked for Bill. As of this morning, Sarah has the title of Director of New Facilities and Planning, and her job duties will be associated with that title. I have asked Sarah to say a few words, and then we will open the meeting up to your questions."

Sarah started by saying, "Change is not always fun or easy. I hope working with you and your people, we can make this change fun and without too much pain. It will be a year before the building is completed. That is, of course, if they can stay on schedule. Ms. White has been working with the building's architects and determined the square footage each area will need. It's up to you and me to determine how you fit into those areas. I will be moving into Ms. White's old office. As I work through the departments and sections, I or a member of my team will be making appointments with you to review the area assigned to your department or section. In these meetings, we will work together on how you want your workers' offices and desks to be laid out.

"You will be seeing me or members of my team in your areas so we can get a better understanding of your needs. If you have suggestions as to how you would like your area laid out, that would be helpful too. Remember, we have a year before the building is completed. It may be a while before it's your turn. When the building is finished, everyone will not be moving in on the same day. Imagine the chaos that would be with everybody trying to move at the same time. A move-in schedule will be developed.

"Now for some fun things. I would like to share a few of the things you can be looking forward to—things that we don't currently have. There will be a childcare facility with an outside playground. An exercise room with all sorts of exercise machines and equipment, and a place to take showers. Two inside handball/racquetball courts. Outside there will be a half-court basketball court and two pickleball/tennis courts. A park area with places to sit and have lunch, if you like, or just enjoy the park. There will be a fountain there too. The plans include a healthcare facility with a full-time nurse. A new cafeteria with all-new kitchen equipment. There will be a conference facility large enough to hold all of our employees and our annual company and shareholder employee meetings."

As Sarah was listing the new things, there were cheers from the people.

Ms. White said, "From what Director Sarah has just said, we are going to have a wonderful place to work. Our company is a medium-sized company, but my vision is to be competitive with other larger companies in our area, where people will want to come work before even looking at those larger corporations for a job."

Applause and cheers came from the people.

Ms. White said, "From what Director Sarah just said, we will need to hire people to work in these new areas—a nurse or two for the health care center, people who can look after the kiddos in the new childcare facility, and people to manage, maintain, and keep everything clean. HR, are you listening? I expect you to be working closely with Director Sarah to coordinate the hiring of the new people. They need to be in place when the areas are ready. I assure you, not everything will be in place on day one. We must all work together to make this happen. Now, Sarah and I will take your questions."

There were several questions, but between Ms. White and Sarah, they all got answered.

Ms. White said, "If there are no more questions, this meeting is over. Thank you for your time."

Several people came up after the meeting to congratulate Sarah on her new position and said they look forward to working with her. They told Ms. White that they liked what she had to say and thanked her for having the meeting. It cleared the air of a lot of the rumors that were going around.

*****

Sarah and Ms. White returned to Ms. White's office. On the way in, Sarah stopped to check Ms. White's phone messages and emails.

Sarah said, "There are a couple of messages and three emails you may want to take a look at."

Ms. White said, "I will get to them in a minute. First, let me say what an excellent job you did. Will you ever cease to amaze me?"

Sarah said, "I hope I can keep on amazing you."

Sarah had a smile on her face you could not remove with dynamite and said, "I'm going to move my stuff from my old office to my new one."

Sarah got a box and packed her personal belongings. She took them down to her new office. She put the box on her desk and said to herself, *Ms. White kept on referring to me as Director Sarah. I have to let that sink in and begin thinking like a director.*

Her phone rang, snapping her back to reality. The caller ID said Jill. Sarah answered, and Jill said, "Hi, boss."

Sarah said, "What did the doctor say?"

Jill said, "The doctor said I looked healthy and if I felt like going back to work now, he had no problem with it. I talked to my mother about me going back to work. She said she had planned on staying here until my leave was up in a couple of weeks and would be happy to watch the kids during that time while I went to work for you. She even said it might be nice not having me around. I don't know how to take that one. I already made arrangements with a babysitter to start in two weeks so I don't have to change anything there. With my mother here, everything is working out just fine. So when do you want me to start?"

Sarah said, "ASAP, but I want you to be up and able to hit the ground running day one."

Jill said, "I will be there tomorrow at nine."

Sarah said, "I will schedule an appointment for you with HR at nine-thirty. See you in the morning. Bye."

Jill said, "In the morning, Director Sarah. Bye."

Sarah said, "I kinda like the sound of that."

They both laughed.

Sarah called HR and set up two appointments: one for Tammy and one for Jill. It was quitting time. Sarah walked down to Ms. White's office and said, "I called HR to set up the new employee appointments for Tammy and my new administrative assistant, Jill. In the morning, I will call down to the print shop and have business cards printed for the new people. Also, I will call IT to have them set up all the access the new people will need to do their jobs."

Ms. White said, "As my assistant, you have been keeping up with my calendar. Get with that support person in IT to set one up for you and make it so I have access to it. Tomorrow will be another big day."

Sarah said, "I think they all are going to be big days for some time to come. Is there anything else you would like for me to do before I go home? If not, I will see you in the morning."

Ms. White said, "No, that is enough for now. Have a good evening."

Karl and Sarah got home about the same time. Margo was just finishing up giving Emily her bath. Kevin already had his. They stepped into the nursery and said to Margo, "How did you and the twins do?"

Margo said, "We are working out a schedule, and it seems to be working okay. They are such good kids. You two did good making them. If there is nothing else, I'm going home."

They both said, "Can't think of anything. Good evening, see you in the morning. Have a good evening. Bye."

Sarah and Karl changed their clothes, and Sarah started getting dinner ready. Karl got the plates and silverware out and set the table. They sat down at the table, and Karl said, "Now slowly tell me about your day. You were so pumped on the phone and talking so fast it was hard for me to take it all in."

Sarah said, "I'm no longer Ms. White's executive administrative assistant. Tammy, the temp lady who filled in while I was on leave and who I talked with from time to time—I hired her to be Ms. White's new executive administrative assistant."

Karl said, "Sarah, you are doing it again. Honey, slow down."

Sarah said, "Okay, okay. My new title is Director of New Facilities and Planning, and I report directly to Ms. White at the vice president level on the corporate organization chart.

"Right now, my duties will be to work with the builder to do the inside decorating but also work with all of the department heads, directors, and vice presidents to help design the areas their people will be working in. That includes ordering all new desks, chairs, filing cabinets, and conference room furniture. In addition, I will still be accompanying Ms. White on her business meetings, same as before, taking notes, doing research, and writing up recap reports.

"My main focus for now is on the new building. You can't tell anyone, but Ms. White is in negotiations to buy additional businesses. I will be involved in merging those companies into my company.

"I have moved into Ms. White's old office. You will never guess who I hired as my administrative assistant, and she starts tomorrow. It's Jill."

Karl said, "Jill? Will that cause problems with your friendship, you telling her what to do?"

Sarah said, "We have talked about that, and for now, we have it all worked out."

Karl said, "You said something about getting a raise. Didn't you just get one before you went on leave?"

She said, "Yes. Ms. White gave me another 33 percent raise for the pay grade of director."

Karl said, "Director Sarah."

Sarah said, "Let's skip cleaning up the kitchen for now, and you can whisper Director Sarah into my ear as you make love to me. I'm back on the pill now."

Well, you know what happened next.

CHAPTER 37

Jill's First Day

It was right at 9:00 when Jill came walking up to Sarah's office and said, "Good morning. Sorry I'm late. I didn't know where your office was and went the long way around to find it."

Sarah said, "Good morning. It's just now 9:00, so you're really not late. Come on into my office. Are you ready for a full, busy day?"

Jill walked in and took a look around and said, "Would you take a look at this place?"

Sarah said, "Yes, it's very nice. It is Ms. White's old office. My job title does not call for an office like this, but my job requires me to have the extra space, and this office was available. It just worked out that way. My office in the new building will not be this nice. It will be in keeping with the other directors' offices. You have an appointment with the HR department at nine-thirty."

Jill said, "I know where that is—I passed it trying to find your office."

Sarah said, "Let's walk down to Ms. White's office, and I will introduce you to her and her new executive administrative assistant."

As they got close to Ms. White's office, Jill said, "Tammy Jones, is that you?"

Tammy said, "Jill Hill, is that you?"

Jill turned to Sarah and said, "She did some temp work many times at my old company."

Tammy said, "It is a small world. Today is my first day. They hired me here full time. So you are Director Sarah's new administrative assistant?"

Jill said, "Yes, today is my first day too."

Sarah asked Tammy, "Does Ms. White have a minute?"

Tammy said, "Let me check."

Tammy keyed the intercom and said, "Sarah is here and would like to know if you have a minute."

Ms. White said, "Send her in."

Sarah motioned to Jill to follow her.

Sarah said, "I won't take but a minute of your time. I wanted to introduce you to my new administrative assistant, Jill Hill."

Jill said, "So pleased to meet you, Ms. White."

Ms. White said, "Pleased to meet you too. Welcome to my company. Pay attention to your new boss. She has a lot to offer, and you can learn a lot from her."

Sarah said, "Tammy and Jill both have appointments with HR, so they better get going, and I know I have things to do."

Ms. White said, "I'm sure you do too."

Tammy and Jill went off to HR, and Sarah went back to her office and called Carol in IT.

Sarah said, "Hi, Carol, this is Sarah."

Carol said, "Hi, Director Sarah. Congratulations on your new position. What can I do for you?"

Sarah said, "You helped me set up a calendar on my first day, but I never used it. You also set me up to have access to Ms. White's calendar at that time. I have been accessing it and have gotten good at navigating the calendar app both on my phone and on my laptop. Ms. White wants me to start using my calendar for appointments, and she wants access to it also. Additionally, I would like to order a laptop for my new administrative assistant."

Carol said, "Can do, no problem. I happen to have an extra laptop here in my office your new person can have. While we have been talking, I accessed your calendar and Ms. White's calendar. Ms. White can now access your appointments."

Sarah said, "You can see our appointments?"

Carol said, "Oh no, not the actual appointments, just the access levels. Only the ones that have the correct access authority can see other people's calendar appointments. All I did was to change the software master table to allow the access. You should be getting a message stating your security access has been changed. The first time Ms. White tries to access your calendar, you will get a message asking you to verify that your calendar can be accessed by this person. Just touch or click the 'allow' button. There is also a button that says, 'Ignore this message in the future for this person.' You will want to touch or click that button. If you don't, you will get that message every time Ms. White looks at your calendar. Hey, maybe you will want to know that she looked at your calendar. Your choice."

Sarah said, "Good to know. Is there anything that Ms. White needs to do?"

Carol said, "No, she has access to several other people's calendars. Yours will appear in her list. I will be up in a couple of minutes with the laptop and will take a look at your calendar to make sure everything is okay."

Sarah said, "By the way, Carol, my new office is Ms. White's old office."

Sarah made a call to the print shop. The print shop secretary answered the phone and said, "Print shop, how can I help you?"

Sarah said, "Hello, this is Sarah. I would like to have business cards printed up for two new employees."

The secretary said, "Congratulations on your new position, Ms. Director. Are you happy with the cards we printed up for you?"

Sarah said, "Yes, you guys do such wonderful work."

Sarah gave her the information for Tammy and Jill.

The secretary said, "While I have you on the phone, I want to ask you, are we going to be stuck in the basement of the new building like we are here?"

Sarah said, "No, the basement will be for the archives and supplies storage. The floor in the area for the print shop will be heavily reinforced to support the weight of your printing presses."

The secretary said, "Today must be your lucky day. We just finished printing some business cards, and the printing press is still set up to print business cards. I will get the guys to print these business cards up before they change the printer to print the next job. I should have the cards sent up to your office sometime this afternoon. The cards will need a little time for the ink to dry. Is there anything else I can do for you?"

Sarah said, "What service. I think that does it. You can have the cards delivered to my office. I have moved into Ms. White's old office."

Sarah went to her calendar and entered the appointment she had this afternoon with Harlow Construction. Just as she finished, Carol knocked on her door and said, "I'm here."

Sarah said, "I just added an appointment to my calendar. It looks like mine is working okay."

Carol said, "Wonderful. Here is the laptop for your new administrative assistant. Do you mind if I take a look at your laptop?"

Sarah said, "No," and handed Carol her laptop.

Carol said, "Just as I thought. There are several updates that need to be made to the software on your laptop. May as well let me check the app on your phone too. This is going to take probably an hour to do. I know how you people rely on your iPads, computers, and phones. I hope it won't inconvenience you too much."

Sarah said, "You can sit at the outer office desk. My new administrative assistant will need to have access to my calendar and the calendar app installed on her phone. She will also need login access to the Internet and an email account set up for her. The same needs to be done for Ms. White's new executive administrative assistant."

Carol said, "It's a good thing I brought my laptop with me. I can do those things while waiting for your downloads and the installs to finish."

Tammy and Jill returned from HR and stopped at Sarah's office. Sarah said, "Tammy and Jill, I want you to meet Carol. She is our IT contact. She is updating my laptop and iPhone. Jill, here is your company laptop."

Sarah said to Tammy, "I talked to Ms. White, and she said you will be using the desktop computer and didn't need a laptop. That might change in the future. That will be up to you two."

Carol said, "Tammy, are you back here again?"

Tammy said, "Yes, but this time as a full-time employee."

Carol said, "You already know how to use the company's calendar, email system, and how to access the Internet. I just need to set those accesses back up again. I will do that as soon as I'm done with Jill. Tammy, good to see you again, and welcome to the company full-time."

Sarah said, "Tammy, it's getting close to lunchtime. As soon as Carol is done, the three of us can all go to lunch together."

Tammy said, "Okay."

Carol said, "I have set up Jill's accesses while we have been talking. I can give her a quick tutorial on the calendar and will work with her to verify her accounts are all working. I think I can do it all before it's time for you to go to lunch. Tammy, good to see you again. Call if you have any problems."

"Your updates are finished. It didn't take as long as I thought. Here is your iPhone and laptop back. I know you have new job duties with the new building. Just saying, you may want a desktop computer with a large monitor and keyboard for this office. We try to keep an extra one in inventory. I have a brand-new one still in the box. It just came in the other day. I could get it all set up and on your desk by tomorrow morning. Your laptop, iPhone, and desktop computer will all be linked together. If one gets updated, they all do."

Sarah said, "You have a good point. Trying to do all of what I'm going to be doing on a laptop will be a challenge. Go ahead and do whatever needs to be done on the computer. I will see you sometime in the morning. Thank you for your help, Carol. I will let you two get on with the calendar tutorial and how to access everything else. Jill, let me know when you are done, and we will go get Tammy and have some lunch."

Carol and Jill finished up just as it was lunchtime. Carol said, "I was even able to get the calendar app downloaded onto Jill's iPhone. Got to go. Congratulations again on your promotion."

Sarah said, "Thanks. I will see you in the morning with that new computer."

Jill said, "That Carol is good. She said I could call her whenever I had a computer problem. I didn't have that level of support at my old company. We accessed your calendar. It shows you have a meeting this afternoon. I'm hungry. Where do we go to eat?"

Sarah said, "Slow down. Are you excited or what? Breathe already! Yes, Carol is something else and knows her stuff. Let's see if Tammy is ready for lunch."

They walked down to Tammy's desk, and Sarah said, "Can you go to lunch now?"

Tammy said, "Yes, just waiting on you two."

The three of them walked down to the double doors that open to the executive dining room. Tammy had eaten there before while filling in for Sarah while she was on maternity leave. Sarah had talked to Tammy just before lunch and said, "Don't let the cat out of the bag. Let's see Jill's reaction."

Tammy opened the door, and they walked in. Jill's eyes lit up as soon as she walked in and looked around. She said, "Is this where we eat or is this just because it's my first day?"

Sarah and Tammy were enjoying Jill's reaction. Tammy said, "We can eat here every day. That is, unless you want to go eat someplace else."

Jill said, "No, this place will do just fine."

They walked down to the other end of the dining room where the staff was supposed to sit and eat. Monty said, "Good afternoon, Director Sarah, Ms. Tammy," and nodded at Jill. "Good to see you again, Ms. Tammy. Are you back with us again?"

Tammy said, "Yes, Monty, but this time I'm now a full-time employee, so you will be seeing a lot of me from now on."

Monty said, "Looking forward to it. Who do we have here?"

Sarah said, "This is my new administrative assistant, Jill."

Monty said, "Pleased to meet you, Ms. Jill. Director Sarah, may I have a word with you?"

Monty stepped away from the table, and Sarah followed. Monty said, "Ms. Sarah, I know you have been eating here for some time, but now that you are a director, you will have to sit at the other end of the dining room with the other executives. I'm sorry, I don't make the rules. Please don't be mad at me. I have enjoyed serving you, and I will take good care of these employees."

Sarah said, "Monty, I understand rules are rules, and the last thing I would want to do is get you, of all people, in trouble. You have been so good to me. I will excuse myself and go to the other end of the dining room."

Sarah returned to the table and said, "Something has come up. Enjoy your lunch. Jill, I will see you after lunch back at the office."

Sarah walked back to the other end of the dining room.

Ms. White was just walking in and said, "Sarah, are you leaving? What's the problem?"

Sarah said, "I was going to have lunch with Jill and Tammy, but because I'm a director, I'm not allowed to eat at that end of the dining room anymore."

Ms. White said, "That rule. I never did like that rule. I understand why my father made it. Employees were complaining that their lunches turned into a work session. Executives should be able to sit with their employees at that end of the dining room if they choose. I am going to change that rule effective tomorrow. I will add that executives can sit with staff at that end of the dining room but cannot talk about business during lunch. I will keep this end the same. Now sit down here and join me for lunch. Let's see if they give you any trouble with you sitting here with me." And she gave Sarah a big smile. Of course, no one would have said anything anyway. After all, it was Ms. White.

Monty brought Tammy and Jill menus and asked, "What would you like to drink?"

Tammy said, "Iced tea."

Monty said, "And for you, Ms. Jill?"

"I'll have iced tea too."

Jill opened the menu and said, "There are no prices. How will I know how much I'm spending? It must cost a fortune to eat here. This place puts some fancy restaurants to shame."

Tammy smiled at Jill and said, "Welcome to the executive world. At this company, eating here is part of your compensation package. You eat here at no charge. You are free to order whatever you like.

Several of the items are offered every day. They do have daily specials and, from time to time, new items."

Jill said, "This menu reads like that of a fancy restaurant."

Tammy said, "It sure does. Since I was on a tight budget working for that temp agency, whenever I got assigned here, this was my main meal for the day. You can put on the pounds if you don't watch it."

Jill said, "I just had my second baby and have not lost much of the weight I put on while I was pregnant."

Tammy said, "You better pick what you want to eat. Monty will be back to take our order soon."

Jill ordered a salad, and so did Tammy. While they waited for their food and during lunch, they caught up on what they had been doing since the last time Tammy had worked at Jill's old company.

When lunchtime was over, Jill and Tammy walked back to their offices. As they got to Tammy's office, Jill said, "Lunch tomorrow?"

Tammy said, "Sure, if nothing comes up and we can't."

Jill returned to her office.

Sarah was in her office. Her door was open, and Jill said, "Can I come in?"

Sarah said, "Yes, and close the door behind you."

Jill asked, "What happened there in the dining room, if you can tell me?"

Sarah said, "It's an old rule that executives can't eat at that end of the dining room with staff. A long time ago, the staff employees were complaining they were having nothing but working lunches when their bosses ate lunch with them. Mr. White had a decision to either make the dining room for executives only or separate the dining room where one end was for executives, and the other end was for the staff. The food and service are the same at both ends of the dining room. Ms. White said she was going to put out a memo to change the rule."

Jill said, "That is some lunch, and the service. Monty kept calling me Ms. Jill. Do you eat there every day?"

Sarah said, "I think you were impressed with our dining facilities? I eat there whenever I can. Lately, I have been so busy I get it to go and eat lunch here at my desk."

While they were at lunch, the business cards were delivered to Sarah's desk. Sarah handed the box of Jill's cards to her and said, "Here are your and Tammy's business cards. Please take Tammy her cards. When you get back, I will give you a briefing on the meeting we will be going to."

Jill said, "We?"

Sarah said, "Yes, we. Now go deliver the cards and hurry on back."

Jill walked down and gave Tammy her box of business cards.

While Jill was delivering Tammy her business cards, Sarah's cell phone rang. It was her old boss, Bill, calling. Sarah answered and said, "What a surprise. So good to hear your voice. How is retirement treating you?"

Bill said, "Hi, Director Sarah. Retirement is great. I have time to do my own yard work, advance my hobbies, and work on this never-ending honey-do list my wife has me working on."

Sarah said, "So you heard about my promotion and new job? Still plugged into the old grapevine, are you? So what are they saying about me?"

Bill said, "Never mind what they are saying about you. I am so proud of you, Sarah. Ever since that interview when you applied to my job ad a few years back, I knew you would be very successful. The reputation you have created is exceptional. When Ms. White was looking for an executive administrative assistant, I had to put your name in the hat.

"She and I go back a long way. But let's not talk about that. I hear you also had twins."

Sarah said, "Yes, a boy and girl. Kevin and Emily. They are growing up so fast. They are out of their bassinets and into their cribs. We have a nanny that watches them during the day while Karl and I are at work."

Bill said, "I heard Karl got a new job too. How is he liking it?"

Sarah said, "You certainly are plugged into the information highway, aren't you? Karl was making good money here but wanted to expand his skills. His college friend started work at an accounting firm at the same time Karl started working here. Well, he made Karl an offer Karl just couldn't pass up. Karl is even on bonus. He loves his job. He is very busy all of the time and has staff working full-time only for him."

Bill said, "We should have lunch sometime."

Sarah said, "You're the busy one, remember? Me? I'm the one that's retired. Bill, let me ask you something. I'm sure you know my job is this new headquarters building project. I know I'm going to need lots of help getting it done. Would you consider coming to work for me as a contractor?"

Bill said, "Ask me when the time comes, but you know I will be there for you. If I do, do I call you Boss or Director Sarah?"

Sarah said, "Bill, you old fart. Go enjoy that retirement. I will call you when the time comes and see to it you work your BUTT off. So get some rest now while you can. You are going to need it. I love you. I have got to go, bye."

Jill waited until Sarah was off the phone before entering her office. Sarah said, "Come on in. Let me brief you on this meeting we are going to. We are running short on time, so I will tell you on the drive over. Grab that new laptop. Get used to having it with you when we are together at business meetings."

Jill said, "I noticed that picture of a cow on the wall. What's that all about?"

Sarah said, "You will find out soon enough. Let's go."

Jill said, "Give me a minute. I have to go pee."

Sarah said, "You can use the bathroom in my office. It's behind that door over there."

Jill said, "Get out of here. You have a bathroom in your office. I can't wait to tell Jack when I get home tonight."

Sarah said, "Hurry up. I don't want to be late for this meeting."

On the drive over to Harlow Construction Company, Sarah said, "This is the first meeting of many we will be having with what they call their inside decoration team. They don't know that I will be taking over more and more of what Ms. White has been doing so far. We don't need to say anything about that to them. It will just evolve as the project goes along. The person we will be meeting with, her name is Judy. She will most likely have a person or two from her team in our meeting. Your role right now is to be a silent sponge. Use your laptop to take any notes that you feel will help you write a recap report to document this meeting and any future meetings you attend with me. I probably will ask you to make a note from time to time. Remember, we are in Boss/Employee mode."

Jill said, "I understand."

They walked in the building and up to the receptionist's desk. Sarah said, "My name is Sarah. This is my administrative assistant, Jill. We have an appointment with Judy."

The receptionist said, "Yes, I have you down on my visitors list. Here are your visitor badges. Please wear them while in the building and don't forget to return them to me when you leave. They are waiting for you down that hall, the third door on the right."

As they walked down the hall, Jill said, "Get a load of this place. It's nicer than a lot of your fancy resort hotels. And that mural on the wall behind the receptionist's desk is something else."

Sarah said, "I thought the same thing on my first visit. I'm going to see to it we have one in our new building."

The door was open, and Sarah recognized Judy from the meeting they had a few days ago.

Sarah said, "Are we late?"

Judy said, "Oh no. We were just having a premeeting before you got here."

Judy introduced her people, and Sarah introduced Jill. On the table were several books and catalogs.

Judy said, "These are yours to take back to your office. You will be picking everything from soup to nuts from these books and catalogs. I know there are a lot of them, and looking at them now is very overwhelming. As you work with them, you will get to the point where you will be able to go straight to what you are looking for. There are a lot of them because they are broken down to a specific area. Take this one, for example."

Judy picked up one of the books and said, "This one only has kitchen items."

They all have very good indexes and section tabs. All of the price lists are in this other notebook. The team and I have put together a slide and video show from some of the jobs we have worked on. If you see a blurred-out place, that is where a company's name is. We have agreements, as we do with your company, to protect the privacy of your company. Please sit back and enjoy our presentation."

After the show was over, Judy said, "What is your first impression?"

Sarah said, "I can see why Ms. White picked your company to do business with."

Judy asked, "Have you developed a plan to proceed?"

Sarah said, "We had a meeting with the department and section heads and the vice presidents. They are on board, and we will be working our way through the different areas, picking out the new office furniture and cubicles.

"I would like to start with the kitchens, followed by the day care facility, including the playground equipment, and then the exercise room equipment and machines. I think these areas have the items that will take the most time to order and get delivered. We will be contracting with a container company to provide onsite storage if the items come in prior to your worker, or the vendors will be ready to install them."

Judy said, "Harry, could you go down to our library and pull the playground and exercise equipment catalogs?"

"Sarah, I thought you were the inside decorating contact."

Sarah replied, "Don't you think the playground and exercise equipment would fall under that?"

"I guess so," Judy said. "Here comes Harry with the catalogs now."

"Am I correct to assume that you will be my contact here at Harlow?" Sarah asked.

"That is my understanding," Judy answered. "There will be other contacts when it comes to landscaping and other things not under my inside decoration duties."

"Here are a couple of my business cards," Sarah said.

Judy took a look at the card and saw it said Director of New Facilities and Planning.

Sarah continued, "Give us a couple of weeks to go through these books and catalogs and work with our people. I will call you to set up appointments for you and whoever to meet with us. For now, I would like to have the meetings at our place. Do you see any problems with doing that?"

Judy replied, "We will work with you and your people however you like. Here are a couple of my business cards." Judy handed the cards to Sarah and added, "Thanks for coming, and I will be looking forward to your call."

"You and your team put together a very impressive presentation. My thanks to you all," Sarah said. "I know how important it is to stay ahead of the construction. We don't want your people standing around because we are behind, causing delays. Please include me on the weekly construction updates that you are sending to Ms. White. Thanks again. Goodbye."

Judy said, "I will have someone help you with all of the books and catalogs."

"That would be helpful," Sarah responded. Then, turning to Jill, she asked, "Do we have everything? And are you ready to go?"

Jill nodded, "Yes."

They turned in their badges and went to the car. Loaded up, Sarah thanked the helper and drove off.

On the drive back to the company, Jill said, "I don't know about you, but I sure am overwhelmed. You have to pick everything from soup to nuts?"

Sarah replied, "First, it's WE who have to do the picking of everything from soup to nuts. We will be working with the people here at our company and Harlow. Remember that cow picture hanging in my office that you asked me about?"

"Yes," Jill said.

"That will be our inspiration," Sarah explained.

Jill asked, "How can a picture of a cow be our inspiration?"

Sarah smiled and said, "You can't eat an entire cow in one dinner."

Jill said, "I understand completely. That will surely be my inspiration when I'm feeling stressed out and overwhelmed. Sarah, I have never seen you act like the way you did in that meeting. You were awesome. I think you have clearly established to Judy that you are the one."

Sarah responded, "They don't teach you that stuff out of a book in college. I have had good mentors. Both Bill and Ms. White have taught me so much. When he first interviewed me, Bill saw potential that I never knew I had. He hired me on the spot. If you choose to watch me and learn from me, who knows where you will end up after this wild ride?"

"Ms. White said the same thing," Jill noted.

They pulled into the company parking lot. Sarah asked, "Is there anything you need from your office?"

Jill replied, "I have my purse, laptop, and phone with me. I have everything."

"Go ahead and go home," Sarah said. "Give those kids a kiss from their Aunt Sarah, and I will see you in the morning."

Jill asked, "How about all of these books and catalogs?"

"You can help me carry them up to my office in the morning," Sarah answered.

Jill said, "I see now why you have that big office. You really do need all of that room. See you in the morning."

*****

Sarah beat Karl home, mainly because she left work a little early. She knew she would be putting in the hours both at work and home. Sarah walked into the house and said, "Hello, Margo."

Margo responded, "You are home a little early. The twins were good as always. They are such great kids. I wish my kids and the others I have looked after were as good as these two."

"Thanks," Sarah said.

Margo continued, "It's true. If you don't need anything, I will just go ahead and head home a little early."

Sarah said, "Go ahead and go. I'm just going to change my clothes and go love on my twins."

About a half hour later, Karl pulled his car into the garage. Sarah had gotten out the stroller built for two and had it parked in the living room. Karl came in, gave Sarah a kiss, and said, "What's this?"

Sarah replied, "Go change your clothes while I put the twins in the stroller. It's still nice out, and I would like to take them for a walk."

Sarah wheeled the stroller into the nursery and put the twins in. As she finished, Karl said, "Okay, I'm ready. Let's go on the walk."

As they began walking, Sarah asked, "How was your day?"

Karl responded, "You know that Doug that works for me?"

She said, "You have mentioned him more than once and said that he has been making lots of mistakes."

Karl continued, "I caught him making a big mistake, and then he lied about it. If I hadn't caught it, it would have cost the client a lot of money and possibly even more in fines and penalties. Surely, it would have cost us the client's trust and their business. I talked to Janet about him, and she said to go ahead and let him go. So I did."

"That must have been stressful," Sarah said.

"Actually, no, it was easy," Karl replied. "I have enough documentation that I have sent to HR over the last month. There is no way he has a legal leg to stand on. I gave him lots of chances to improve. Put him on probation. It was like he wanted to be fired."

Karl asked, "Tell me about your day."

Sarah said, "Today was Jill's first day. I took her with me to the construction meeting. She listened to my instructions going into the meeting. She did well. I think she is going to do a good job for me. I think we will work great together. You should have seen her at lunch. I think her reaction to the executive dining room was better than mine when I first saw it."

Karl asked, "What do you think we should do for dinner?"

Sarah suggested, "Are you in the mood for pizza? I could call now, and by the time we are done with the walk, it will be delivered."

"Excellent idea," Karl said.

As they were walking back to the house, Sarah said, "Karl, we are both making good money. We have the houses as our only debt. I think we should both get new cars. I will get one to be used as the family car. One big enough for us, the twins, and all of the things they need anytime we go anywhere. You can get any car you want. We could trade in both cars and pay the balance in cash for one and carry the other one on a loan. That way, we would only have one car payment. You are the accountant, do the math, and tell me what you think. If you don't want a new car, I still want one."

Karl said, "I think that's a good idea. Both cars are getting old and are starting to need more repairs. Okay, let's do it. Do you have an idea for a car you want?"

Sarah replied, "I have been looking at cars and SUVs on the highway but don't have one picked out."

Karl suggested, "Let's go car shopping this Saturday. We can look around. It's a want, not a need at the moment. We could get by with what we have for now. I think that would make it easier to walk away from a deal we don't think is right."

Just as they were walking up to their house, the pizza delivery person pulled up. Sarah paid when she ordered, so they took the pizza and went into the house. The twins were sound asleep, so Sarah just left them sleeping comfortably in their stroller while they ate their pizza.

After dinner, and after the twins were fed, Sarah gave Kevin a bath while Karl rocked Emily in one of the big wooden rockers. Then Sarah gave Emily her bath while Karl rocked Kevin. After Emily's bath, Sarah rocked her, and Karl continued to rock Kevin. The twins were sound asleep. Karl and Sarah placed the twins in their cribs and went into the living room to see if there was anything on TV they wanted to watch before going to bed.

CHAPTER 38

Getting Started with the Picking and Choosing

On Sarah's way up to her office, she carried as many of the books and catalogs as she could. Jill was at her desk and saw Sarah just about to drop a couple of the books. She took several books from Sarah and carried them into her office.

Sarah said, "Good morning. Thanks for the help. I was just about to drop a couple. I guess I'm not that bad of a boss after all. You came back to work."

"Good morning. I guess I'm just a glutton for punishment. Besides, I need the money," Jill replied.

They laughed, and Sarah said, "Here are the keys to my car. I would like for you to go get the rest of the books and catalogs and bring them up to my office."

Jill took the keys. While Jill was getting the stuff out of her car, Sarah cleared the conference table. She had rolled up the blueprints and set them aside. Jill returned with her arms loaded. She put the books and catalogs on the conference table and said, "That's all of them."

"Let's start getting familiar with the books and catalogs," Sarah said.

Sarah and Jill each picked up one and started paging through them. When one or the other came across something interesting, they would show it to the other.

Sarah said, "Put a sticky note on the item, and I will do the same," and handed Jill a pad of sticky notes. They spent most of the morning going through the material. There was a lot to look at, and they knew they had a tremendous job ahead of them.

Jill looked up at the cow picture and said, "You know, every time I look at that cow picture, I either get a peaceful feeling or I get hungry. It is about time for lunch, right?"

Sarah said, "Go ahead, I'm going to make a couple of phone calls, and then I'll go to lunch."

Jill walked down to Tammy's desk and said, "Can you go to lunch now?"

Tammy said, "I was just about to call you when I saw you walking this way."

They went off to eat.

Sarah made her couple of calls and headed down to the company cafeteria. She thought she would talk to Lisa and eat something there. As soon as she walked in, Lisa saw her and walked right up to her and said, "Director Sarah, what brings you down here? Are you planning on eating here?"

Sarah said, "It's okay for me to eat here, isn't it?"

"Yes, executive people are allowed to eat here, they just hardly ever do," Lisa replied.

Sarah asked, "I know you must be busy because it's lunchtime, but can I have a couple of minutes to talk to you?"

Lisa said, "If you are going to eat here, go ahead and bring your food back to my office where we can talk. If any of my people need me, no hiding from them, they always find me."

Sarah got something to eat and went to Lisa's office.

Lisa said, "I always have a messy office, but I cleared a spot for you to eat."

Sarah said, "You being a department head, I saw that you attended the meeting the other day. I have selected your department to be the first one to work with. How flexible are your days? The reason I am asking is we will need to meet and go over the planning and equipment for the new building. I don't know how long our first meeting will take, but I do know you will have your work cut out for you selecting and planning. You have longtime employees working for you. They will be of help. I am not going to be abandoning you. At Harlow Construction, they have people that are experts. You will be working not only with me but with them too."

Lisa said, "The best time for me is after lunch. My team can do the after-lunch clean-up with not much supervision. Most have been doing it for years. I have a great staff."

"Would one-thirty tomorrow, in my office, work for you?" Sarah asked.

Lisa replied, "I will be there."

As Sarah finished her lunch, they visited. Lisa asked, "Do you ever get to talk to Bill?"

"Funny you should ask. He called me yesterday. We had a nice conversation. He congratulated me on my new job. Have you talked to him?" Sarah responded.

"Yes, we talk about once a week. We have known each other for a very long time. I think he is having a hard time adjusting to retirement," Lisa said.

"Good to know. Thanks for taking the time to meet with me, and I will see you tomorrow," Sarah said.

Sarah went back to her office. Jill had finished her lunch and was back at her desk.

Jill asked Sarah, "Did you have lunch? I didn't see you in the dining room."

"I had lunch in the cafeteria. Please add a meeting with Lisa, head person of the cafeteria, to my calendar tomorrow at one-thirty. Then I would like for you to research some local day care facilities," Sarah said.

"I'm on it," Jill replied.

Jill knocked on Sarah's open office door.

"Come on in. What did you find out?" Sarah asked.

"There are a few day care facilities around here, but they had low ratings and some bad comments. There are two facilities not too far from here, and they both have four out of five and five out of five ratings. I have the addresses and phone numbers in my laptop. What do you have in mind?" Jill said.

Sarah responded, "Road trip. This will be a data-gathering outing for our company day care facility. We are both new mothers looking for a place for our kids. That's the role we will be playing. Leave the laptop here, but take good mental notes. Ready to go?"

Jill said, "I guess I better be. Let me grab my purse."

They arrived at the closest place Jill had picked. They were not too interested in what the place looked like from the outside. They were interested in what was inside and the playground. They stepped inside and were greeted immediately. The person asked, "May I help you?"

Sarah said, "My best friend and I both had kids not too long ago. We are needing to go back to work soon, and we are looking for a place to care for our kids."

She asked, "How many, and what are their ages?"

Jill looked at Sarah to see if she was going to answer the question, and Sarah gave Jill a go-ahead nod to answer. Jill answered the question for both of them.

The lady handed them both a brochure and said, "Most of the questions new moms have when looking for day care are answered in here."

She handed them both a sheet of paper and said, "This is our price list. As you can see, the prices change based on the level of care your child requires. The more care needed, like feeding and diapers for an infant, costs more than that of an older one who is potty trained and can feed themselves. There is also a late pick-up fee. Kids are to be picked up no later than six-thirty.

"Allow me to give you a quick tour. This side is for the infants. On the other side, it is for the toddlers. We do not take any after-school kids. Feel free to look around."

Sarah asked, "Do you have a playground? Not that my kids are going to be ready for one anytime soon, but I'm looking at the long term."

The lady said, "Since you said how young your kids were, I didn't think it would be of interest to you. Remember, we don't do after-school kids, so the playground is geared toward toddlers."

She pointed to the door leading to the outside and said, "Right through that door."

Sarah and Jill went outside. The playground was small and didn't have much in the way of things to play on.

Sarah said, "I know she said no after-school kids, but there is not much for toddlers either. Have you seen enough and are ready to go?"

Jill said, "I wouldn't pick this place for Jack Jr. and Steven. I don't know how they got such high ratings. I'm ready, let's go."

Sarah said, "No more baby Jack, it's Jack Jr. now?"

On their way to the next place, Jill said, "That place has high Internet ratings and lots of good comments. I was not impressed, and that lady didn't seem all that nice."

They arrived at the other place on Jill's list. They basically said the same thing as at the last place: they were looking for a place to care for their babies while they went back to work. They took the information pamphlet. The playground was better equipped than the last place, mainly because this day care watched after-school kids too.

As they left, Sarah said, "I think the city has a children's park not far from here. See if you can look it up on your cell phone."

Jill did an online search and said, "It shows that it is located a mile down Tenth Street. Turn right at the next street. It should cross Tenth right at the park."

Sarah turned right, and soon they were at the park.

Sarah said, "This is more like what I had in mind and is more in keeping with the playground catalog Harlow Construction gave us."

Sarah said to Jill, "Take several pictures of this place. We can compare your pictures to the catalog."

Jill took about a dozen pictures.

On the way back to the office, Sarah said, "When we get back to the office, I would like for you to print off a copy of the recap report I wrote on the meeting Ms. White and I had with Harlow

Construction last week. Read it, and it should give you a 'how-to' for writing company recap reports Ms. White likes for the files. You never know when one of those reports will become an important piece of information. You now have two to write: one from yesterday's meeting and one for this fact-finding mission today."

Sarah spent the remainder of the workday looking at the kitchen equipment book and the blueprints of the kitchen and cafeteria areas. She wanted to make sure she would be ready for her tomorrow's meeting with Lisa. What she didn't get done today, she could finish in the morning. The meeting was not until one-thirty, but things do come up, and she didn't know if something just might come up in the morning and she would not have time. Sarah's time is not always hers when Ms. White needed something.

Jill had printed off a copy of the recap report Sarah talked about. She read it and then read it again. She said to herself, "I wonder if I could write recaps as good as this." Jill started keying the recap report from the notes she had taken during the meeting. Most of the meeting was the slide and video presentation. She did her best to summarize what it was about. She read it over and made some additions and corrections and said to herself, *This will just have to do.* She saved it and printed out a copy. It was coming up on quitting time, and she thought she would hardly get started on the day care places before it was time to go home and would do it in the morning.

Jill took the recap report she just wrote in for Sarah to read.

"Here is the recap report from yesterday's meeting," Jill said.

Sarah read it and said, "Not bad. You should have seen the first one I did for Ms. White. It was really terrible. I had to rewrite it three times before Ms. White would accept it. I thought she was thinking she had made a big mistake in hiring me and was going to fire me. The problem was I didn't have a format or a sample to work from. Thinking back, I could have gone to the files and looked at a report or two. Lesson learned. If you don't know how, do some research. That's why I had you print out my last recap report, so you could see how they like the reports done. Like I said, not bad for your first one. I know you will do better. These reports are all done in the third person, factual, without feelings. Keep that in mind when you rewrite this one in the morning along with the day care one. Let's call it a day. I will walk out with you."

Jill said, "Are all of the days going to be this way?"

Sarah replied, "Oh no, some are going to be much worse."

Jill didn't know if Sarah was joking or not.

CHAPTER 39

Start of the New Cafeteria

The morning was going by quickly. Jill had rewritten the recap report on the Harlow meeting and wrote the one on the day care facilities fact-finding mission. Sarah had a scheduled meeting and then lunch with Ms. White.

During lunch, Ms. White said, "I see several of the executives are eating lunch with their staff. I guess that change to allow the two to eat together was a good move. I just hope I don't start getting complaints about working lunches."

Sarah said, "If the two agree to have a working lunch, that would be entirely up to them. It really could be a win-win situation. I think it will work out just fine. It's a different time than it was back when your father made that rule. It's an informal place to have a conversation. Sometimes it's hard not to talk shop when we get together."

Ms. White said, "That rule is for executives to staff and doesn't apply to executives to executives. We will still have our business lunches."

Sarah said, "I guess this is going to be one of those business lunches. We just had a meeting. What more is it you are wanting to know?"

Ms. White just smiled at Sarah and said, "Calm down, Sarah, just eat your lunch. I'm just having some fun with you."

The relationship between the two of them was growing. Sarah still addressed her as Ms. White and probably always will.

Ms. White asked, "How are the twins and Karl doing?"

"The twins are now sleeping in their cribs. They have an over-size playpen and are starting to turn over on their own. Karl still loves his job. He had to fire one of his employees the other day. It was a disciplinary action. With the weather still being so nice, the four of us have been taking walks most every night. The twins love being outside. Thanks for asking. Karl and I are looking to buy new cars. Both are getting old and are needing more repairs. I would like to get one with more room, especially since we have to take so much with us everywhere we go," Sarah said.

Ms. White said, "I have connections with several car dealerships in the area. When you get ready to buy, let me know. Maybe I can get you a good deal."

Sarah said, "Thanks, that is so kind of you."

Ms. White added, "Don't let that get around. The offer is for you only."

Sarah said, "I understand."

*****

It was one-thirty, and Lisa walked up to Jill's desk.

"My name is Lisa. I have a one-thirty meeting with Director Sarah," she said.

Jill replied, "She is expecting you. Please go right in."

Lisa walked in and said, "I have been up to this floor many times, but that was mostly to HR. I have never been on this side of the building. So this was Ms. White's office before she moved into her father's office?"

"It was. After she moved, this office sat empty. When I took on my new job, Ms. White knew I would need a place to work and would need lots of room for my meetings. All of the new building information sure takes up a lot of room. We didn't want to tie up a conference room for a year. It just made good sense for me to move in here," Sarah explained.

"Come, let's sit over at the conference table. Sit next to me so neither one of us is looking at things upside down. On the table, you will see the blueprint floor plan for the new cafeteria seating area and the cafeteria kitchen. The architecture people at the construction company have laid out the placement of the walk-in freezer and walk-in refrigerator—you see here and here. The stoves, ovens, fryers, sinks, and dishwasher are here, here, and here. The serving line is here," Sarah said.

Lisa asked, "What is there left for me to do? It looks like I'm going to have to live with what has been done."

Sarah said, "Not so fast. This is on paper. The architecture people at the construction company have been doing this for some time and for many different companies and restaurants. This is, as they say, not their first rodeo. What I would like for you to do is take a copy of this layout. The dimensions are clearly marked, as you can see here and here. My suggestion to you is to clear a spot on your cafeteria floor. Tape to the floor, using this layout and the dimensions to create your new kitchen. Move around with your kitchen staff as though you are working. See if the architecture people got it right. Now is the time you can make changes."

"I can make changes?" Lisa asked.

"Yes, but first see if what has been done can work for you and your people. Give it a try. If changes are needed, we will get with the construction company and see what can be done to make the changes. Everything is on paper, and changes can be made," Sarah said.

"That's not all you are going to have to do. The equipment and machinery for your new kitchen will all be new. I know you probably have some that you hate and would like to replace and some you love and would like to take to your new kitchen. Sorry, this is a nonnegotiable area. All of the equipment and machinery in your new kitchen will be new. You can take the hand tools, pots, pans, skillets, and cooking utensils that you like. The ones that need or should be replaced, look in the kitchen catalog and book, and we will order more of what you want and need.

"For the equipment and machinery, you will need to pick the brand and model from this book and catalog. I have looked through them both. They have top-named brands and models. Here's the catch: you have a budget to work within. Right now, I'm not going to tell you what your budget is. I want you to pick by what you need and want and not by how much things cost. If you go over budget, we can revisit everything and make adjustments. Besides, the price list is not in your book or catalog, so you won't be able to see how much things cost anyway. The prices we can get are heavily discounted. So looking them up on the Internet will be of no value. Are we okay so far?"

Lisa said, "So far? There's more?"

Sarah gave her a big smile and said, "Yes. We have been talking about the kitchen. You will need to pick the new cafeteria tables and chairs. It might be helpful to you if you pick a theme for your new eating area and decorate around it."

Lisa said, "That's a good idea."

Sarah said, "After we have finished, I will present the final rendition to Ms. White for her approval."

"You have time to do this, but don't sit on it too long. It takes time to order the equipment, machinery, tables, and chairs and have them delivered and installed. Don't forget the paint and wall coverings the builder will need to order. The last thing I want to happen is for the building to be delayed because they are waiting on us. Don't think for one minute that you are all alone on this. Use your staff to help you. After all, they are the ones who will be working with and around the equipment and machines. Just don't promise anything. Remember everything is subject to budget and approval. Lastly, I'm here to help too. I also have the staff at the construction company at my disposal."

Lisa said, "That is a lot to think about and a big responsibility too."

Sarah said, "Yes, it is, but you have been in the business for a long time and have a lot of knowledge and experience. I think once you get started, you will get excited and enjoy doing it. Would you rather have everything done for you and then just have to live with it?"

Lisa said, "You are right. I'm just overwhelmed right now."

Sarah, pointing to her picture of the cow, said, "You can't eat a whole cow in one dinner, but if you break it down, one meal at a time, you can eat it all."

Lisa said, "I will break it down and get it back to you as soon as I can. Sarah, it has been enlightening and a pleasure working with you. I now see why Ms. White put you in charge. Good luck."

Sarah walked down to the executive dining room to see if Pierre, the head chef, was still in his office. She had not been back to the kitchen before and didn't know where Pierre's office was. She did know where the servers came in and out of the kitchen.

Sarah entered and said, "Pierre, are you back here?"

Pierre said, "One moment, I will be right with you."

He stepped out of his office and said, "Director Sarah, what brings you here?"

Sarah said, "I would like to set up an appointment for you to come to my office so we can visit about your new kitchen and dining areas in the new building. When would be a good time for us to meet?"

Pierre said, "Oh good. I thought you were here to talk about what happened the other day with Monty."

Sarah said, "Monty is the best server you have. I hope he didn't get in trouble. He was most professional, just following the rules. I was the one out of order. Besides, it got the rules changed for the better, don't you think?"

Pierre said, "It does seem to be working out okay."

Sarah said, "How is your schedule? What is the best time for us to meet? I think I'm more flexible with my schedule than you are with yours."

Pierre said, "I'm available now."

Sarah said, "Then let's walk down to my office and see how much we can accomplish before quitting time."

The two of them went down to Sarah's office. Just before she went in, Sarah said to Jill, "Hold my calls. I will be meeting with Pierre."

Sarah said, "Go ahead and sit down in that chair. I will pull the blueprints for the executive kitchen and dining room."

Sarah basically went through the same scenario as she did with Lisa. She had requested a second kitchen book and catalog from Judy at Harlow.

Sarah gave the book and catalog to Pierre and said, "Take your time but not too much time. I don't want to delay being able to move into the new building because we were not ready."

Pierre said, "I will move on it and get back to you as soon as I can."

Sarah said, "When you are ready to meet again, give my administrative assistant, Jill, a call and set up an appointment."

Pierre said, "Yes, I know who Ms. Jill is. She loves to eat our salads."

It was time to go home. Sarah gathered up her things and said to Jill, "Are you ready to walk out?"

Jill said, "I sure am."

Sarah said, "If you didn't know who that guy is, he is Pierre. He is the department head and also the head chef of the executive dining room. You have quite a reputation going for you. He said you love the salads."

Jill said, "He said that? I do eat a lot of salads. I'm still trying to lose the weight I put on carrying Steven."

Sarah said, "How's that going?"

Jill said, "Oh, don't ask. It's an uphill battle. I'm not losing it as fast as I hoped."

Sarah said, "It does take time and effort. You did put it on over nine months. Keep working at it."

Jill said, "Look at you. You had twins and look like you never even had a kid. Your breasts still look firm. How do you ever do it? You know I hate you."

They laughed and walked to their cars.

CHAPTER 40

Car Shopping

It was Saturday, the morning they picked to go car shopping. Both Sarah and Karl had been researching cars and SUVs on the Internet and looking at cars and SUVs being driven around town. Sarah had narrowed her choices down to two. They were both from the same manufacturer, so they only needed to go to one dealership. Karl still had not made up his mind. They put the twins in their car seats and headed to the dealership. They took Sarah's car because if they decided to do a deal, that would be the car they would be trading in. Originally, they thought they would trade both cars in and then pay the balance in cash for Sarah's new car. Since Karl had not made up his mind about the car he wanted, they decided they would work the deals separately.

Arriving at the dealership, they put the twins in the stroller and started looking for the SUVs that Sarah wanted to see. Karl was also looking around at cars he might like for himself.

One of the salesmen, looking out across the lot, said, "Hey, boss, there is a redheaded lady with two kids in a stroller and a husband in tow. You think that might be the ones you wanted me to keep an eye out for?"

Gus, the sales manager, said, "That just might be the ones."

Gus walked up to Sarah and Karl and said, "Hi, folks, my name is Gus. I'm the sales manager at this dealership. Would you two happen to be Karl and Sarah?"

Sarah was taken totally by surprise that this total stranger knew their names. Neither she nor Karl had contacted the dealership.

Sarah said, "Yes, I'm Sarah, and this is my husband, Karl."

Gus said, "I can see by your reaction that you are surprised. Ms. White told me you would be coming in sometime today and for me to make you the best deal possible. Here is my offer: I will knock $10,000 off the sticker price and also give you top book value for your trade-in. Go ahead and look around. If you want to test drive any cars or SUVs, just let me know. Oh, by the way, Karl, if you decide you want to buy a car too, I will knock $7,000 off the sticker price and also give you top book value on your trade-in. If you have any questions, I will be in my office."

Gus walked back to his office.

Karl looked at Sarah in disbelief at what they had just heard and said, "Ms. White sure does like you a lot, and she sure has a lot of connections. That is a deal you can't pass up, and I think maybe I should get more serious about getting myself a new car too. I'm sure the offer is limited. With that much off of a deal, are you still think-ing about the same two SUVs you were looking at?"

Sarah said, "Pretty sure, but let's look around a little bit anyway."

Sarah said, "I don't see anything I like better."

They went back to the ones Sarah had picked.

Sarah said, "I will stay here with the twins. Could you go in and see if we can test drive these two? If you saw any you would like to test drive, ask for the keys to them too."

Karl walked up to the office and said to Gus, "We would like to test drive those two SUVs."

He pointed out to the car lot.

Gus said, "Let's walk out there, and I can get the information off the SUVs to make sure I get the right keys."

Gus said, "These are two of our top-selling models. I guess you are wanting more room for the family you now have?"

Karl said, "Sarah's car will do for now, but it won't be long before we will be forced to buy a bigger one."

Gus said, "I will need to make a copy of your and your wife's driver's licenses before you can do a test drive. I will bring them back with the car keys."

As Gus was getting the information he needed, Sarah and Karl got out their driver's licenses and handed them to Gus.

Gus said, "I will be back in just a couple of minutes."

Sarah and Karl got the car seats out of their car so they could put them in the SUV for the test drive.

Gus handed them back their licenses and the keys to the SUV. He helped Karl put the car seats in the SUV. Sarah and Karl then put the twins in their car seats. Karl thanked Gus and then got into the passenger's seat. Sarah, behind the wheel, adjusted the seat, the mirrors, and started the engine. She liked that she could clearly see all around without any major obstructions blocking her view. The SUV had lots of options that her old car didn't have. It drove nicely, had good pickup, and got up to speed quickly.

She pulled the SUV over to the side of the road. She and Karl switched seats so Karl could drive. Sarah would be the primary driver, using the SUV to drive back and forth to work and running errands, but when they would go as a family, Karl would be doing the driving. He adjusted the seat and mirrors to fit him, and they took off driving.

Karl said, "I really fit in here, and it's easy to get in and out of."

He drove back to the dealership and said, "Do you still want to drive your other choice?"

Sarah said, "I like this one a lot, and yes, I would still like to drive the other one just to compare the two and make sure I am making the right choice."

They took the twins and car seats out.

Karl said, "Let's put the twins in the stroller. I will stay here with them, and you can test drive this SUV by yourself. If you like it better, I will take it for a spin when you come back."

Sarah drove off and was back at the dealership in no time. Sarah parked the SUV and said, "I definitely like the first one the best. I'm ready to buy. What do you say we go in and talk to Gus?"

Karl said, "You are that sure?"

Sarah said, "Ms. White sure has set the groundwork for a great deal. I don't think we should pass on a deal like this. I do like the SUV I picked."

They went to Gus's office, and Karl handed the keys to Gus and said, "Let's do the deal on the first SUV we did the test drive."

Gus said, "That would have been my pick too. Let me get the paperwork started."

In anticipation that they might be making a deal, Karl had cleaned out Sarah's car of all their personal belongings. Gus called on his phone to the service department to come get the keys and do a make-ready on this SUV. It was just a few minutes before a young guy came by and got the keys.

Gus said, "After I get the contract finished, I will turn you folks over to our finance person."

Soon they were on their way over to the finance person's office. The twins were getting fussy, and Sarah asked Karl to get their bottles out of the bag. She said, "I know Emily needs her diaper changed. Could you check Kevin?"

Karl said, "He could stand to be changed too."

Sarah asked the finance person where the bathrooms were. She took Emily and said to Karl, "I will be back for Kevin. Don't wait on me. Go ahead and work with the lady while I'm gone."

The lady said, "Gus gave me the copy of your driver's license. I can get most of the information off of it. Do you want the SUV titled in both of your names?"

Karl said, "Yes, and all of the information on the license is correct."

Sarah returned and took Kevin to be changed. Karl gave Emily her bottle. She took it right away. She must have been really hungry. Sarah returned and gave Kevin his bottle. The paperwork on the new car showed $10,000 off the sticker price and the trade-in amount of Sarah's car.

The lady said, "If you choose to finance with our credit, I can give you another $500 off. You can pay it off any time after the first month with no early prepayment penalties. Just don't miss a payment. The penalties are severe, even if you just miss one payment.

I can give you another $500 off if you choose to go with autopay. There are also a couple of rebates that you qualify for that will also reduce your cost by another $1,000. Both of you have outstanding credit. I will be able to offer you the lowest interest rate available on your loan. If you choose, you can purchase the extended warranty and service maintenance policy. You get free oil changes and service for 100,000 miles or 60 months."

Sarah said, "Go ahead and include both of them, and let's do the loan too."

All of the paperwork was done. They did the e-signatures and got a printed copy of all the paperwork.

They stopped by Gus's office to thank him and to find out where their new SUV was parked.

Gus said, "Did you folks get all taken care of?"

Karl said, "We did. Your finance person was very professional and polite, a pleasure to work with."

Gus said, "Karl, that deal I made for you on a car is only good for today."

Karl said, "I know you can't offer it to me indefinitely. You have given me something to think about."

They all walked out to where Sarah's new SUV was parked.

Gus said, "The plates should be in here in a couple of weeks. We will give you a call. Just stop by, and someone will put them on for you."

Sarah and Karl put the car seats in the back seat, secured them, and put the twins in and buckled them up. The stroller fit nicely, and there was plenty of room left.

Sarah said, "Are you sure you don't want to walk around and look for a car for yourself while we are here? I hate to pass up such a deal."

Karl said, "Let's go home and get some lunch or stop by a drive-through. I'm really hungry."

Sarah adjusted everything that needed adjusting for her to drive, and they drove off.

She said, "There is a place to eat. Let's go inside to eat. I don't want to eat in my new SUV. If we use the drive-through, by the time we get home, everything will be cold."

Karl said, "That's okay with me. Remember our Midway Café we ate in when we would go back and forth to your folks' house? I sure wish it was around here."

Sarah said, "That is a fantastic place to eat."

They ordered their food, found a seat, and sat down. The twins were being good for having such an outing.

Karl said, "I have been thinking. After we get home, I want to go back to the dealership and seriously take a look at what they have. Like you said, that is a nice deal, and I hate to pass it up."

When they got home, Karl cleaned out his car of his personal belongings just in case he did make a deal.

Sarah said, "Do you want or need me to go along?"

Karl said, "No, the twins have had enough of an outing already. If I need you, you can drive down, but I don't think so. They have all of your information. If you need to sign anything, you can do it using your computer. It's an e-signature anyway."

Karl got into his car and drove back to the dealership. He found Gus and asked, "Is the deal you quoted me still good?"

Gus said, "Yes, until the next time you drive your old car off the lot."

Karl said, "Since that's the case, I would like to look around."

Gus said, "I'm here until six o'clock. If you want to do a test drive or have questions, I will be in my office."

Karl said, "Thanks."

Karl had an idea of the car he was wanting. What he really wanted was a middle-age-crazy car. Karl never had a brand-new car before. All he could afford were used ones. Karl was both conservative and practical. He looked at the very sporty-style cars and thought to himself, *is that really me or my alter ego me?* He was married now and didn't need a car like that. He went looking at what he felt better suited his personality—something that would get really good gas mileage, maybe a hybrid. He was doing a lot of driving to his clients' places of business. He needed a car that fit his body, one that he could get in and out of easily and take his clients to lunch.

After looking at several cars and SUVs, comparing options and the gas mileage ratings, he decided to take this one for a test drive. He felt that it was a car that fit his needs and wasn't just settling on one because he could get a good deal. Karl went back in to find Gus.

Gus was with someone and said to Karl, "I will be with you in just a minute."

Karl took a seat in the lobby. A few minutes later, Gus said, "What did you come up with?"

Karl said, "I would like to take a test drive in that car" as he pointed out the dealership's window.

Gus said, "Let's go out, and you can show me which one." Gus took the information he needed and said, "I will be right back with the keys." Gus gave the keys to Karl and said, "Let's take a ride."

They both climbed into the car, and Karl drove off.

As Karl was driving, Gus pointed out the features of the car and said, "How do you like it so far?"

Karl said, "I do like it, and it performs well."

Gus said, "Take a right at the next street and slow down to almost a stop. There is hardly any traffic on this road. Now I would like for you to give it the gas."

Karl stepped on the gas, and the car took off.

Gus said, "That's the power you need to get on the freeways around you. Power when you need it, and this being a hybrid car gets the best gas mileage in the hybrid class."

Karl said, "It sure has the get-up-and-go. I like the roominess." Karl pulled the car over and said, "I sometimes take clients out to lunch. If you don't mind, could we both sit in the back seat? I want to see how much room there is back there."

Gus said, "Sure, no problem."

Karl was surprised at just how roomy it was. Karl said, "Thanks for doing that. There is lots of room in that back seat."

On the way back to the dealership, Karl said, "I would like to trade in my old car and buy this one."

Gus said, "As soon as I get back into my office, I will get the paperwork started."

Karl called Sarah and said, "Honey, I will be a while. I found a car to buy and will be doing the paperwork here shortly."

Sarah said, "I was hoping you would find something. I hated to pass up such a deal. See you when you get home."

Later, Karl drove into the driveway just as Sarah was returning from taking the twins for a walk. Karl got out of the car and said, "Well, what do you think?"

Sarah said, "That car says YOU all over it. I like it a lot, and it's a hybrid too."

She took a closer look at it.

Karl pointed out some of the features and said, "It sure has the power for having a small engine and is best in class for mileage. It has the roominess I need for when I take a client out to lunch. Go ahead and sit in the back seat."

Sarah could tell Karl was excited about his new car, and that made her very happy. They both sat in the back seat, and Sarah said to Karl, "You do have nice leg room."

They went into the house. Karl got a beer and sat in his chair. It was Sarah's turn to cook, so she started fixing dinner.

They talked about now having two car payments and what they would do. Sarah wanted to pay off one of the cars after the first month so they would only have the one car payment. Karl said, "Let me work the numbers, and we can figure it out."

CHAPTER 41

Monthly Meeting with the Builder

It was time for the monthly meeting with Harlow Construction Company. On the way down in the elevator to the limo, Sarah said to Ms. White, "Thank you so much for what you did for us with the car dealership. We ended up buying Karl a car and me an SUV."

Ms. White said, "Gus owed me a favor. Knowing old Gus, he gave you fleet price and didn't have to pay a salesman commission. He still made money on the deal, but I'm glad I could help you two."

Charles greeted them and had the door open for them. Ms. White said, "I know you have been giving me status reports, but give me a quick update on the way over."

Sarah said, "I have met with both Lisa and Pierre."

Ms. White interrupted Sarah and said, "You didn't do it with them together, did you? They don't get along with one another, AT ALL. Actually, they are brother and sister. Lisa went to a culinary school here in the States, and Pierre went overseas to some French school. Pierre's real name is Peter. He says Lisa is just a cook, even though she has a culinary degree from a top US school."

Sarah said, "Lucky for me, I met with them separately and had requested Judy, over at Harlow, to send me a second set of kitchen information. They both have their own set of information and should both be done by the end of the month. I'm pleased with our meetings. I will set up a meeting with you for review and approval. After the approval, I will get with Judy to schedule an appointment for her and her team members to go over our equipment and machinery needs and get them ordered.

"I have asked Jill, my administrative assistant, to head up the day care and playground facility development. I plan for us to meet with HR to get a feel for what our true needs will be for the nursery size and number of cribs and playpens we will need. Also, just how big the toddler and outside playground areas will need to be. Since we are going to have after-school care, we will need to have playground equipment for the bigger kids and room for them to do their homework. I know Harlow's people have given us their estimates, but they are based on an average of an average. I just want to get a feel for what our HR sees as being our needs. I want HR to put together some kind of survey to give us a better idea. With that information, Jill should be able to finish that up, and we can move on with the approval and get the equipment ordered."

"There is a guy who works here at the company named Ralph. He and his wife own a small gym over off of Second Avenue. He does personal training after work and on weekends. He has agreed to take the lead in our exercise facility. I talked to his boss, and she agreed to provide him time from his job to do the project. With his knowledge, it shouldn't take too much time to complete.

"I think the exercise and day care facilities should both be a break-even cost center. The ones that use them should be the ones to pay."

Ms. White said, "I don't disagree with you on that, but let's put it on the list of things to decide upon later."

Sarah went on to say, "I'm going to contract with Bill to head up the part of the headquarters building that will be occupied by the workers and managers. Bill will be a great asset. He knows this company like the back of his hand."

Ms. White said, "I can't think of a better person to do that job. Do what you have to do to make that happen."

Sarah continued, "My major concerns right now are the wellness center and the building's decoration theme. I think the theme should start in the main lobby and carry throughout the entire building, blending with the theme we go with for each floor. The lobby at

Harlow is so impressive I would like to have one too. If you have any suggestions, I sure would like to hear them."

Ms. White said, "Sounds like you are progressing right along. On your lobby question, go ahead and ask Judy who did their lobby. On the wellness center, let me think about it. I just might have something that may help."

Just as Sarah finished her update, Charles was pulling up to the building's entrance. Charles opened the limo's door to let Sarah and Ms. White out. Ms. White said to Charles, "I don't know how long we will be. I will call you when the meeting is about over."

They walked into the lobby, and the receptionist said, "Good morning, Ms. White, and good morning to you too, Sarah. Here are your visitor's badges. You will be meeting in the same conference room as before. Remember to return your visitor badges to me as you leave."

As Ms. White and Sarah walked into the room, greetings and introductions were made. Mr. Harlow himself was in this meeting. Sarah had not met him before. He looked a lot younger than she expected and later found out he was the older Mr. Harlow's son.

He said, "We ran into some permit and code inspection problems, but I think they have been all taken care of. Working with this city has its challenges."

He went on to say, "The building construction is moving along. It might not appear that way to you, seeing it every day. There are things that we have to let sit and cure before work can continue in that area. We did have a few scheduling problems with some of the subcontractors. Not your problem, but we have the unions that we have to work with too. Certain unions will not work in the same area with other ones. We just have to watch our work scheduling, is all. We did have a bit of trouble with the supply chain in getting some of the materials and products delivered. That seems to be freeing up. All in all, I'm happy with our progress so far and don't see any major delays on our end. I know your team has been working with Judy. How do you feel things are going, Ms. White?"

Ms. White said, "I know every building construction has its problems. I do look at the construction every day. Sarah has been

241

working in the areas needing the most lead time to get things ordered and delivered. The kitchen equipment and machinery, the dining tables and chairs, the exercise and day care facilities are all works in progress. Sarah has informed me that by the middle of next month we should be ready to place the orders, well ahead of the schedule you set for us. Plans are in the works to start on the employees' workstations, managers' and executives' offices. If you have any questions, Sarah can answer any you may have."

Sarah said to Judy, "The people responsible for kitchen and eating areas are working from the plans and blueprints and are going over the equipment and machinery book and catalog. I don't know if they will have changes to be made to the layouts until they get back with me. I just wanted to give you a heads-up and would like to know how flexible you are in providing us with your support."

Judy said, "The more lead time, the better. I will do whatever it takes to keep us ahead of schedule."

Sarah said, "One other thing. Your lobby is very impressive. Could you provide me with the name of the company that did it?"

With a big smile on her face, Judy said, "It was the first project I did when I came to work here. We were in our old facilities, and Mr. Harlow Sr. asked me to take on that project. I'm so happy you like it. We do get lots of compliments."

Sarah said, "Judy, I look forward to working with you, one-on-one, on our new lobby design."

The next month's meeting was scheduled, and the meeting ended.

*****

Returning to the office, Jill asked, "How did the meeting go?"

Sarah said, "We got a nice update on the construction progress. It was a good meeting. Are you planning on eating lunch in the dining room?"

Jill said, "Tammy and I have been eating together most every day. I don't see any reason you can't join us."

Sarah said, "I thought we would go out to eat, and I would give you a ride in my new SUV."

Jill said, "Get out of here. You got a new SUV? Let me give Tammy a call to tell her I won't be eating lunch with her today."

Sarah said, "It's a little early to go to lunch. I have a phone call I would like to make, and then we will go."

Jill said, "Whenever you are ready."

Sarah called Bill's cell phone. Bill answered and said, "Well, if it isn't Director Sarah calling me."

Sarah said, "William, now cut that director stuff out. You may call me Ms. Sarah."

They both laughed.

Sarah said, "You know the last time we talked, I asked if you would like to come work with me on the new building. Bill, I don't know of anyone who knows this company better or is more well-liked than you. You know every nook and cranny of this building, including all the hiding places. I need your help to work with the department and section heads, directors, and executives to plan out their areas. The picking of the office furniture, worker cubicles, or workspaces, getting it ordered, and overseeing the move into the new building. It sounds like a lot, but you have had harder projects while you were working here. What do you say?"

Bill said, "Let me think on it."

He did a long, dramatic five-second pause and said, "Okay. I will leave the land of retirement and come work for you, Ms. Sarah."

Sarah laughed and said, "No Ms. Sarah, no Director Sarah, no boss. Just Sarah, and I won't call you William. Deal?"

Bill said, "Boy, you are getting to be no fun. Every time I talk with you, you are sounding more and more like that Ms. White. When do you want me to start?"

Sarah said, "How about Monday?"

Bill said, "I will be at your office at nine on Monday. Are you still in Ms. White's old office?"

Sarah said, "Yes, I look forward to seeing you. Say hi to your wife. I hope this doesn't cause problems with you working and not being retired, doing all of those honey-dos."

Bill said, "I don't think it will be a problem. You may have just saved a marriage."

They both laughed again and then said their goodbyes.

Sarah said to Jill, "Done with my phone call, are you ready to go?"

Jill said, "Yes."

They walked out to the parking lot, and Jill said, "Is that it?"

Sarah said, "It sure is. Here, let me unlock it for you."

Sarah pressed the unlock button on her key fob, and the doors unlocked. She said, "Go ahead and get in. Do you have a place you would like to eat?"

Jill said, "Look at all of this space. And is that a special setup for the child seats? I don't care where we eat."

Sarah said, "I will take you to this place Karl and I would go to when we didn't want to eat in the company cafeteria and just wanted to get away from the office."

Jill said, "Your SUV sure rides nice. I think it will be a while before Jack and I get a new car. He has been wanting to get a truck. I asked you earlier about how the meeting went. You didn't give me any real information."

Sarah said, "Are you turning this into a business lunch?"

Jill said, "We are not in the executive dining room, and besides, you are buying. Right?"

Sarah pulled into the parking lot away from the other cars and said, "I'm still getting used to driving the SUV. It is bigger than my old car. I surely don't want to dent it the first week I have it. Okay, I'm buying lunch."

They were seated and ordered their lunches. Sarah went on to recap the meeting. She also told Jill about her old boss, Bill, coming to work for her and getting Ralph to help with the exercise facility.

Jill asked, "Is that going to feel strange for him that now you will be his boss?"

Sarah said, "I don't think so. Bill and I have had a great working relationship. He is going to be such an asset to our team." Sarah went on to say, "I want you to take the lead on the day care facility development. When we get back, I will call HR to set up a meeting to see if they can help us come up with some numbers for the babies, toddlers, and after-school kids they think will be using the facility. Harlow provided us with their guess. Their guess is based on an average of an average. I want a better handle on what our numbers will be. That will make it a lot easier for you to plan for the number of cribs, playpens, and changing tables we will need in the nursery. The size allocation for the toddler area and their toys and the number of tables or desks the older kids will need to do their homework. Also, the ratio of younger kids to older kids for the playground equipment."

Jill closed her eyes and said, "Sarah, I am imagining that cow picture in my head right now. Did I hear you correctly that you want ME to take the total lead on the day care facility?"

Sarah said, "I did. From the floor to the kiddo wallpaper, to the fence surrounding the facility."

Jill said, "Oh my god."

Sarah said, "Jill, you have it in you. Believe in yourself. Don't try to eat that entire cow for dinner. Besides, I will be here to help you, and so will the people from Harlow. I wouldn't have given it to you to watch you fail. If you fail, I fail, and that's not going to happen."

They finished their lunch, and it was time to return to work.

Jill said, "I guess you wouldn't consider letting me drive your new SUV back to the office now, would you?"

Sarah said, "Jill, honey bunch, you know I love you dearly, but NO as in HELL NO. Now get in, we need to get back to work."

As soon as they got back from lunch, Sarah called HR and set up an appointment for two o'clock. Just before two rolled around, Sarah and Jill went over to HR.

Sarah said, "Hi, Kim."

Kim said, "Hi, Sarah. Hi, Jill. I guess it's not fair to ask you how your job is going in front of your boss, but how is it going?"

Jill said, "It's going great. The greatest boss one could have. I'm loving my job. Did I answer that one correctly?"

They all laughed.

Kim said, "Come on in and take a seat. The company really is a great place to work, and it's the people that make it that way."

Kim went on to say, "Sarah, you called and said you need some help getting some information. What kind of information are you looking for?"

Sarah said, "We have some estimates from the Harlow people. They have based their numbers on company size and come up with an average of an average. I don't think they really factor in the demographics of our people. I just don't have a good feel for their numbers. I could be wrong. I just have a feeling."

Jill is taking the lead on the day care facility development and will need good data on the numbers of who will be using the day care facility. That's where she needs your help. What we would like is for your department to develop a survey to see how many employees' kids might be using our new day care facility. The information needs to be broken down by the number of babies, toddlers, and after-school kids. Ms. White and I are working out the details on whether there will be a fee or if it will be free. If for a fee, what would be a fair amount? It would be helpful if you could somehow work that question into your survey. While you are doing the survey, you may as well include questions about the exercise facility too. No sense in doing two surveys."

Kim said, "I can't think of another way to get the data you are requesting. I will definitely have to work up a survey. How soon do you need it?"

Jill said, "ASAP. I can't do any planning without good data. I need the numbers to be able to order the cribs for the nursery, how to divide the area needed for the toddlers, and also the after-school kids. Desks for kids to do their homework on. Tables for the younger ones to do crafts. We might need a few computers too. Also, there is the outside playground equipment. The equipment needs to be age-appropriate. Some equipment for the little ones and other equipment for the older kids. We could come up with some numbers and just set limits on how many we can facilitate, but to make it work, we need to accommodate as many as we need to. The other problem I have is getting the equipment ordered and delivered, so as not to delay opening or delay construction. The timeliness of the survey is very important to getting the project done."

Sarah said, "I already have a manager in mind to work in the day care facility, but you will need to process the applications and do the background checks. Your survey will help you determine how many will be needed. So you see how important your survey will be."

Kim said, "I understand, and I will start working on a survey right away. After I finish, I will pass it by you for review. If you approve it, I can get the print shop/copy center to print it out and get it to the mailroom for distribution. As soon as I get some of the results of the data gathered, I will see that you get a copy. After talking with you, you have gotten my curiosity up on just how many kids our employees have. I have access to the health insurance information that lists the number and birthdates of the kids. We can compare these totals with the totals from our survey."

Sarah said, "That would be interesting."

Sarah and Jill thanked Kim for her time and returned to their office.

Sarah said to Jill, "You did alright in that meeting. You jumped right in and at the right time. You really made it clear what you need."

Jill said, "You really do think I have it in me, don't you?"

Sarah said, "I believe in you. Now is the time for you to start coming up with a plan. I would like to see a draft the day after tomorrow."

Jill said, "I'm on it. Do you want me to do a recap report on the meeting?"

Sarah said, "That's a good idea. You could use the practice."

CHAPTER 42

Bring Bill on Board and Getting Started

On Saturday, George invited Karl, Sarah, the twins, and several others from the office over to his house for a cookout. Karl loaded up the SUV with the twins' playpen, while Sarah packed what the twins would need for a day away from home. At George's house, Karl set up the playpen in a shady spot to protect the twins from getting sunburned. The twins were now crawling and were able to pull themselves up and hold on to the side of the playpen. Far from walking, but their legs were getting stronger. George had set up the cornhole game, and it was game on. Teams were formed, and the competition was fierce. They all had fun, and the BBQ dinner George and his wife prepared was delicious.

On Sunday, Karl spent most of the day in his workshop. He was working on something and would not tell Sarah what it was. She was thinking it was going to be some kind of gift he was making. Sarah spent the day reading, relaxing, and playing with the twins. Her days at work were busy, and she worked many evenings too. The weekends were her time to fully relax as she refused to let herself work on these days.

At nine, Monday morning, Bill walked up to Jill's desk saying, "I'm Bill, here to see Sarah."

Sarah, hearing Bill's voice, came out of her office to greet him. She said, "Bill, this is my administrative assistant, Jill."

Bill said, "Pleased to meet you."

Jill said, "Hi, Bill. Sarah has told me a lot about you. Welcome to the team. Let me know if there is anything you need."

Sarah said, "Come on in, Bill. Would you like a cup of coffee?"

Bill said, "I think I might need one."

Jill said, "How do you like your coffee?"

Bill said, "Black, no cream, no sugar."

Jill asked Sarah, "Are you wanting anything?"

Sarah said, "No, I'm fine, thanks."

Jill went off to get Bill his coffee.

Bill stepped into Sarah's office and said, "Ms. White's office looks just like it did when she was here, except not as messy."

Sarah said, "You have been in this office before?"

Bill said, "Elizabeth and I have been friends for a very long time, even before I got married. In the early days of this company, things were rough. We would talk things out and plan how we could make things better and still work with her father. We were never romantically involved, but we did go out as friends. Had more than a few drinks together. Her father was okay at running the company, but not a risk-taker. This frustrated Elizabeth to no end. Back then, she wanted to grow the company, but he held her back. It looks now like she is in full steam ahead mode. I guess she is trying to make up for lost time. Keep this between you and me."

Sarah said, "You know me. I know how to keep my mouth shut."

Jill returned with Bill's coffee and handed it to him. Bill thanked her, and she left.

Jill said, "I will hold all of your calls until you are finished."

Sarah said, "Thanks, Jill."

Sarah and Bill were seated in the lounge area of Sarah's office. Bill said, "How did you luck out to get this office?"

She said, "After Ms. White moved into her father's office, this one sat empty. When I got my promotion, she knew I would need the extra room to lay out the plans and blueprints, the extra storage for the books and catalogs, and conducting meetings. She didn't want to tie up one of the conference rooms. So it just made sense for me to move in here. I checked, and your old office is available. I think that's the best place for you to work from."

Bill said, "I guess it will be like returning home."

"Let's move over to the conference table."

Bill and Sarah went over to the conference table, and Sarah said, "Sit here beside me so neither of us has to look at things upside down. Here are the plans and blueprints for the different office areas. Each one has been increased in size by 15 to 20 percent over the area they now occupy."

Bill, pointing on the blueprint, asked, "What is this big blank area on each floor going to be used for?"

Sarah said, "I can't tell you right now, but I will give you a hint. Remember what you just said about Ms. White wanting to make up for lost time?"

Bill said, "Enough said."

Sarah said, "That is a question you will need to come up with an answer for when someone asks. I'm sure you will come up with something. These are your copies of the blueprints. If you need additional copies to give to the people you will be working with, The print shop can make them for you. Here are the books and catalogs for the furniture. I would like weekly update reports. I know how you hate doing reports. I don't have it in the budget for you to have an administrative assistant. What I can do for you is this: If you give your notes to Jill, she can create a recap report and type it up for you. Sort of like you used to do for me when I worked for you. We will still have a face-to-face meeting once a week. You know Ms. White will want me to tell her how things are going. Hey, you just might be called into some of those meetings."

Bill asked, "So what will be all of my responsibilities?"

Sarah said, "Good question. Thought you would never ask. You will need to work with each of the department and section heads and the executives to work out how they would like their area laid out. They will need to stay inside the area, lined out in the blueprints. A lot of work has gone into laying out the areas to have related areas next to one another. Ms. White and people at Harlow Construction Company worked this out long before I got involved. Harlow not only builds buildings, but they have an entire staff of consultants that are tops in their field. They do all sorts of time and motion studies that have saved companies hundreds of thousands of dollars just by rearranging their production lines and workflows. I was very impressed with the layouts they suggested for our kitchens. It will be in your best interest to keep the areas located as is."

"That takes care of the areas. Now comes the fun part. You get to work with the people to find out how much furniture will be needed and ordered. If they are wanting cubicles or a more open workspace. That would include desks, chairs, tables, and file cabinets. And don't forget the conference rooms. There are lots of planned offices in each area. It would be helpful to identify the people who will be occupying those offices when it comes time for the move. It would be total chaos if everybody were to move on the same day. So when the building is finished or we get the okay to occupy an area, we will do phased move-ins. You will be involved in that too. Coordinating with the packing, moving, and unpacking."

Jill knocked on the door and said, "Sarah, sorry for the interruption. It's time for your meeting."

Sarah said, "Thanks, Jill. I lost track of time. Bill, leave that stuff here. I will have it sent down to your office later. We have to go now. We have a meeting with the department and section heads and the executives that you will be working with. I'm going to announce that you are THE ONE*."

They went down to the cafeteria and were greeted by several who came up to Bill and said, "You just couldn't stay away, could you?"

Another one said, "I think I won the lottery on how many days it would be before Bill came back."

Bill could not believe the reception he was getting.

Sarah said, "If I could have everyone's attention, please."

The place quieted down, and she said, "Thanks for taking time out of your busy schedules to meet with me today. As you know, I am the Director of Facilities Development and Planning. Today, it is my pleasure to announce that Bill has joined my team in helping us all get into the new building. With Bill's help, you will be picking out the desks, chairs, tables, file cabinets, and everything else needed in your areas. Yes, that means you will be getting all new furniture. No old desks, chairs, or file cabinets will be going to the new building. Today is Bill's first day, so it will take him some time to develop a plan and start meeting with each individual area. You people that know Bill, that will probably start sometime later this afternoon."

The people laughed, and one person said, "You got that right. Bill has always been a 'get after it' kind of guy."

Sarah said, "Bill will be occupying his old office. I guess some things really don't change after all."

"A quick update on the building. Everything is still on track as construction continues. Ms. White and I are having monthly meetings with the construction company. My staff and I have already started working on getting some areas finalized, and we are in the process of picking out equipment and machinery for approval and order."

"Expect to see a survey coming out from HR, asking for input for the new day care and exercise facilities. It's important that you and your people respond to the survey as soon as possible. It will take time for HR to process the surveys and develop the data needed to plan for and select the equipment for these facilities. We just don't know how much and how many to order until the surveys are processed. We want to have enough equipment and machines so there is not a long wait to use them or we have to turn people away. Also, enough of everything to accommodate all the children who will be using the day care facility. Again, that's why this survey is important, and you get them returned quickly. Return it, even if you don't have kids or will not be using our day care or have no plans to use the exercise facility. Mark the box that says 'not going to use.' Please help us by returning your surveys. If you have any questions, I will try to answer them."

One asked, "Will there be a charge for using the day care and exercise facilities?"

Sarah said, "That will be one of the questions on the survey. If there is a fee, it will be less than the going rate being charged by places around town."

Another asked, "Are there plans for a swimming pool?"

Sarah said, "Not at the moment."

One more person asked, "When will the building be finished?"

Sarah said, "That's a question I ask at each of the monthly meetings we have with the builder. I will give you the same answer as I get from them. We are working hard to get the building finished. I can tell you this: I, for one, want to get into the new headquarters building as quickly as you. Thank you for coming. Your input is important, so complete the survey and get it returned back to HR."

The meeting ended, and Sarah walked with Bill to his office.

Bill said, "Thanks, Sarah. This means a lot to me. I really look forward to us working together again."

Sarah said, "Me too."

When Sarah got back to her office, Jill said, "I scheduled you a meeting today at one-thirty with Lisa. She wants to give you an update and has a few questions. I also scheduled a three o'clock meeting with Kim. She has the survey worked out and wants us to take a look at it. You also have a four o'clock meeting with Ms. White. She didn't say what that meeting would be about."

Sarah said, "Things are starting to hop. At least I still have time for lunch today, RIGHT?"

Jill said, "At the moment." Jill pressed the intercom button and said, "Lisa is here for her one-thirty meeting."

Sarah said, "Send her in, please."

Lisa walked in, and Sarah said, "Let's sit over here in the lounge area of my office."

Sarah could see that Lisa was excited. They sat down, Lisa on the couch and Sarah in one of the overstuffed chairs.

Lisa said, "Sarah, that suggestion you made to tape the layout on the floor was the best. I wish you could have been there. My people had so much fun with that. One would say, 'Hey, I'm cooking here.' Another one would say, 'Hot pot, coming through, watch your backside.' One even said, 'Do you know you are standing where the dishwasher is supposed to be?'"

She went on to say, "Oh, Sarah, we all were having so much fun pretending that we were cooking for a lunchtime meal. The new kitchen is a lot bigger than the one we have now. It must be at least 10 percent bigger."

Sarah said, "Actually, it's 20 percent bigger."

Lisa said, "Now for the serious part. You said to see if the layout Harlow's people suggested would work. Everyone said the layout was so much better than what they have now. No one, and I mean NO ONE, said they would change a thing. Even the serving line was going to be so much better, and putting the checkout register away from the serving line and having two of them off by themselves will improve the serving line flow. I'm having the checkout register moved away from our current serving line this week. The electricians are doing the wiring now so we can have power to run the register. Sarah, I see no need to meet with the Harlow people. Please pass on for me the wonderful job they did."

Lisa continued, "We all sat down and poured through the book and catalog you gave me. I told everyone that none of the existing equipment or machinery would be moving to the new building, and that was a nonnegotiable thing. Not one said they had a problem with that. Sarah, some of that equipment is older than you. They are so happy to be rid of some of it. They asked about handheld tools. I said they were okay to take to the new building, and they could take the pots, pans, skillets, and utensils too. You said that would be okay. They did pick out a few new pots and pans and a few new handheld tools. I said I think that would be okay. I hope I didn't overstate and cause you problems."

Sarah said, "I don't think so. I guess we could just trade the cost of the automatic dishwasher for the cost of the new pots and pans."

Sarah could see the surprise on Lisa's face and said, "Lisa, I'm just having fun with you. I'm sure everything will be all right."

Lisa said, "Sarah, you had me really going there."

They both laughed.

She said, "Here is the list of our equipment and machinery picks. Some of the equipment is smaller in size than the ones we currently have, but they have a bigger capacity and are more energy efficient. I sure hope I'm within the budget with our picks. I did say to them that everything would be up for review and approval."

Sarah said, "How about the dining area?"

Lisa said, "I got so excited, I forgot to tell you about it. As you suggested, I started off by coming up with a theme. I had a little contest for who could come up with the best one. Some of their suggestions were a bit off the wall, but we did come up with a couple the team liked. We took a vote, and this is what we came up with."

Lisa handed Sarah a picture of a cafeteria that was cut out of a magazine. She also handed Sarah the catalog with a page showing the style of tables and chairs they chose. I estimated, by the number of people who are currently eating in the cafeteria, the number of tables and chairs we will need. Of course, they all don't eat at the same time, so the tables can be used again as people finish eating."

Sarah said, "I like the theme you and your team have picked, and the table and chairs fit right in with it. We might want to add a few more tables and chairs to the order. Lisa, you and your team have done an excellent job. I know you are proud of them. Tell them 'good job' from me, will you?"

Lisa said, "I sure will."

Sarah said, "Let me get the numbers together, and I will be getting back with you before I take your package to Ms. White for her final approval. It will be a while because I want to get a few areas completed and present several to Ms. White at one time. After she has approved them, I will get with the Harlow people and place the order."

Lisa left. You could tell she was feeling very good and proud of the work she did. It's nice to have that feeling when you have worked hard to get a job done. It just makes it feel all that much better when someone tells you, "You did a good job."

Jill stuck her head into Sarah's office and said, "It's almost time for Kim to be here for the three o'clock meeting. Can I get you anything?"

Sarah replied, "Check the mini-fridge to see if there are enough drinks in there."

Jill responded, "I restocked it when you were having your meeting announcing Bill. Here she is now."

Sarah said, "Come on in, Kim."

Jill followed Kim into Sarah's office. "Let's sit down in the lounge area. Would you like water or soda?"

Kim said, "A water, I'm a little dry."

Sarah asked Jill, "Could you please get us two waters and, if you want, something for yourself?"

Kim said, "I have come up with this as our survey," and handed Jill and Sarah a copy. Kim gave them a few minutes to read it and then asked, "What do you think? Do you think it will get the results you're looking for? I had some trouble coming up with the questions regarding the possible fee for the day care and exercise facilities. You know people will want it to be free."

Sarah said, "I think that's true, but I think the facilities should break even. The ones who use it should be the ones that pay for it. Let's see if we can put our heads together and come up with some wording for the fee questions."

They kicked around several different ways to word the question and settled on one. Sarah said, "I saw that you were at the meeting this morning, and you heard me say the survey would be coming out. I see you added the check-a-box that says, 'Will not be using this facility.' At least I know one person was listening. That question about a swimming pool was really a good question. I think I will look into it. We should add a place for comments on the survey. The numbers for people not using the facility should be reflected in the survey totals too."

Sarah asked, "How long do you think it will take to get this out to the people?"

Kim said, "As soon as I get back to my office, I will make the changes we talked about. I think I will add a stronger statement in the cover letter on how important it is that we get the surveys back quickly. I will take it down to the print shop/copy center. It shouldn't take too much time for them to get it copied. I will request a rush job. It won't be the first time. I will have them deliver the copies to the mailroom for distribution tomorrow morning."

Kim continued, "We will have to give people time to respond. As the surveys come in, I will have one of my people start keeping running totals and will give you periodic updates. When the number of surveys comes to a trickle or stops, I will provide you with the final results. Even with a 'respond by' date, people still will wait until the very last minute."

Sarah said, "Sounds good. Jill, do you have any last-minute questions?"

Jill said, "No, I think we covered everything I can think of. I am looking forward to the results so I can get on with my project. Thank you, Kim."

It was rolling on to four o'clock and time for Sarah's meeting with Ms. White. She didn't say to Jill what the meeting would be about. Sarah didn't like it when she felt unprepared going into a meeting, especially a meeting with Ms. White. Sarah stopped at Tammy's desk and asked, "How are things going? And are you liking your full-time job?"

Tammy said, "I do and really like the steady income. In my old job, I didn't know if I would be working a temp job the next week or even the next day."

Sarah whispered to Tammy, "What kind of mood is Ms. White in?"

Tammy said quietly, "She has been in a good mood all day."

Sarah said, "She didn't say why she wanted to meet. Could you buzz me in?"

Tammy pressed the intercom button and said, "Director Sarah is here for her four o'clock appointment."

Ms. White said, "Send her in."

Ms. White's door was closed, and Sarah opened it. She didn't know if the door being closed was a good or bad thing. Sarah opened the door and stepped in.

Ms. White said, "Go ahead and close the door behind you. Let's sit down in my lounge area. Come sit down, and NO, you are not in some kind of trouble."

Sarah said, "What made you think that I thought I was in trouble?"

Ms. White said, "Sarah, you should never play poker. I could see it in your face and your body language. Relax. You want something to drink? I have some beer in the mini-fridge."

Sarah said, "No, but I would like one of those fancy waters you keep in there."

Ms. White said, "Help yourself and get me a beer. It's close enough to after work hours for me to have one."

Ms. White said, "You know I bought that company downstate."

Sarah said, "I remember you telling me about it. Nothing was ever announced here at the company, and I have wondered about it. I figured if you wanted me to know, you would tell me."

Ms. White said, "I checked your calendar and didn't see any important appointments scheduled for tomorrow. I would like for you to take a ride downstate with me. It's been a while since I was last down there. I have a feeling about that place and would like another pair of ears and eyes with me."

Sarah asked, "Are you having remorse about having bought it?"

Ms. White said, "Oh no, nothing like that. It was a good buy and a good move to expand the business. I just have a feeling."

"I have been on the phone with Mr. Goodson, the president of that company. He is the person we will be meeting with. No formal announcement has been made to the people working there either. The purchase has been kept quiet. I can't tell you right now why it has been done that way. Do you feel you can get away for the day?"

Sarah said, "I have a bunch of follow-up work planned for tomorrow, but no real appointments. If anything comes up, I will have Jill schedule them for later."

"I will just tell Jill I will be on a joy ride with you."

With that statement, Ms. White sat straight up in her chair and almost choked on her beer. Sarah said, "I see by your body language that you are not in agreement with that answer."

Ms. White knew she had been had and started laughing, and Sarah joined in.

Sarah said, "What time would you like to leave?"

Ms. White said, "Eight o'clock. It will be a long day. It's about a two-hour drive."

Sarah said, "I will be ready."

Ms. White said, "On second thought, I will have Charles drive to your house and pick you up there. It will be on the way and save you from having to drive all this way here. That will give you more time at home. Say, pick you up at eight-fifteen?"

Sarah said, "Eight-fifteen at my house. I will call Charles to make sure he has my address."

Ms. White said, "Just use my phone. Press 3 on speed dial."

Charles answered, and Sarah said, "This is Sarah. You know you are driving Ms. White downstate tomorrow."

Charles said, "That is supposed to be on the QT. How did you find out about it?"

Sarah said, "Because I'm going too, and it's still on the QT. You and Ms. White will be picking me up at my house. Do you know where Pony Express Estates is located?"

Charles said, "I do."

Sarah gave Charles her address and said, "See you in the morning at my house at eight-fifteen."

Sarah went back to her office and said to Jill, "I will not be in tomorrow."

Jill started to say something, but Sarah gave her that look, and Jill knew not to ask. Sarah said, "Hold down the fort. If something comes up that REALLY needs my attention and can't wait, call me on my cell phone. If someone asks where I am, just say, 'She is out of the office today and will be back tomorrow.' I'm going home now. Good night."

*****

On their evening walks with the twins, Sarah and Karl would share what happened during each other's day. Sarah said, "Bill was really received well. I have to tell you the story that Lisa told me about her team pretending they were preparing a lunch in their imaginary kitchen taped to the cafeteria floor."

Sarah told Karl the entire story, and Karl said, "That would have been something to watch. Sounds like things are really starting to come together for you."

She told Karl, "I'm going to be picked up at the house in the morning and will be accompanying Ms. White to a meeting at the company she purchased downstate. I don't know how late I will be getting home. As soon as I know, I will either text you or call you."

Karl said, "That sounds interesting. Do you know what the meeting is all about?"

Sarah said, "All she would tell me is she wanted another pair of ears and eyes there."

Karl said, "I made bonus again and should be seeing a sizable check in a few days. George and I are the top two performers in the firm. The firm is growing again, and they brought in another senior accountant to help with the new accounts the sales staff is bringing in. I got more business coming my way from two of my clients. They want us to handle more of their accounting functions. I do like my job."

Sarah said, "And you are good at it too."

CHAPTER 43

Visit to the Company Downstate

You could set your watch by Charles's promptness. Right at eight-fifteen, he pulled into Sarah's driveway. Sarah had her purse and laptop in hand and was walking out to get into the limo. Charles stepped out and had the door open for Sarah to get in. She wondered if any of her neighbors were watching and what they were thinking. It put a smile on her face.

Sarah said, "Good morning, Charles. This is for you—I just finished making it," and handed him a breakfast taco wrapped in foil.

Charles said, "A breakfast taco? Thank you. How did you know I loved breakfast tacos?"

Sarah replied, "In this part of the country, who doesn't?"

Sarah got into the limo and said, "Good morning, Ms. White. I made you one too."

Ms. White said, "Gloria made me a big breakfast this morning, and I don't think I could eat another thing. Maybe Charles would like to eat it."

Sarah said, "Here is another one, Charles. Ms. White said she had a big breakfast."

Charles said, "Happy to take it off your hands. This one is delicious. Thanks."

The drive would be on the freeway all the way. Where they were heading was mostly a lot of nothing. The best thing to do was sit back, relax, and enjoy the ride. Ms. White was reading something, though Sarah couldn't really tell what it was. Sarah said to Ms. White, "You look very busy. I can't read in the car—I get motion sickness. If you don't mind, I'll put my earbuds in and listen to a podcast on my phone. Just give me a nudge if you need to say something."

Ms. White just nodded and went back to reading.

Ms. White finished what she was reading and asked Charles, "What is our estimated time of arrival?"

Charles looked at the GPS and said, "About ten after ten, another half hour from now. I've been making good time."

Ms. White said, "Thank you, Charles," and she turned to Sarah, saying, "We will arrive with plenty of time to go to the restroom and freshen up a bit before our ten-thirty appointment. I wasn't given an agenda for this meeting, Sarah. I wanted you along to get your feeling and maybe pick up on something I missed. I'll introduce you as my administrative assistant. As with all the meetings you've accompanied me on, I ask that you take notes and, if need be, do some research on that laptop of yours. We've worked together enough, and you're really good at following my lead. I had a tour of the company before, but I'll request another one so you can see for yourself. They may have one planned for us anyway. I don't know."

Sarah could feel Ms. White's uneasiness with this meeting—something she had never seen before in Ms. White.

Right at 10:10, Charles pulled the limo up in front of the building and opened the door. Sarah and Ms. White stepped out, walked into the building, and up to the lobby receptionist's desk. Ms. White said, "My name is Ms. White, and this is my administrative assistant, Sarah. We have an appointment with Mr. Goodson, but we'd like to freshen up first."

The receptionist pointed across the lobby and said, "The restrooms are over there, and I'll let Mr. Goodson's secretary know you're here. I see you on the appointment list but not Sarah. I'll have to get clearance for her to enter our facilities. Return here for your visitor badges."

When they returned, the receptionist said, "I talked to Mr. Goodson's secretary and got clearance for Sarah. Here are your badges."

By the time they were finished signing in and getting their badges, Mr. Goodson's secretary came to escort them to Mr. Goodson's office. Mr. Goodson said, "Hi, Elizabeth. Nice to see you again. You sure are looking fit."

Ms. White said, "Why, Harry, you old fool. I look just the same as I did the last time you saw me. I want to introduce you to my administrative assistant, Sarah."

Mr. Goodson said, "I wasn't expecting anyone else to come down with you and didn't add anyone else to the visitor's list. Sorry for any inconvenience. Pleased to meet you, Sarah," and shook her hand. "Please, sit down. I scheduled a meeting for eleven. Let's visit until then. Can I get you something to drink?"

Ms. White said, "Coffee."

Sarah said, "A bottle of water, please."

Mr. Goodson pressed a button and said into the intercom, "Two coffees and a bottle of water, please."

Mr. Goodson's secretary brought in the drinks and left.

Mr. Goodson said, "Is it okay to talk with Sarah here? No offense to you, my dear."

Ms. White said, "Sarah is one of my most trusted employees. She has a secret security clearance."

He said, "I'm ready to make the announcement that I've sold the company to you. To the best of my knowledge, no one here knows that the company has been sold. It will be a shock to everyone in this meeting. As we've been planning ever since we first talked, you agreed to a one-year hands-off policy regarding the way we're doing business now, and it was written into the contract. That year is almost up, and I'm ready to step aside. Elizabeth, we go back a long way—all the way to high school. I've seen what you've done with your dad's business and trust that my business will also grow under your leadership."

Ms. White said, "Harry, we do go back a long way. You were a couple of years ahead of me in school, and thanks for your kind words. I've given lots of thought to how to go forward with this company. I've been thinking about whether to keep it as a stand-alone company or merge it into my company, but I haven't decided on the best way yet. Of course, you'll stay in place until the end of the agreed-upon year. I may need to consult with you from time to time after you retire. I know you very much want to take an early retirement with that wife of yours. How is Catherine?"

He said, "She's doing great and is involved with her charity work."

Ms. White said, "Do you have someone you'd like to take your place after you retire?"

He said, "I do, and you know him—my son, Bruce. Now don't think that just because he's my son, you have to have him replace me. Put him in as acting president. If he proves himself to you, then good. If not, go ahead and find someone else. I know you'll do what's right and make a good business decision. Making this announcement today kind of puts you on the spot, I know, but I think it's the right time."

Ms. White said, "Harry, you could have told me that the last time we talked on the phone or called me before I came down today. I'm not happy that you did it to me this way. I didn't prepare for you to make the announcement today, but I'll deal with it. After this meeting, I'd like another company tour. I want Sarah to see the company's manufacturing facilities."

Mr. Goodson said, "That is part of today's agenda. I didn't plan for you to have someone with you, but since she works directly for you and has a secret security clearance, I'll make sure she can take the tour."

Mr. Goodson made a phone call to add Sarah to the tour. He said, "That takes care of that. The meeting is scheduled with just the senior staff. After the meeting, a few of us will have lunch together. I have reservations at a restaurant not too far from here. When we return, we'll go on the tour. Let's go on down to where the meeting will be held."

Ms. White looked at her phone and said to Mr. Goodson, "Please excuse me for a couple of minutes. I received a message that I need to take care of. Is there a place I can make a phone call?"

Mr. Goodson said, "You can use that office just down the hall. That person is on vacation."

Ms. White placed the call and said, "That son of a bitch did just what I had a feeling he would do. The press release we worked on about buying this company—get it out as soon as you hang up the phone. Make sure everyone gets a copy and the local news too."

Ms. White took a really big deep breath to try to calm down. Oh, was she mad. She walked out of the office and back to Mr. Goodson's office, where he and Sarah were waiting.

Mr. Goodson asked Ms. White, "Is everything all right?"

Ms. White said, "It will be. The problem is being handled as we speak."

The three of them went down to where the meeting would be held. The room was small, and not everyone had a seat. Several were standing around the walls. Mr. Goodson said, "I'd like to introduce Ms. White and her administrative assistant, Sarah. Please go around the room and introduce yourselves, say your job title, and the area you're responsible for. Let's start with Bruce."

Each of the men and women took turns introducing themselves. Sarah was taking mental notes on each person as they introduced themselves. Ms. White had told her she was taking her on this trip for her eyes and ears.

When they were finished, Mr. Goodson said, "Almost a year ago, I sold my company to Ms. White." The place got really quiet. He continued, "Even Bruce didn't know. I didn't enter into this decision lightly. I've put my blood, sweat, and soul into this company, long before some of you were out of diapers."

He paused and said, "That's where you people were supposed to chuckle. Come on, folks, that was funny. This should be a happy day for all of us. I feel I've taken this company as far as I can. I know Ms. White will be able to take this company to new heights, more so than I ever could. Her company has the capital and with her and her team, and most of all, your support, you can do it. She and I have a contractual agreement that she would have a hands-off management style for one year from the time of the sale. That year will be up in six weeks. At that time, I'll be stepping down, and my son, Bruce, will become the president of this company. I'll now let Ms. White say a few words, and then we'll take your questions."

Ms. White said, "Your company is the best in the country at what you do. Your numbers are up over last year, and that's due to your management and the skills of the people making the products. The contract you have with the government doesn't expire for six more months. I hope that we'll be able to renew it. My purchase of your company has been on the QT for reasons I can't address due to the contract's nondisclosure agreement. At my company, my board of directors and a few high-level executives are the only ones who know about this purchase. They all have signed nondisclosure agreements. Because Mr. Goodson has made this announcement at this time, all of those nondisclosure agreements have now expired. It will be up to Mr. Goodson as to how he announces the sale to the rest of your company. Because of the limitations placed by the contract, little has been done as far as going forward. As it has been almost a year since the purchase, I do not foresee any major changes. At the end of the agreement, members of my management team will be meeting with you to start planning our future. Thank you."

Mr. Goodson said, "We will now take your questions."

Everyone was so shocked by the announcement that there were only a few questions asked, mostly about what Mr. Goodson would be doing after he left the company. A few questions were asked of Ms. White. Her answers were noncommittal and mostly consisted of, "That will be determined as we go forward."

Mr. Goodson said, "There is an announcement letter being distributed to the employees as soon as this meeting is over. So everyone will know soon. Thank you." He said, "Let's go eat."

There were about a dozen people at the luncheon, including Bruce. Sarah studied each and tried to study their body language. She listened closely to what they were saying. She wanted to get a feel for each one of them. She got a real feeling for the one sitting next to her—he was hitting on her. Sarah made it a point to hold her hand just right so he could see her wedding band. He didn't take the hint, so Sarah said sternly, so only he could hear, "I'm married, cool it."

That seemed to put an end to that. Each of the people at the table was wearing their company ID badges, so she could clearly put a name to the face. Orders were placed, and soon the food was served. When lunch was over, they all returned to the company.

Mr. Goodson said, "If you ladies would like to freshen up a bit before we take the tour, the restroom is right here."

Sarah and Ms. White stepped in. This was the first time she and Sarah were alone together. Ms. White said, "Not here. Wait until we're in the limo and on our way home."

Sarah could tell Ms. White was still upset, and she didn't dare say a word.

They started the tour. Mr. Goodson walked Ms. White and Sarah through the office areas, explaining the function of each. He said, "In this area is where the orders are taken. Over there is accounting, and on the other side is where the government contracts are processed."

That was one of the areas they did not enter. Next, they went outside and into the building next door. When they entered the building, they were met by a safety officer. He gave them all white overcoats, hard hats, safety glasses, and ear protection. Mr. Goodson led the way with the safety officer following them. Mr. Goodson pointed and said, "Over there is where the parts and raw materials are delivered and enter the factory. They move through the various processes and end up over there."

He pointed to the corner of the building and said, "From there, they are taken to the next building. There is where the parts are packaged, stored, and shipped. That building is not as noisy as this one. Let's go over there and take a quick look in that building. It shouldn't take too long."

In the building, there were lines of conveyor belts with people packaging the parts for storage and delivery. Mr. Goodson pointed and said, "That's our shipping department over there."

All through the tour, they were kept far away from the people. Sarah could hardly see what the workers were doing, let alone what they were handling.

They walked back to the first building, returned all the safety gear, and thanked the safety officer. Then they returned to the main building. Ms. White called Charles on his cell phone and said, "Come pick us up," then said to Mr. Goodson, "Thank you, Harry. I'll be in touch. Goodbye."

Sarah said, "Thank you for lunch and the tour, Mr. Goodson."

He said, "Nice meeting you, Sarah. Thanks for coming. Goodbye."

Charles drove up and opened the limo's door. They got in and were on their way. Traffic seemed light for this time of day. Ms. White closed the window between Charles and where they were seated. Ms. White said, "Remember I said I didn't have a good feeling? I didn't know just what to expect. Before the meeting, when I said I had to take care of something—"

Sarah said, "You looked at your phone and said you had a message."

Ms. White said, "I just used that as an excuse to call the office. I had them release the press release announcing the purchase. I think my press release will take care of any damage that could have come out of this. There's nothing in the release about the purchase being almost a year ago—just that the purchase was made for a nondisclosed amount and some stock options. We had worked on the press release months ago so it could be ready for release at the end of the hands-off year. That expired when Harry made his announcement. Okay, Sarah, permission to unload."

Sarah thought to herself, *This is the first time Ms. White has ever asked for my opinion.*

Sarah said, "I could tell you didn't like what you heard as much as I did. I so admire the way you handled yourself in his office. That is something I will have to work on."

Ms. White said, "Talk about body language—your face turned fire-engine red after he said it."

Sarah said, "I did buy a book on body language and have been reading it."

Ms. White said, "You're smart and will pick up how to read people's body language with more study and practice. You do a good job of reading people by what and how they say things. By adding body language, it will provide you with additional information, including if they're hiding something or lying."

Sarah said, "I have been practicing. Still feel I have a long way to go. By the way, you said I have a secret security clearance?"

Ms. White said, "We can talk more about that later."

"We both know Harry is a snake in the grass. Let's get past that."

Sarah said, "One more thing, if I may. I didn't care for the way he put his son in place as his successor. He didn't allow you to choose, and he said President, not Acting President."

Ms. White said, "I think Bruce would have been my choice to start with. I would have had people problems if I went outside of that company to fill that position. Bruce is well-liked. A bit spoiled, too, but well-liked. Now tell me your impressions about the company."

Sarah said, "I'm not familiar with the products being built and really didn't understand what they're used for. We were kept far away from seeing what the people were doing and what they were handling."

Ms. White said, "There are several different products being built here. Some domestic but mostly governmental. This little company builds a lot of military components. That guy who was the safety officer? He's really a gun-carrying federal agent posing as a safety officer. You wouldn't have been able to go on the tour without a security clearance. So I told a little lie about you having one. I was happy that they didn't do a check or ask to see your ID. However, you will need to fill out the paperwork, get fingerprinted, and pass an extensive background check to get a top-secret security clearance. After all, Ms. Director of Facilities and Planning, you will need one to do what I have planned for you. Now, back to my original question. Off the top of your head, what would you do?"

Sarah said, "Some of the equipment and machinery looked really old. It seemed to me that their assembly line could stand to be rearranged and streamlined. I believe time and money could be saved with a better flow. It looks choppy and redundant in places. There's a lot of distance between some of the operations, requiring a lot of movement by forklifts or people carrying boxes. I'm not the expert. I would get the Harlow's time and motions people to do a study on the flow."

Ms. White said, "For security reasons, we can't have the Harlow team on site. What you will have to do is get blueprints drawn up if there are not any. You may need to spend a couple of days down there identifying the activity being done and the flow direction of the material without identifying what the products are."

Sarah said, "What about the new building project?"

Ms. White said, "Sarah, that company has been getting along for some time now with how they're doing things. Nothing can be done for another six weeks anyway until the hands-off part of the contract expires. When you have time to work it in, you will. Remember your cow picture."

Sarah pulled out her phone and showed the picture of the cow she had on her phone to Ms. White. Ms. White said, "That's my Sarah," and they both laughed.

Ms. White lowered the window and asked Charles, "How much longer until we get to Sarah's house?"

Charles said, "About forty-five minutes."

Sarah said, "I'll be getting home about the same time as I always do. By picking me up at the house, it really did cut my travel time. Thank you. Would you like to come in and see my house?"

Ms. White said, "Some other time. I'm tired and would like to get home."

Sarah said, "Some other time, then."

For the rest of the trip, they both just sat back and looked out the window. It looked like Ms. White was deep in thought or maybe just zoned out. Sarah said to herself, *I really need to study body language a lot more, especially when it comes to Ms. White.*

Time passed quickly, and Charles was pulling into Sarah's driveway. He got out and opened the limo's door and helped Sarah out.

Sarah said, "Thank you, Charles. Ms. White, I'll see you in the morning. Have a good evening."

As she walked toward the house, she looked to see if any of the neighbors saw her get out of the limo, and she just smiled as she walked into the house.

Margo met her at the front door and said, "I like your ride."

Sarah said, "Ms. White and I had a business meeting downstate. It was convenient for them to pick me up here. How was your day? And how are the twins?"

Margo said, "Karl said you might be late. Oh, we had a normal day. The twins were fine. They're in their playpen. They're getting more active every day. Karl called to say he was running a little late and asked if I could stay until one of you got home. Since you're home, I'll be on my way. See you in the morning."

Sarah looked in at the twins. They were playing with their toys. She went on in to take a shower. She felt dirty after the day she had. After the shower, she put on Karl's favorite softball jersey. She went into the kitchen and poured herself a glass of wine. She heard the garage door open and knew Karl was home. He walked in the house and said, "What do we have here?"

She smiled at him and hiked up the jersey to show Karl she had nothing on underneath and said, "Does this give you any ideas?"

Karl said, "I guess we're not going to take our evening walk right now."

There was a race down to the bedroom.

CHAPTER 44

Just Another Day at the Office?

Jill was sitting at her desk when Sarah got to her office. Jill said, "Good morning. I know where you were yesterday. The press release came out during lunch about the downstate company purchase. A copy is in your inbox. Also, first thing yesterday morning, the surveys were delivered. There's a copy of it in your inbox too. So how was the meeting?"

Sarah said, "Good morning. Very interesting. You'll know more in time. How were things here?"

She said, "Busy. Pierre dropped off his kitchen equipment and machinery requests. He said the layout and new kitchen and dining room sizes were fantastic. His information is in your inbox. Ralph dropped off his equipment and machinery information. He said it's broken down by the number of people to equipment and machinery ratio. He also said if you want him to redo it after the surveys are processed, he'd be happy to do it. That spreadsheet you asked me to do for Lisa's kitchen and cafeteria—I have columns for quantity, model number, description of the equipment or machinery, and the price. I've entered all the items. I didn't see the price lists and didn't want to go digging around in your files or desk."

Sarah said, "All of the price lists for all items are in one book that is on the shelf in my office."

Sarah said, "Sounds like you were busy. Get the information left by Pierre and Ralph back out of the inbox and go ahead and make separate spreadsheets and enter the data for each. While you're at it, make one for the day care facility too. After you're done, we can work on putting the item prices in and see where we stand on the budgets. I'm still at a loss for what to do with everything related to the health care center. Ms. White said she had some ideas. Let's see what she comes up with. We have lots to do and don't need to focus on the health center right now. I'm going down to her office. I shouldn't be gone long."

Jill said, "I'll get right on doing the new spreadsheets."

Sarah said, "Hello" to Tammy and walked right into Ms. White's office, closing the door behind her. She said, "Good morning."

Ms. White said on the intercom to Tammy, "Hold my calls until Sarah leaves."

Sarah said, "How are you feeling? Have you had to do any damage control follow-up from yesterday's announcement or the press release?"

Ms. White said, "Let's sit over there."

They went to the lounge area of her office and sat down.

Ms. White said, "Surprisingly, no need for any damage control. I don't think there will be a need for any either. We got the release out as the meeting was going on. The company's stock took a big jump in the market yesterday and again as the market opened this morning. That's a good indicator. My phone has been ringing off the hook with well-wishers."

Sarah said, "I read the press release online last night. It was well written. It had a familiar style I recognized. I hope to be that eloquent in my writings. I won't take up any more of your time. I just wanted to see how you were doing and if there was something you wanted me to do."

Ms. White said, "There is. I'd like for you to go to HR and get the paperwork needed to apply for your top-secret security clearance. It takes a long time for the government to process those things, and I want you to have it when you need it. Also, if you don't have a passport, I want you to get one. It would be nice if Karl and the twins have one too."

Sarah said, "We have passports, and I'll check to see what needs to be done for the twins."

Sarah had that look on her face.

Ms. White said, "Just go do it. Now get out of here so I can take more well-wishers' phone calls."

Just as Sarah was leaving, Tammy buzzed the intercom and said, "Mr. Goodson is on line one."

Ms. White answered and said, "Harry, you son of a bitch. You thought you could get me with your little plan? You saw my press release, didn't you?"

Mr. Goodson said, "Elizabeth, you've always been able to keep a step ahead of me. So where do we go from here?"

Ms. White said, "First, you have to end your little games with me. You have a little less than six weeks. You need to plan your exit strategy for your retirement. Since you've already said Bruce is going to be the acting president after you leave, he needs to be brought up to speed to run the company. I know you, and you keep everything to yourself and don't share information. Bruce will also need to have someone take over the responsibilities he's handling now. He can't do both jobs, and you know it. Don't set him up for failure. I want to see your exit plan and a turnover plan for Bruce taking over the company on my desk by the end of the week. Did I make myself clear?"

Mr. Goodson said, "I understand, and I'll start working on it now."

Mr. Goodson understood he had made a big mistake and should have coordinated his announcement with Ms. White. He thought in order for his son to get off on a good footing, he'd better come up with very good exit and turnover plans.

Sarah walked over to HR. Kim was standing just outside her office.

She said, "I was just about to come over to your office. Come on in."

Sarah followed Kim into her office. In Kim's hand was a stack of returned surveys.

She said, "Look at this. We're having such a good response to the survey. It was just sent out yesterday morning, and look."

My secretary is entering the data and totaling up the responses as they come in."

Sarah could clearly see that Kim was excited. It was a great response.

Sarah said, "Good work gets good results, and Kim, you did great."

Kim said, "You and Jill were a big help. Thank you. If you want, I can give you the totals we have right now. I will have my secretary print off and send you a copy of the totals every few days."

Sarah said, "That would be nice."

"Kim, I need the government paperwork to apply for a top-secret security clearance. Ms. White said you have them here."

Kim went to her file drawer, pulled out the forms, and said, "The instructions are clear. You will need to go to the police station and get fingerprinted. There is a special form included in this packet. The government will not accept the form the police use. Carefully read everything and follow the instructions to the letter. Make sure you answer every question. If a t is not crossed or an i is not dotted, they will reject the application and send it back. It is helpful if you have a current passport."

Sarah said, "I have a passport. I was wondering, do you know if babies need a passport?"

Kim said, "I have no idea. That question has never come up before. Good luck with filling out the paperwork. It takes a while to process, and there is no way to expedite it. I hope you don't need it right away."

Sarah said, "Thanks, and again, good job on the survey. Looking forward to the updates."

Sarah returned to her office. Jill said, "I have all of the spreadsheets created with the equipment and machinery information entered. When do you want to start working on the prices?"

Sarah said, "Give me a chance to go over a few things. I need to do the recap report from yesterday's meeting. I will give you a call when I'm finished."

Sarah wrote the recap report and read the government forms over. She put the forms in her briefcase, then called Jill into her office.

Sarah said, "These price lists are sorted by model number. Go ahead and do a sort on your spreadsheets by model number. That will speed up getting the prices entered."

Jill was very knowledgeable with spreadsheets, and for her to do a sort was no big deal. She said, "Done. Which do you want to start with?"

Sarah said, "Lisa turned hers in first. Let's start with hers."

Jill read the model number, and Sarah looked up the price, and then Jill entered it into the spreadsheet on her laptop. They were making good progress, and it was coming up to lunchtime, a good time to break.

Sarah said, "Let's go to lunch. We could use a break."

Jill said, "Good, my eyes were starting to cross, and I'm getting hungry. Can I use your bathroom before we go to lunch?"

Sarah said, "Go ahead. Why are you so hungry, eating for two again?"

Jill said, "No, I just finished having my period and don't plan on having another kid anytime soon or maybe ever."

Sarah said, "What about that girl you want?"

Jill said, "No guarantees that the next one would be a girl. I'm still trying to lose weight, and it seems that I'm hungry all the time."

They stopped by Tammy's desk and asked her if she would like to join them, and she said she did. The three found a table, and Monty said, "Ms. Sarah, how nice to be able to serve you again. Hello, Ms. Jill. Hello, Ms. Tammy. Everyone want the usual iced tea?"

They all said, "Yes."

Monty said, "Ms. Sarah, Pierre said if you were to come in, I was to tell him you are here. Should I?"

Sarah said, "It's okay, go ahead and tell him. You know if he found out I was here and you didn't tell him, you would get into trouble?"

Monty said, "You got that right. Thanks."

Soon Pierre came over to the table and said, "Sorry I missed you yesterday. Have you had a chance to go over my information?"

Sarah said, "Jill and I just finished entering your data and have not processed it yet. I want to get the data from all the different areas entered and processed before I present them for Ms. White's review and approval. If I find any major problems, I will set up a meeting with you, and we can go over them, but so far, it looks good. I will also give you and the others an update, but that will be at least another week. Did you and your staff respond to the survey?"

Pierre said, "I did. I don't know about my staff, but I will follow up on that for you. Enjoy your lunch. I suggest the salmon."

Seeing Pierre leaving the table, Monty walked up and said, "May I take your orders?"

Sarah said, "Pierre is pushing the fish. What say you? Come on, Monty, this is Sarah you are talking to. You can tell me."

Monty said, "We have a wonderful chef's salad today, and the pot roast beef plate looks very delicious. It comes with mashed potatoes, gravy, and peas."

Sarah said, "I will have the chef's salad."

Tammy said, "I will have the same."

Jill said, "Monty, I'm hungry. I would like the pot roast."

Monty said, "Excellent choices. I will place your orders."

Sarah said to Jill, "That's some diet you are on."

Tammy said, "I know we are not supposed to talk business during lunch, but how is the new building coming?"

Sarah said, "I'm pleased with the construction. They are really moving along, and with this good weather we have been having, they may be a little ahead of schedule, but you know the construction business—ahead today, behind tomorrow. Jill and I have just started processing the equipment and machinery information. We are waiting for the survey information to be collected and summarized to finish the day care and exercise facilities. We are going to get really busy real soon as Bill finishes his areas. Then there will be another big push as we get the areas moved over to the new headquarters building. There may be a time where we will need to hire couriers to move work back and forth between the two buildings for the department to continue to work together but apart. Something that needs to be worked out. I think Bill and I will come up with a move-in plan that will minimize that. How are you doing in your job?"

Tammy said, "I made the best decision of my life coming to work here. The best job one could have. Ms. White keeps me busy, and I like that. I'm mostly answering the phone, keeping her calendar up to date, and doing her correspondence. You are still doing the heavy lifting. I have a steady income I can count on and company benefits too."

Their food was served. Jill said, "You should have ordered this pot roast. You can cut it with a fork."

Tammy said, "My salad is fine. I was not as hungry as you."

Sarah said to Tammy, "Mostly when we have talked to one another, even when I was on my maternity leave, we only talked business. I know little about you."

Tammy went on and told Sarah about her life and how she was the oldest of seven kids, that she had grown up on a ranch with lots of cows and a few horses. Several of her younger brothers and sisters still lived at home. She said how she was part of a 4-H club and showed cows and chickens but did not miss that life. She said, "I'm a city girl now." She said she was not married but had been living with a guy for about a month.

They finished their lunch, and Monty said, "Would you ladies like some dessert?"

Jill was tempted, and Sarah and Tammy looked at her, and Jill said, "No, thank you."

Tammy said, "You eating for two?"

Jill said, "No, I was just hungry today. I will be back on my diet tomorrow."

They all had a laugh.

Jill and Sarah returned to Sarah's office and continued to look up prices and enter them into the spreadsheets. Sarah said, "I need to check with Bill to see if he has finished any of his areas. We will do each area separately as we have done so far for his. They will need to be kept separate for budget purposes, but for ordering, we will need to merge and consolidate them before giving it to Harlow."

Sarah called Bill and said, "How about coming up to my office at nine-thirty tomorrow morning, and you can let me know how you are doing? If any of the areas are completed, bring them along."

Bill said, "I have a meeting scheduled at nine-thirty. How does your afternoon look?"

Sarah said, "It's open right now. What time is good for you?"

Bill said, "Two-thirty would work for me. I have another meeting at one and another one at four."

Sarah said, "I will see you at two-thirty then."

It was getting on to going-home time. When she arrived home, Karl was already there. Margo had gone home. He had changed his clothes and was getting the twins ready for the evening walk. Sarah gave him a kiss and said, "Hi, I will do a quick change of clothes, and then we can go on the walk."

It was a beautiful evening with just a bit of a light breeze. Karl said, "How was your day?"

Sarah said, "You go first."

Karl said, "You know Doug, the guy that I fired?"

She said, "Yes."

Karl said, "Well, I got a reference check call on him today."

Sarah said, "What did you do?"

He said, "I followed the firm's procedure and told the caller all of that is handled by HR. At least he is out looking for a job and got to the point of a reference check."

Sarah said, "What do you think HR will do?"

He said, "With the way laws are today, all they can really do is verify dates of employment and if they are eligible for rehire."

Sarah said, "I have never had to fire anyone before."

Karl said, "I'm sure that day will come when you will have to. Okay, your turn, how was your day?"

Sarah said, "It seems that Ms. White didn't have to do any damage control over Mr. Goodson's announcement. In fact, the announcement made the stock jump up. The press release had been worked on and would have gone out when the hands-off agreement ended in six weeks. Nothing really at all had to be done but release it. Ms. White needed to see that it got out as soon as she found out what Mr. Goodson's meeting was all about. The surveys are starting to come in already. Kim is excited about that. Jill and I are working on getting the equipment and machinery information and prices entered into spreadsheets. Lastly, Ms. White is pushing for me to apply for my top-secret security clearance and wants all of us to get passports, including the twins. I know we have passports, and they should be okay, but I want to check the expiration dates. It would be helpful if you could find out what needs to be done for passports for the twins or if they really need to have passports.

"Tomorrow, I'm going to the police station to get fingerprinted. This top-secret security clearance has me wondering just what it is that the downstate company is making and why Ms. White wants me to have one.

"After dinner, I would like for you to help me fill out this application. Kim in HR said to make sure all questions were answered and the t's were crossed and the i's were dotted. She said the government will reject the application and send it back for the slightest of errors."

Karl said, "I will do what I can to help you."

CHAPTER 45

The Twins' Birthday Party

It was hard to believe Emily and Kevin were a year old. That gave Karl and Sarah a reason to host a party at their new house. They both were so busy with their new jobs, and one thing led to another, they didn't have a housewarming party. They were going to have one now. The invitations went out and said, "The twins are one year old. Time for a party. No gifts, please. Party to start at 11:00 until... If you plan on getting in the hot tub or swimming pool, bring a towel."

Karl got a keg of beer and a Margarita machine, a dozen or so bottles of wine from a local winery, a tub full of bottled water, and a variety of soft drinks. He set up, in the corner of the patio, an area for the bar. Sarah got the name of a friend of a friend who had a BBQ trailer and smokes meats. The guy arrived around ten to set up the trailer. Sarah had ordered up the works. He had smoked briskets, sausage links, ham, turkey legs, pork shoulder, lamb chops, and both beef and pork ribs. Sarah thought, if we are going to have a party, it was going to be one heck of a party. He parked the trailer on the grass in the backyard beside the patio. He told Karl and Sarah nothing had to be done except stir the baked and pinto beans every once in a while. The potato salad was in the cooler; just check that the ice has not all melted. "I will return in the morning to get my trailer. Enjoy your party," and he left.

Ben and Andrew had come down and spent the night. They planned on staying another night and would go home the next day. Karl and Sarah had invited Jack and Jill, their kids, Jack Jr., and Steven. Several neighbors and their kids, George and his wife, Tammy and her fiancé, Charles and his wife, but she was not feeling well and didn't come. Charles came driving Ms. White in the limo. Bill and his wife, several of Karl's softball friends, Margo and her husband, and a few more. Sarah said to Margo, "You are invited to the party, not to take care of the twins."

Karl had built all of the patio furniture and a playpen in his workshop. That was the surprise he had been working on over the last few months. The twins were walking now, and the patio's super-size playpen was the best place for them to be during the party. Jill put Steven in there with the twins. It was full of toys, and they had plenty of room to move around and play. Karl and Sarah had an inground pool built and an above-ground hot tub installed on the pool deck. The entire swimming area was fenced to keep the kids from accidentally falling in. Sarah had taken Emily and Kevin to baby swimming lessons, and even at such a young age, they already could swim.

The house sat on a three-acre lot with plenty of mature trees. Lots of room for Sarah's vegetable garden and chicken coop. She was growing squash, both yellow and zucchini, beans, cucumbers, lettuce, tomatoes, and a few different melons. She had six Rhode Island red hens. Karl built a chicken coop and put up a fence so they could free-range and keep the other animals out. Karl also put up a fence around Sarah's garden, mainly to keep the rabbits, deer, and other wild visitors from eating everything.

It was coming on to noon, and most of the guests had arrived. Karl said, "Could I have your attention, please? Most of you have found the bar, the dip, and the chips. Please serve yourselves or each other. The potato salad is in the cooler. The deviled eggs are made from the eggs laid by Sarah's chickens. In the pots at the end of the smoker, there are baked beans and pinto beans. When you are hungry, eat, and when you are thirsty, drink. We have a net set up over there if you want to play badminton or volleyball, and over here is the cornhole game. There is a soccer ball around here someplace if you kids want to play soccer or anyone else for that matter. In the corner of the patio, I set up a table for a friendly penny/nickel/dime Texas Hold'em poker game. If you are planning on going swimming or in the hot tub, to open the gate, just pull up on the ball at the top of the gate and make sure it closes behind you. Andrew said he would like to give the blessing."

Andrew gave one of the best blessings Sarah had ever heard. Karl said, "Thank you, Andrew, for that wonderful blessing. Let's eat."

There were several who wanted to play poker, and the table soon filled up with players. Ben acted as the banker and traded the money for chips. Sarah said, "Anyone up for a little volleyball?"

Teams were formed, and soon the game began. Some of the kids found the soccer ball and were out back kicking it around. There were a couple of grown-up players too. As the day went on, several got in the pool and hot tub, especially the kids.

Later that afternoon, Sarah brought out a lemon-filled sheet cake with two candles. Written on the cake was "Happy 1st Birthday Emily and Kevin."

Sarah got the cake from the same bakery that made Jill's and her wedding cakes. Sarah cut the cake; Tammy and Jill helped with the serving.

The BBQ food was out of this world. People were eating and snacking on it all day long. The keg of beer seemed to be a big hit. Karl was happy that it would be mostly gone, if not completely gone, when he returned it. Several bottles of wine were consumed. He refilled the Margarita machine a couple of times. It was not cold, but Karl lit a fire in the patio's fire pit. People gathered around and told stories of campfires from the past, some from when they were in the Scouts and some from recent outings. The kids and adults made s'mores or just toasted marshmallows.

It was getting on to late evening time, and people were starting to leave. Andrew, being Andrew, was going around cleaning up, putting trash in the trash can, and asking Sarah where she kept the storage containers so he could put away the leftover food. Sarah and Jill pitched in and were helping Andrew. Ben was still playing cards with Ms. White and some others. Charles had joined the game after some of the others had left to go home. Even though the invitations said no gifts, several still brought them. Margo couldn't help herself; she had to check on the twins several times throughout the day. She changed their diapers and even changed Steven's. She said to Sarah, "I have not had this much fun in years. Thank you for inviting me and my husband."

Sarah said, "I told you, you were here to party and not take care of the twins."

Margo said, "I know, I just couldn't help myself, but I did party, and so did my husband. He won $3.10 playing poker."

Only Sarah, Karl, Ben, and Andrew were left. They were sitting on the back patio. The evening was so nice, and none of them wanted to go into the house. Ben said, "It is so peaceful out here. If I fall asleep, just leave me here."

Karl asked Ben, "Who was the big winner at the poker table?"

Ben said, "Guess."

Sarah said, "Ms. White."

Ben said, "That's right. That woman won over $12.52. She is amazing. She had no poker face whatsoever, and she could read everyone else like they were a large-print book."

Sarah said, "That's my boss. Yes, she is amazing."

Sarah said, "I'm going in to put on my swimsuit. Going to sit in the hot tub and maybe take a swim. Anyone care to join me?"

They said, "Maybe later."

Ben leaned over to Karl and said, "Let me tell you a story. Sarah and I were about twelve years old. We had gone down to the stream not too far from the house. That part of the stream is not there anymore. When they put the freeway in, they installed large cement pipes to route it under the freeway. Well, anyway, as I was saying, we were walking down by the stream. There was a small swimming hole. We were the only ones around, and Sarah said, 'Let's go skinny dipping.' She took off all of her clothes. It was the first time I had ever seen a girl naked. She was just starting to develop. She said, 'What are you waiting for? Take your clothes off.' She jumped into the water. I took my clothes off and got in. We were not in for more than a few minutes. We got out and dressed again. I think that's when I thought I may be gay. Don't you dare tell Sarah I told you that story."

Karl said, "She was wild back then too."

Ben said, "You don't know the half of it."

Sarah came out wearing a very small two-piece swimsuit and said, "I guess no one is going to join me."

Karl said, "Okay, I will go in and put my swimsuit on and join you."

CHAPTER 46

The Construction Is Finished, Time to Move In

Construction on the new building has been completed. All of the builder walk-throughs were completed, and only a few corrections were needed. The mural depicting the history of the company in the lobby was amazing. The color theme that carried from the lobby to each floor made the entire headquarters one of the best-looking buildings in the city.

Sarah took Lisa over to see her new kitchen and let her check it out one more time. Lisa is a very excitable person, and when she saw her kitchen for the first time, well, it was like a kid in a candy store. She said, "Everything is so clean. I am going to make sure my team keeps it this way."

Even though everything had been checked out during the building's walk-through, Lisa still turned on each piece of equipment, every one of the machines, and checked the temperature in a refrigerator and a freezer. She made doubly sure everything was working. She took a look at every table and chair, checked the burners on the serving line, and even rang up a sale on each of the cash registers. Sarah had Lisa sign off for her approval that everything was okay. The new cafeteria would be one of the first areas opened in the new building.

Sarah went through the same scenario with Pierre and the new executive dining room. As it was with the cafeteria, the executive kitchen and dining room had been checked out, and Pierre signed off for his approval that everything was okay.

Jill and Sarah went over the day care and the exercise facilities. As the cribs, desks, tables, and chairs were delivered, the orders were checked at that time, so they didn't have to do that again. The city had inspected the facility and the playground and found it to be within code. The equipment and machines in the exercise facility had been installed and checked out a couple of weeks ago, so really nothing more had to be done there.

After Sarah did some research, she found it would be better to subcontract out the health care center. Talking to Ms. White, she was in agreement and said, "That makes sense. Let's do it that way."

It made Kim in HR happy that she didn't have to hire staff to work the center. The health care subcontractor people would supply all of the equipment and needs for the center.

Bill and Sarah had set aside the entire day to go through the workers' areas of the new building. As the various deliveries were being made, Bill worked with the managers, department, and section heads responsible for each of their areas. Together, every desk, chair, file cabinet, cubicle, and every piece of conference room furniture was checked against the actual delivery, the order, and the blueprint layout. As an area was completed, Bill had each person responsible for their area sign off for their approval. Both Sarah and Bill wanted to make sure everything was perfect for the move, so they took the time to do that one last walk-through. All areas were ready for the people to move in.

Sarah went over to Ms. White's office. She had made an appointment for her and Ms. White to do the walk-through of the executive area of the new building. As they were walking over, Ms. White said to Sarah, "This has been one hell of a ride building this new headquarters facility. When I started with this part of my dream, I knew it would be expensive, long, and difficult, but I had no idea it would have been like this. Sarah, I knew I could not do it alone, and you know me, I like to do things by myself and my way. I could not have picked a better person than you to take along with me on this journey. Thank you, Sarah."

Sarah began to cry. Through her tears, she said, "If it weren't for you, Ms. White, believing in me, encouraging me, and supporting me, I would not have been able to do it. I have learned so much from watching and listening to you. If it was not for you and Bill, I don't know where I would be today. Thank you, thank you so much."

Sarah said, "Everything in the new building is ready to start the move in. If you have the time, let's take a walk around the floors before the people are moved in."

Ms. White said, "Yes, I would like that."

As you walked into the building, you could not help but have your eyes drawn to the mural on the back wall of the lobby. Ms. White suggested they start with the executive floor. They took the elevator up, and as they stepped out, Ms. White said, "Let's go this way."

Sarah said, "Don't you want to see your office first?"

Ms. White said, "We can end up there."

As they walked around, they looked into some of the offices. The name and title of the person to occupy the office was hung on the wall by the door. Ms. White stopped and said, "I believe this is your office, Sarah."

Sarah said, "My office is on down with the rest of the directors' offices."

Ms. White pointed at the office nameplate. It said, "Sarah Brown, VP of Facility Development, Planning and Maintenance."

Sarah stood there, trying to process what she had just read. She could feel her heart pounding, she was trying to catch her breath as tears began flowing from her eyes yet again today.

Ms. White said, "You are the youngest VP this company has ever had. Sarah, you have earned every bit of this position. Go on into your office. I helped design it myself."

They sat down in the lounge area of Sarah's new office. Sarah was trying to compose herself. Ms. White pulled out a tissue, gave it to Sarah, and said, "With this job, you will have a lot more responsibilities and about two hundred people working for you to start with.

You are now responsible for the day care and exercise facilities, all of the maintenance of the new building, the old building, and the one downstate too. The planning part of your title—I expect you to help me with the planning of the growth I want for this company."

Sarah pulled out her phone and searched through her pictures to find the cow picture and hugged it to her chest.

Ms. White said, "What are you doing?"

Sarah showed her the picture. They both started to laugh.

Ms. White said, "Sarah, you are one of a kind. I have never met anyone like you. You know that someday I will retire. You are on my short list to replace me."

Sarah said, "You really think so? You think I could?"

Ms. White said, "Hold on, girl, I'm not ready to retire anytime soon. You have plenty of time to screw up and fall off that list."

She said it with a big smile on her face.

Sarah said, "Somehow, with you as my mentor, I don't see that you will let me screw up."

*****

That night, during their evening walk, Karl said, "How was your day?"

Sarah said, "Ms. White and I did a walk-through of the executive area of the new building. We walked around and looked in most of the offices. We stopped in front of this one office, and I took a picture of the office nameplate. Here, look at this."

Sarah handed her phone to Karl. He looked at it and said, "VP? You are now a VP? Sarah, I don't know what to say. I am so proud of you. I'm married to a VP. We need to celebrate."

Sarah said with a big smile on her face, "What do you have in mind, big boy?"

Karl said, "How fast can you push that stroller home?"

*****

The next morning, Sarah said to Jill, "Come with me to the new building. I want to check out our new offices one more time before the move-in."

They went over to the new building and up to the executive floor. Sarah started walking toward their new offices, and Jill said, "Sarah, are you turned around? Our offices are down this other way."

Sarah said, "Not anymore."

She pointed to the office nameplate hanging on the wall outside her new office door.

Jill said, "Get out of here! I'm working for a VP now?"

Sarah said, "WHAT, no congratulations for me? All you can say is YOU are now working for a VP."

They both burst into laughter and gave each other a big hug.

Jill said, "Congratulations, boss lady."

Jill looked around Sarah's new office.

Sarah said, "What are you looking for?"

Jill said, "The bathroom."

Sarah said, "Those days are gone, girlfriend."

A security system had been installed throughout the entire building. Kim and her team had been working for the last month to get all employees their ID badges. ID badges would be needed to enter the building as soon as the first employees moved in. They were to wear their badges at all times. Kim worked with IT to get the employee information entered into the security system. As new employees joined the company, Kim's department would be adding and deleting them from the system.

Before any of the employees moved into the new building, there was a day set aside for an employee open house. In the main lobby, there were poster boards for each floor. The departments were clearly marked on each one. Sarah set aside the entire day to welcome the employees as they entered the building. The department and section heads were encouraged to give their employees time off to tour the new facilities. They were asked if they could be in their new area to show their employees where they would be working. One of the departments organized a group tour. The entire staff went on a field trip–style tour. The employees were free to tour the cafeteria and the kitchen where Lisa was. She and her team had made some cookies and snacks. Lisa made herself available to answer any questions people had, and the team made sure there were plenty of cookies and snacks for the employees.

The building's security system was disabled so everyone could tour the building, except the executive floor. The elevators were programmed not to stop on that floor.

Jill was in the day care facility to give tours and answer questions there. Sarah had Ralph in the exercise facility to give tours and answer questions. After all, he was now working for Sarah to manage that area. Sarah had asked him if he would like the job. Ralph said, "That would be great. I can work here doing what I love and make good money. My wife could still run our little gym."

Sarah went home that night. Karl had not gotten home yet, so Margo was still at the house. Margo asked, "How did the open house go?"

Sarah said, "I think it went really well. Lots of good compliments were given."

Margo asked, "How long before everyone will be moved?"

Sarah said, "We will start the move soon and should have everyone moved and everything up and running in about two weeks."

Margo said, "The day care facility too?"

Sarah said, "The day care facility too."

Margo said, "I guess you will be having the twins there in the place with you and won't be needing me anymore. I have become so attached to them. I will miss them so much. I probably will never see them grow up." Margo started to cry.

Sarah said, "Wait just a minute, listen to me. I want you to come work for me. I need someone to run the day care facility. I can't think of a person more caring or more qualified to do that job. You will be on salary and company benefits, including health care. I have laid the groundwork for you with HR to hire the people who will be working there for you. HR will do the background checks. I know you have a day care license, so that's no problem. What do you say? Do you want the job?"

Margo said, "My husband and I dreamed one day of having a day care center of our own. We never had the startup capital or could get a loan to do one. Oh, Sarah, I would love to come work for you. I could watch the twins grow up."

Sarah said, "I was hoping you would say yes. Here is the paperwork for you to fill out. You will be a direct report to me. I know HR has been taking résumés for people who want to work in the facility. I will bring them home, and you can do some phone interviews while you are here watching the twins. We will have to work out someone to help watch the twins while you get things set up at the day care facility. You will need to do your face-to-face interviews at the facility. If you plan and schedule your time, we will not have to have someone else watch the twins that long."

Margo said, "I know the perfect person to watch the twins. I will call her and see if I can work something out with her. Sarah, you have made my day."

Sarah and Bill worked together and developed a move-in plan. The cafeteria and executive kitchens would be the first ones to be moved. Employees would have to go over to the new building if they wanted to eat, including the executives. They thought this would be a good way to get the employees to start using their ID badges to enter the building.

Bill and Sarah's moving plan was to move departments that worked closely with one another on the same day. It wasn't just the move from one building to another; the packing and unpacking had to be planned for too. If the departments could work their jobs in the morning and pack in the afternoon, they would only lose a half day of work. The movers would move the boxes overnight. The next morning, the people could unpack and go back to work in the afternoon, again only losing a half day of work. This way, the workers would not end up being too far behind in their work schedules. The movers could only move so much at a time. They would be competing for the elevators to get the boxes to the correct floors. The movers would be working at night so as not to disturb the workers during the day.

To coordinate with the areas to be moved, the plan was for Sarah and Jill to work the days. They would make sure the boxes were clearly marked so they would be moved to the correct floor and area that night. Bill would work the night shift to monitor and answer questions the movers might have. If their plan was followed, within a few days, everyone would be moved in.

The morning after the last area was moved in, Bill went up to Sarah's office. He saw "VP" on the office nameplate and said, "VP now?"

Sarah said, "Yes, and I owe it all to you. If you had not hired me and told Ms. White to make me her executive administrative assistant, this would never have happened."

Bill said, "I may have hired you and recommended you to work for Ms. White, but it was you and your hard work that got you here. I guess my job here is over?"

Sarah said, "Bill, you sure made this adventure a lot easier on a lot of people, especially me. I can't thank you enough. If I ever have more work for you to do, are you interested?"

Bill said, "Sure, give me a call, I will think about it at that time."

Ms. White called Sarah to her office. Ms. White said, "Now that we are all moved into the new building, I want you to start focusing on the downstate company. It's time for you to take a trip down there and use the facility development and planning parts of your job. The hands-off period has expired. Bruce is doing an okay job as acting president. I can see from the status reports he sends me that he lacks vision and could use some help. I want you to find out what needs to be done and get it done. You once said that you think the production line could stand to be reconfigured, making the factory more productive and products could be processed faster at a lower cost. See if you were right. Also, I want you to bring back all of the file information on the governmental and nongovernmental contracts. The big governmental contract is due to expire soon. I want work started on getting it renewed and possibly an additional contract. There is a lot of money that can be made there, also the success of that company."

Sarah said, "I will make an appointment and head down there."

CHAPTER 47

Sarah's Trip to the Down State Company

Everyone had settled into the new building, and things were going great. Lots of people were eating in the cafeteria, and Lisa and her staff loved their new kitchen. There were plenty of kids using the day care facility. Margo was in her element. She was happy with how things had turned out and could still see the twins every day. She worked with Kim in HR to get the best people to work. It did turn out that there was a fee to have the kids stay in the facility, but the fee was less than what people were paying elsewhere. Having the day care facility at the company made it extremely convenient for them too. Ralph, in the exercise facility, made sure that people using the equipment and machines were using them correctly. It, too, was on a fee-use basis. The ones using it were paying less than what they were spending at other health clubs in the area. Ralph also had the courts and outside areas to manage.

As Ms. White requested, Sarah had turned her attention to the downstate company and made an appointment to visit the Goodson Company. She packed an overnight bag just in case she needed to spend more than a day there. Arriving earlier than expected, she decided to take a little drive around town until it was about time for her appointment.

Sarah walked up to the receptionist's desk and said, "My name is Sarah Brown, and I have an appointment with Bruce Goodson."

The receptionist said, "I see your name on the visitor's log. Here is your badge. Please remember to return it to me before you leave. I will let Mr. Goodson's secretary know you are here. Feel free to take a seat in the waiting area."

Mr. Goodson's secretary, Polly, entered the lobby and said, "Please follow me. I will take you to Mr. Goodson's office."

Sarah remembered Polly from her previous trips with Ms. White. She was polite but very cold in her reception.

Polly said, "Can I get you anything to drink?"

Sarah said, "Yes, please, a bottle of water."

Polly got Sarah a bottle of water and said, "Go on in, Mr. Goodson is expecting you."

Sarah stepped in and extended her hand to shake his hand and said, "Hello, I'm Sarah Brown. We met at the meeting when your father announced his retirement."

Bruce said, "I know who you are."

He did not shake her hand nor did he step out from behind his desk. He said, "I'm the president of this company and don't need some redheaded bitch, who gets driven around in a limo, snooping around here telling me how to run my business. I send my weekly status and my monthly financial reports to that Ms. White up in that fancy office up state. Just because the hands-off has expired you people think you can come down here and push me around."

Sarah thought what kind of hornet's nest did she just walk into and figured that is why she got the cold shoulder treatment from Polly. Sarah said "Do you know why I'm here?"

Bruce said, "Yes, to find out what you can about me. Tell me how to run my business and report it back to headquarters."

Sarah asked, "What do you know about me?"

Bruce said "You are the one that did the move to that new building. Got yourself a promotion. You probably sleep your way to the top."

Sarah knew she had to neutralized this situation right now. She stood up and turned the two side chairs to face one another about four feet apart and said calmly, "Come over here and have a seat. We need to talk."

Bruce reluctantly came from to behind his desk, plopped down in the chair, leaned back and folded his arms and said, "What now?"

Sarah said, "I listened to you. Now it's your turn to listen to me. I had an academic scholarship to college and paid for the rest it didn't cover. I only attended for a year. I had to quit because my husband was killed in an accident. I was on my own and had to get a job to support myself. Unlike you whose father paid for you college education. It didn't cost you a dime. You didn't have to work and go to school at the same time. You were smart enough to be a B+ and A- student but goofed off and settled for a C average, knowing that when you got out of school you had a job waiting for you here at your father's company. All you needed to do was get a degree and a diploma.

"This company would not exist if it wasn't for THAT Ms. White, as you call her. You see, your father and Ms. White went to the same high school. It was she who convinced her father to help your father start this company. You said I slept my way to the top. I have you know I worked hard for every promotion and break I got. Being a woman in a man's world didn't make it any easier. My father did not own the company and gave me promotions because I was his son and then named me president. Those weekly status and monthly financial reports that you say you sent to that Ms. White. Well, she gives them to me. Most of the time the envelopes are not even opened. The reason is this entire company is my responsibility. Everyone working here, including you, works for me.

"That's right I'm your boss. I am here to make this company more successful. If this company fails, I fail, and I'm going to let that happen. I'm going to let your comments about me being a redheaded bitch and sleeping my way to the top slide for now. I have a job to do here and I'm not leaving until it's done. Are we clear? Do you want to work with me or pack your stuff up and get the hell out now? If you try to hide anything from me, I will find out. If you ever lie to me, there is no second chance. I will fire you and have you escorted out of this building. Don't you ever make a comment like that to me again. Are we clear?"

Sarah stood up and extended her hand and said, "Let's try this again. I'm Sarah Brown. We met at the meeting where your father announced his retirement."

Bruce stood up and shook Sarah's hand and said, "I'm such a fool. My behavior was totally unprofessional. Please accept my apology. I would like very much to start over and work with you."

Sarah didn't know if he was telling the truth or if he was just a snake in the grass as is his father. She decided on giving him a chance.

Sarah said, "Let's see how much we can get done before lunch. When I toured the production area, I think with a few changes we could improve productivity. More product could be processed. We could do more business and make more money. Do you have layouts or blueprints of the production areas in all of the buildings?"

Bruce said, "I will need to check. If we do, they may not be up to date."

Sarah asked, "Would you know where they are kept?"

Bruce said, "Let me check. They most likely would be in this file cabinet or this closet."

Bruce sorted through some of the files and the closet. "I think this might be all of them."

Sarah said, "If that's the case, what I need for you to do is verify their accuracy. Be sure it doesn't say anything about what the parts or products are or what they're used for. I know there is a lot of governmental work being done here."

Bruce spread the blueprints on the table and said, "Let me take a look at these."

Sarah walked over to look.

Bruce said, "Just a minute, I haven't looked to see if there is any security-sensitive information."

Sarah said, "That is not a problem. I have a top-secret security clearance," and showed him her ID card.

Bruce said, "Really? Top-secret! My clearance is only at the secret level."

Sarah said, "I would like for you to apply for a top-secret security clearance as soon as you can."

Bruce said, "Okay. I will do it."

He looked at the date the blueprints were created and said, "That was a long time ago. The parts and products have changed, but not much has changed in the areas or the production line flow since these were created."

Bruce took a closer look and said, "I don't see any changes at all. Before going off to college and every summer, I worked on the production line. Thinking back, my father didn't want to spend the money to change the line."

Sarah said, "It is very important that the blueprints are accurate in all of the buildings. You or someone else will have to verify, just to make sure. When you are done, we can take the next step. At my disposal, I have a team of time and motion specialists. I will set up a meeting. You and some of your people will need to attend to explain the flow and answer questions. I will schedule the meeting to be held at the headquarters building. We will try to keep the number of trips you need to make at a minimum. We will work that out as we go along. During these meetings, you and your people are not to divulge any information about the products being manufactured. The people in these meetings that you will be working with will not have the proper security clearance levels. Another reason to have the meetings in the new building."

Bruce said, "It's time for lunch. Are you hungry?"

Sarah said, "Yes, I am. I got an early start this morning and didn't have much of a breakfast. I could eat anywhere other than that place your father took us to."

Bruce said, "You too? That place is my father's favorite place to eat. I can't stand that place. How about Chinese?"

Sarah said, "Great, lead on."

*****

On the way over, Bruce said, "I'm so sorry about my actions this morning."

Sarah said, "Remember we started over. That didn't happen."

The restaurant was typical Chinese with all the Chinese decorations. They had a choice to either order from the lunch menu or the buffet. Sarah said, "I am going to do the buffet."

Bruce said, "Right behind you."

While they ate their lunch, Bruce did most of the talking. He was saying how much the city had changed. Sarah didn't talk about herself or her family. Bruce asked about the new building. Sarah gave some facts about the building but not a lot of details.

Bruce said, "What is going to happen to the old building?"

Sarah said, "As soon as I get it renovated, it will be turned into leased property."

Bruce said, "You are responsible for that too?"

Sarah said, "Yes, that's in my area of responsibility. Just the renovation, not the leasing. I will still be responsible for the maintenance."

Bruce asked, "How many people do you have working for you?"

Sarah said, "In total, at various levels, a little over a hundred, not counting the ones working here."

*****

They finished their lunch and returned to Bruce's office.

Sarah said, "I would like a copy of active governmental and nongovernmental contracts."

Bruce went to the door and asked his secretary to come into his office. He said, "Polly, I would like for you to pull and copy all of the current governmental and non-governmental contracts, have a copy of them made, and give them to Ms. Brown."

Polly said, "Mr. Goodson, the governmental ones have all sorts of military information and require a secret security clearance to look at them."

Mr. Goodson said, "Thanks for stating that. Ms. Brown has a top-secret security clearance."

Polly said, "It will take me some time to pull them and get them copied. I have the clearance level that allows me to copy them, but no one else will be able to be in the copy room while I'm doing the copying. That will back up others from doing their copying."

Bruce said, "Don't slow-walk this. Do your best and as quickly as you can."

He turned to Sarah and said, "Is there anything else we need to discuss?"

Sarah said, "Not at this moment."

Bruce said, "On the tour you took when you were here before, you were restricted and not allowed on the production line floor. If you would like, I can take you on another tour where you can get closer and see what is being done. I will explain what the parts are and how the finished products are used."

Sarah said, "I think that would be helpful and a good use of time while waiting for Polly to gather and copy the contracts."

Bruce made a call to say they were coming to take a tour.

Bruce and Sarah walked over to the first building. Each was given a white overcoat, a hard hat, goggles, and ear protection. Sarah showed the safety officer her top-secret security clearance ID. He looked surprised and figured that Sarah knew who he really was. Sarah gave him a big smile and, with her back to Bruce, held her finger to her lips. The safety officer smiled back at Sarah and nodded his head. He did not accompany them.

Bruce walked with Sarah down to where the people were working. He picked up one of the parts and explained what the part did and what it went into. He explained this just happened to be what they were working on at this time. He explained there were several different parts they made, but the production lines did not change. If that product did not require something to be done at a station, it just went on down the line, skipping the station. They went through each of the buildings, and Bruce gave detailed explanations. Sarah got a better understanding of what was manufactured here. She felt her instincts were correct—that the assembly flow could be improved.

They returned the safety gear and were on their way back to Bruce's office. As they passed the copy room, Polly stepped out and said, "All of the requested information has been pulled and is being copied. It should be about another ten to fifteen minutes."

Bruce said, "Ms. Brown and I will finish up our meeting and can pick up the copies as she leaves. Just let me know when the copying is done."

Polly said, "Okay."

Bruce said, "I feel I'm on board with what you are wanting and do want to work with you. I hope you will give me a chance to prove I can be the person for the job. To be perfectly honest with you, Sarah, I am scared that I'm really not ready for this job. I have reached out to my father on several occasions. He pretty much has washed his hands of the company and may as well have said I was on my own. He really did nothing to prepare me for this job. I feel I can handle the day-to-day operational stuff. I grew up doing a lot of what these people are doing. As I said before, my summer job was working the production line. It's the creating and planning, staying ahead of the game that I need help with. I realize why you want copies of the contracts. I had forgotten our major governmental contract is due to expire soon. Losing that contract could have financially destroyed this company."

Sarah said, "What happened with the execution of exit and turnover plans?"

Bruce said, "My father said doing them was BULLSHIT. He only went through the motions and lied to Ms. White about the updates that the plans were implemented. He said you people, up in your ivory tower, would never find out. I guess he is not as smart as he thinks he is."

Sarah said, "Bruce, we are in this together. As long as you are working with me and doing the best you can do, you can keep your job. It's going to take a lot of work on your part. You can no longer skate along. Don't wait until you are drowning to ask for a life ring. I will do my part to help you, but you must believe in yourself and work hard. No one is going to give you anything from now on. You will have to earn it, all of it. I will do whatever it takes for this company to be more successful. I will not fail. I think you understand that from our meeting today. If you let me down, lie to me, or try to cover up your mistakes, and most importantly act like your father, you will no longer be working here."

Bruce said, "Sarah, I can see why you are where you are in the organization and that you earned every bit of it. I know you to be hard, honest, but most of all fair. You can count on me to do my best. I will never be like my father."

Sarah said, "To recap our meeting: You are going to review the blueprints for accuracy and send them to me. I am going to set up a meeting with the time and motion people. You are going to come up and attend that meeting to answer questions the team may have. Don't worry about the governmental contracts for now. We will take care of them from headquarters. Bruce, is that your understanding? Are you clear on everything? Or do you have some questions?"

He said, "I will get right on the blueprints and have them sent up by courier no later than the day after tomorrow. I will start by working late tonight. I can't think of any questions I have right now."

Sarah said, "Let's see if the copying is finished so I can get back home."

They stepped out of the office, and Polly said, "Here is everything, Ms. Brown."

Sarah said, "Thank you, Polly. I know this was a lot of work and was dropped on you at the last minute. I don't normally work that way, but under the circumstances, this was the only way it could be done. I hope it didn't put you too far behind in your work or the other workers either. My administrative assistant's name is Jill Hill. I'm sure she will be calling you from time to time, and feel free to call her. Thanks again."

Bruce said, "Let me walk you to the lobby."

Sarah returned her visitor's badge, said, "Goodbye," and walked out to her SUV.

The drive home was one of reflection. Sarah, in many ways, felt sorry for Bruce—the way his father was treating him, hanging him out to dry like that, and what he did to Ms. White by what he did in the announcement meeting. She thought things must have been different back when Mr. Goodson and Ms. White were in high school and afterward. How she went to her father and persuaded him to help Mr. Goodson get started. He must not have always been that way and had somehow changed over the years. She replayed the day and thought about how she would write up the recap report, thinking just what she would say in that report. She had a feeling that Bruce would work hard to become what he said he wanted to become. At least that's what she wanted to believe. She was good at reading people, but with the history of his father, she was unsure of herself. She was hoping Bruce was not going to be like him and would use how his father was as an example of what not to do and how not to act.

Sarah pulled into the garage and went inside the house. The house was empty. Karl was not home yet. The twins were at the day care facility. Jill said she would drop the twins off after work. It was a different experience for her being alone in this house. She changed her clothes and went out to her garden to see if anything was ready to be picked. She picked some vegetables and thought she would give them to Jill. She collected the eggs the chickens had laid. There were a couple dozen in the refrigerator, and she thought she would give the ones she just collected to Jill. Sarah went back into the house, turned the TV on just to put some noise in the quiet house, poured herself a glass of wine, and wondered what Karl was going to cook for dinner. After all, it was his turn to cook, and she had had a difficult day and was in no mood to cook.

Sarah heard the garage door open and knew Karl was home. He came in, gave her a kiss, and said, "How was your day?"

She said, "There is work to be done there."

To change the subject so she didn't have to talk about it, she said, "It's your turn to cook. What's for dinner? How was your day?"

Obviously, Karl didn't want to talk about his day and just said, "Same old, same old. I'm going to change my clothes and get dinner going. How does breakfast for dinner sound? What did you have for lunch?"

Sarah said, "I had a Chinese buffet for lunch. Breakfast for dinner sounds yummy."

While Karl was changing his clothes, Jill pulled into the driveway. Sarah went out to help bring the twins into the house.

Sarah said, "How were things at the office?"

Obviously, Jill didn't want to talk about her day either. It seemed everyone was having the same day. Was it a full moon?

Jill said, "Nothing that you can't take care of in the morning. I can't stay. I have to get home. The sitter said she had to be somewhere and hoped I would not be too late."

Sarah said, "Just a minute, I have something for you."

Sarah handed Jill the vegetables and eggs and said, "I just picked the vegetables and collected the eggs. The eggs are still warm."

Jill said, "Thanks. See you in the morning."

After dinner, they did their evening routine of taking a walk, feeding and giving the twins their bath and getting them ready for bed, watched a little TV, and went to bed.

CHAPTER 48

Back to Work After the Visit

Sarah returned to work early the next morning after her visit to the Goodson Company. Jill was not at her desk; it was not nine yet. Sarah knew Ms. White would be in her office and would want to know how the visit went. Sarah walked to Ms. White's office and, while standing in the doorway, said, "Good morning."

Ms. White said, "Good morning, Sarah. Come on in. How was your visit?"

Sarah said, "It got off to a rocky start. Bruce thought I was there to take over the business and start telling him what to do and how to do it right from the start. We had a meeting of the minds and an attitude adjustment, so to speak. The bottom line is he is scared. He feels he can handle the day-to-day operational things but doesn't feel he knows the planning end of the business. I don't think that he can't do it. I just think he never had to do it. Over the years, he has been given everything and just went away and did what he was told to do. The turnover he and his father were supposed to do never happened. He said the plans that were sent to you were just eyewash. He told me his father said you would never find out about it here in your ivory tower."

Ms. White said, "Were you able to get anything accomplished?"

Sarah said, "Yes, after I told him I was now his boss and could fire him on the spot. I was there to help him and make the company more successful. He could work with me or pack up his things and get out right now. That seemed to get his attention. He said he wanted to work with me. I don't know if he was just saying that or if it was what he thought I wanted to hear. Time will tell. He is his father's son. Putting that aside, I think he deserves a chance to prove himself."

"The rest of my time there, he worked to provide me with what you requested and the information I wanted. He gave me a detailed tour of the facility. He is very knowledgeable about the operational end of the business. I am more convinced that improvements in the production flow are needed. Bruce will be very valuable in working with the Harlow's time and motion team. I know that will cost some money upfront, but I think we can recoup it in a short period of time and be able to take on more business. I need to work up a business plan after we have the meeting with the Harlow people. There is the capacity to do a second shift if we get more business."

"I wrapped up the visit by telling him if he needs help, not to wait. If he tries to hide anything from me, I will find it out. If he ever lies to me, there will be no second chance. I will fire him and have him escorted out of the building. I think he got the message."

Ms. White said, "Sarah, you are sounding more and more like me. Is that the copy of the contracts you have there?"

Sarah said, "Yes. That was next on my list. I did take a brief look at some of them. I didn't really understand the legal wording."

Ms. White said, "It took me a while to learn it. Besides, that's why I have a legal department. What are your plans now?"

Sarah said, "I told Bruce he needs to go through all the blueprint layouts of the production areas, make notes of the flow, and make sure there was no security information written on them. After he verifies everything, he is going to send them to me. He said he would send them up here via courier by the end of today. I will make an appointment with the Harlow people and have Bruce come up for the meeting with the Harlow time and motion team to answer detailed questions about the production line flow. Based on what comes out of the meeting, we will act upon it."

Ms. White said, "I think you might have your work cut out for you on this one. I know you will do what needs to be done. I have all the confidence in the world in your ability to get the job done."

Sarah said, "Thanks, I think. I will keep you posted like I always do."

They both started laughing.

CHAPTER 49

The Old Building Walkthrough

Sarah said to Ms. White, "I have a meeting scheduled for later today with the people from Harlow to go through the old building. I need to get estimates for getting the building renovated and ready to be leased. The sooner we get it fixed up, the sooner it can start making some money. Bill has agreed to go on the walkthrough but has not made any commitment beyond that. I think he really wants to see what he is getting into before he says yes this time.

"Johnny, the head of maintenance, will also be going along. As you know, he started working for me when I got my new job responsibilities.

"In my spare time, I am working on new organization charts I want to present to you. Now that the hands-off agreement has expired, I'm trying to figure out how to merge the departments from the Goodson Company with the departments at our headquarters. I need some direction and help from you. Do you want to keep them as a satellite stand-alone company or bring all the accounting functions from down there to our accounting people here at headquarters? That would eliminate the need to have any accounting people down there."

Ms. White said, "For now, let's continue with the hands-off approach. Do work up the new organization charts and the report on bringing all of the accounting functions to headquarters. Depending on the workload increase, we may offer some of the people a chance to relocate here. What you have pointed out will also hold true for the additional companies I purchase. The exercise will be good for you in the planning part of your job duties. You seem to have a good approach to doing your job, and that's a good thing.

"I have decided to remove the maintenance part of your job title and duties associated with it by promoting one of the maintenance people and having them report to me. Besides, you will have your hands full for the next several months with the old building renovation, getting it ready for leasing, and also the new production line flow at Goodson. Oh, one more thing—after I get with legal on the government contract that is about to expire, I will make an appointment to visit the Pentagon and see if I can get that contract renewed and maybe get some more business. Getting an appointment with the government takes time. Sarah, have you ever been to Washington, DC?"

Sarah said, "Washington, DC? No, never."

Ms. White said, "That's where the Pentagon is located. Don't go packing your bags just yet. I always take you with me to my business meetings, don't I?"

Sarah said, "I have work to do."

She turned and walked out of the office, shaking her head. As she passed Tammy's desk, still shaking her head, she said, "Good morning, Tammy," and just kept on walking.

Tammy said, "Good morning?"

By the time Sarah had gotten back to her office, Jill was sitting at her desk and said, "Good morning. I saw your SUV in the parking lot, so I knew you were here. I figured you were in Ms. White's office. Bill called and said he may be a couple of minutes late. There was a big accident, and the road was all backed up."

Sarah said, "The people from Harlow attending the meeting should be here soon. When the receptionist phones to say they're here, please escort them up to my office. We will be touring the old building, and you are to come along. The Harlow Company will most likely be doing the renovations. I want you to bring along your laptop to take notes. I asked Bill to come along too. He hates to be late. That's why he called. Bill knows his way around, so when the receptionist phones to say Bill is here, ask her to give him a visitor's badge and send him on up. I think the walkthrough will take the better part of the day. We will break for lunch, eat in the company cafeteria, and continue working after lunch."

Jill asked, "How did your meeting go yesterday?"

Sarah said, "The meeting yesterday was productive. The secretary down there, her name is Polly. I'm sure you two will be talking to one another from time to time. Have you submitted your paperwork for your security clearance?"

Jill said, "I have, but have not heard anything back yet."

Sarah said, "It takes a while. They do a thorough background check. Was there anything questionable that you did in your wild days?"

Jill was now concerned. She did do some wild things and did party a lot. She thought that shouldn't be a problem, but it did start her thinking. Sarah got her all shook up, and she was now trying to think if she had done any really questionable things. Sarah saw Jill deep in thought and said, "Got you," and walked into her office. Jill knew that Sarah was having fun with her. Jill sat in her desk chair and started to reminisce about some of the wild things she had done, which put a smile on her face.

Sarah was thinking about the recap report she had to write about her meeting yesterday. She figured she would write the recap report and also write an addendum for the comments Bruce had made before their reset. She wanted to document that for her private file and not include it with the recap report. Just as she finished the report, Jill said on the intercom, "Bill is here."

Sarah said, "Send him in and let me know when you are on your way down to the lobby to get the Harlow people."

Bill walked in and said, "Hi. What a wreck, they closed the highway down right behind me. I think my car was the last one they let through. I see the Harlow people are not here yet. Maybe they will be late too. So what are your plans? And what is it you think you want me to do?"

Sarah said, "Hi, Bill. And how are you? Now you are sounding more like Ms. White, wanting to get right down to business. The

Harlow Construction Company has been selected to do the renovations on the old building. What I would like for you to do is be the contact focal point between them and me. You won't be doing any of the heavy lifting. I need someone there full-time to answer questions and keep me posted on the progress. I don't know how long it will take. Maybe we can get a feel after today's walkthrough."

Jill said, "The Harlow people are here. I'm going to the lobby to escort them up to the conference room. Johnny is here in my office."

Sarah said, "Thanks. Have Johnny wait there at your desk. He can walk over with Bill and me. We will be out in just a minute."

Bill asked Sarah, "How are things going with the downstate company?"

Sarah said, "I had a meeting there yesterday. I think I will be able to handle everything there. We better head on over to the conference room."

They all filed into the conference room. Introductions were made. Even Mr. Harlow the younger was there. Sarah said, "Welcome and thanks for coming to our new headquarters building. I'm guessing several of you have been here before during construction. Allow me to recap the purpose of this meeting so we are all on the same page with no misunderstandings. Since the Harlow Company did such an outstanding job of building this building, the Harlow Company has been selected to do the renovations on our old building. Today has been set aside for us to do a walkthrough and for you to do a preliminary assessment of the work that needs to be done. It would be foolish for me to think you could possibly come up with any estimate numbers, cost, or time today. I'm sure you will want to do a follow-up return or two and do a more thorough inspection. Come lunchtime, we all will go to our company cafeteria for lunch. After lunch, we can finish what we didn't cover on the tour before lunch. Do you have any questions?"

There were no questions, and they all walked over to the old building.

Each of the people Mr. Harlow brought has a specialization, whether it be plumbing, electrical, structural, or heating/air conditioning. They also brought along one person who was a specialist in city code and compliance. As they walked through, the code guy said, "All of the exit signs will need to be replaced. They are the old style, and since the building is being renovated, they need to be in compliance and have emergency lighting too."

He asked, "Johnny, does any part of the building have a fire sprinkler system?"

Johnny said, "No."

The code guy said, "The city has been pushing for it. It's not a requirement today, but it will be soon. It is a safety thing and maybe something you want to think about during renovation."

Sarah said, "That is a good point. Note that in your report. On this tour, let's walk through the building and keep it at a high level, not getting too bogged down with details right now. Go ahead and make your notes, and after lunch, you can get to a more detailed level in your area of specialization. If need be, Johnny can bring more of his people to help if needed."

Sarah said, "Our intent is to lease out this building. What we are wanting on the inside is the old flooring removed, restrooms upgraded with new fixtures, and the infrastructure heating and air-conditioning updated as needed. The executive kitchen and dining room will be removed and converted into office space. The old cafeteria will need major attention. On the outside, repairs are needed and a new paint job. The landscaping needs some attention too. As we get companies wanting to move in, that's when you will need to build to their needs. I know that would be impossible to esti-mate what you don't know. Let's call that phase 2, with individual estimates to build office areas as we get companies to lease parts of the building."

Mr. Harlow said, "In the old cafeteria area, you might want to think about a restaurant. With this many people that are going to be working here, they will need a place to eat. Most of the infrastructure is in place. Just something to think about."

Sarah said, "That is something to think about. I will pass that on to Ms. White. She is working with the leasing people."

One asked, "How about all of these desks, chairs, and file cabinets?"

Sarah said, "We plan on keeping the newer ones that are in good condition and providing them as part of the lease if the customers want them. Anything that is in disrepair and can't be fixed will be discarded. Any leftovers will be sold. We will have a professional cleaning company come in to thoroughly clean the furniture. You will just have to move it around or store it on another floor you are not currently working on."

They were just about done with the high-level pass, and it was getting on to lunch. Sarah said, "I'm hungry. Is anyone else hungry?"

Mr. Harlow said, "Lead the way. I'm hungry too."

They all walked back over to the headquarters building and into the cafeteria. Sarah said, "Lunch is on me. Just get in the serving line and select whatever you want to eat. Sit wherever you like."

Lisa saw Sarah entering the cafeteria and asked, "This must be the group you are buying lunch for?"

Sarah said, "Yes. Lisa, are you still liking your kitchen?"

She said, "Oh, yes. Is the top Harlow guy among these people?"

Sarah said, "Yes, come with me and I will introduce you to him."

Lisa and Sarah walked up to Mr. Harlow, and Sarah said, "Mr. Harlow, I would like to introduce you to your biggest fan, Lisa. She is our cafeteria manager. She and her team did the picking of the equipment and machines and all of the tables and chairs and the cafeteria theme."

Lisa said, "Mr. Harlow, it's an honor to meet you. Your team did such a wonderful job designing my kitchen. Maybe after you have your lunch, and if you like, I can give you a tour."

Mr. Harlow said, "Lisa, it is my honor to meet you. Sarah told me how happy you were with what we had done. She even told me the story of how you laid out your kitchen with tape and fixed lunch in your imagination kitchen."

Lisa said, "Oh, we had so much fun doing that. Sarah was the one who suggested that we do it. Oh, I'm taking up too much of your time. Enjoy your lunch. I better get back to work. Remember, I will give you a tour."

Mr. Harlow and Sarah got in the serving line and got their food. He said, "She is as excitable as you said she was."

Sarah said, "She sure does have the energy. If you don't mind, I would like for us to sit by ourselves. I'm happy you came along with your people. I have something I want to talk to you about. It will save us from trying to schedule another meeting."

They took a table that was just for two and away from the others.

Mr. Harlow said, "What is it you would like to talk about?"

Sarah said, "I assume you read the press release where Ms. White purchased the Goodson Company."

He said, "Yes, I did read about it."

Sarah said, "That facility falls under my responsibility. It is a manufacturing and assembly company. I have seen their assembly line and have the feeling that with some help from your time and motion people, they can work up a better flow that will increase productivity and save us money."

Mr. Harlow said, "I'm sure we could arrange to send a team down there to take a look."

Sarah said, "That will not be possible. We have contractual agreements that prohibit non-company employees from being in the facilities. Your team will have to work from the plans and blueprints. I will provide people who are familiar with all of the areas on the production line to answer the questions your team may have."

Mr. Harlow said, "Sounds like the government is somehow involved."

Sarah said, "I won't comment on that."

Mr. Harlow said, "I understand. We have worked under those conditions before. I don't see that as a problem. As long as the plans and blueprints are accurate and we have access to a knowledgeable person who knows the production flow. We have done projects this way with some of our overseas clients when the cost to send a team is too high. When do you think you would like to start?"

Sarah said, "The plans and blueprints are to be delivered to me by day's end. I don't think they will be much good to you without a detailed flow explanation. I can have knowledgeable people here to

314

answer your team's questions. Just give me a day or two for them to arrange a trip to come up here."

Mr. Harlow said, "That sounds like something we can do. I don't think I really need to stay here any longer. The team can do their thing without me, and I can get their briefing tomorrow. Besides, as you said in your opening remarks, it's going to take multiple trips to get all of the data gathered to make the final estimate. I will go back to the office and see when we can put a time and motion team together for you. I assume you want to do this ASAP."

Sarah said, "Yes. There is a sense of urgency."

He said, "I will give you a call later this afternoon as to what I have come up with. Thank you for lunch, and tell Lisa this was the best cafeteria food I have ever eaten. I will have to take a rain check on that tour."

"Sarah, you sure did a great job on your headquarters facility, and you now have two major projects that you are currently working on. If you ever need to take a vacation, come work for me."

Sarah said, "Thanks for the vacation offer. I'm having too much fun right now on this wild ride. Here is my business card. I have written my cell number on it. If you can't get ahold of me, tell my administrative assistant, Jill, that it's important and you need to talk to me. I will call you back as soon as I can. Thank you for coming over today."

Sarah rounded everyone up, and they walked back to the old building. Sarah said, "How was everyone's lunch?"

They said, "Great, and thank you."

She said, "You people are experts at what you do. Johnny and Bill will answer whatever questions they can or get the answers you need to do your job. I know the one who is the electrician said he wanted to look at the electrical panels, and the HVAC person wanted to take a detailed look at the equipment. Jill and I are going to return to the other building. Thank you for all of your hard work, and I look forward to working with the Harlow Company."

At lunch, Johnny had arranged for several of his lead people to come to the old building and help answer questions. The Harlow team split up and were joined by one of Johnny's people and did a more in-depth look at what needed to be done. Bill and Johnny supported the teams by answering questions the others couldn't. The Harlow people took all sorts of notes. After several hours, they all met in the old building lobby and said, "We have collected as much information as we could today."

Bill said, "When you need to return to gather additional data, let us know, and someone will be here to let you in the building. Thank you for coming."

They all shook hands and said their goodbyes.

Bill returned to Sarah's office. Sarah said, "How did the rest of the day go?"

Bill said, "Those people really gave the building the once-over. They said it really is a sound building—no foundation problems and no structural problems. The original construction was very good. It really could stand a facelift, as you had already said. It's going to take some time for them to compile all of the data they collected. The code guy was having a day pointing out all of the things that would have to be done to bring the building up to current code. I thought Johnny was going to punch that guy out. I don't see the renovation starting anytime soon. If you want me to babysit the renovation, I will do it. Like I said, it will be a while before anything gets going. Let me know when you want me to start. Thanks for lunch. Say hello to Karl and give the twins a hug from me. I'm tired; I'm going home, making myself a drink, and putting my feet up."

Sarah said, "Thanks for coming today. I will keep in touch."

Jill said on the intercom, "Bruce Goodson on line one."

Sarah said, "Thanks, Jill."

She picked up the phone and said, "Hello, Bruce."

Bruce said, "Hello, Sarah. First off, the carrier said he was unable to get the blueprints to you before your quitting time today. The delivery truck had left before I could get the package to him. He promised no later than midmorning tomorrow."

Sarah said, "How did the old blueprints match the production line?"

Bruce said, "Perfectly. I think you are on to something about the production line flow. I talked to several of the line workers, and they had some good ideas. As I was writing up the flow descriptions, I could see where changes could be made. I don't know why my dad didn't do something years ago."

Sarah said, "That's great news. I have made contact with the time and motion people. They are checking their schedule to see when we can meet. As soon as they get back to me, I will schedule a meeting. I want you and anyone else you think could answer questions about the production line flow to come up here to the headquarters facility. You have operations going on in more than one building and in the yard too. I would rather have too many people than not enough. Once a new production line is identified, you and your people will be busy getting equipment moved around and possibly having to get new or replacement equipment installed.

"Bruce, I know you are excited about changing the flow up. You are not to do anything until our meeting and we are all in total agreement that the new flow is the right one. Do you understand?"

Bruce said, "Yes."

Sarah said, "Good. I have to trust you on this. Don't go rogue on me."

Bruce said, "I know this will prove to you that I can be trusted and that I want to work with you. Do you know how long it will be before we have the meeting?"

Sarah asked, "How much time do you need to get ready to come up here?"

Bruce said, "Should not need more than a day. I will work on who I would like to bring with me."

Sarah said, "Right now, I don't know if everything can be done in one day. That will be based on how many questions are asked and how long it will take to answer them. It will be a long day for you and your team for sure. You may want to prepare for an overnighter. Is there anything else?"

Bruce said, "I don't think so. I promise I will not do anything until we have agreed upon a plan."

Sarah said, "I'm going to hold you to that promise. I will let you know I have received the blueprints and hope to hear back as soon as tomorrow as to when we can have the meeting. Thanks for calling to let me know the package will not be here today. Bruce, I can tell you are trying, and that's a good thing. Goodbye, and have a good evening."

Bruce said, "Thanks for saying that, Sarah. Goodbye."

CHAPTER 50

After the Old Building Tour

The next morning, Jill was in Sarah's office, and Sarah said, "This is going to be another big project, but nothing like what we just finished. No picking of equipment or furniture. Everything will be done by the construction company. Bill has agreed to do the job."

Jill asked, "Does Ms. White have anybody lined up to lease the building?"

Sarah said, "The only thing she has said was that there is a lot of office space to be leased. I think several companies or businesses, including doctors and dentists, would occupy different parts of the building. The cafeteria could be renovated or some restaurant might want to lease the space. Harlow will build to the needs of the ones wanting to lease if they sign a long-term contract. We might need to build generic offices to fill the areas not filled by larger companies or businesses. Ms. White is working with a leasing and property management company. Your guess is as good as mine right now as to who might occupy the building. Ms. White is handling that.

"Harlow will have to come up with the estimates to renovate and bring the building up to current city code. I think that will have a big factor in how the decisions will be made. I just don't have a feel for how much time will be required from the two of us as Bill will take the lead on that. I will still be the main focus between White

Enterprise and Harlow Construction Company. For us, right now, we need to concentrate on the Goodson Company."

*****

The following week, Sarah received the detailed report from the Harlow team on the old building renovations. All of the code issues had been identified, including the fire sprinkler systems. The electrical checked out, and the HVAC was in working order but would need to be replaced within the next year or so. Johnny had earlier said they were having to do a lot of maintenance on the units and have had some major problems in the past. He suggested that they should be replaced with new, more energy-efficient ones during the renovations. He thought that would save money over the long term. Nothing needed to be done with the current plumbing, water, and sewer pipes. The old bathroom fixtures needed to be replaced with new ones that automatically turn on and off and self-flushing toilets.

Ms. White was working with a leasing company to find a company to occupy the building. They tried to find one company, but the building was too large for the companies that showed interest. The leasing company told Ms. White she would have better luck filling the building if she were to lease to many companies and businesses. Ms. White agreed with the idea, and the leasing company went to work getting companies and businesses lined up.

Craig, from the leasing company, had a meeting with Bill and Sarah. Craig had a list of companies and businesses who showed interest in occupying the building along with the square footage they wanted.

Sarah said, "Give us some time to work out some details, and we will get back to you."

Craig left, and Sarah said to Bill, "I guess you are going to have your work cut out for you after all. You will need to work with the architects at Harlow and the new companies and businesses that will be moving into the building to create their office space."

Bill said, "There went my cushy babysitting job."

They laughed.

Sarah said, "So that's a yes, you will do it?"

Bill said, "You sure do have the power of persuasion. Yes, I will do it. I'm looking at buying a fishing boat. With the money you are going to pay me, I will be able to pay cash for it. The only problem I see is you keep asking me to do these jobs. I will never have time to go fishing."

CHAPTER 51

The New Production Line Flow

Karl's and Sarah's morning routine had changed. When Margo was their nanny, she took care of the twins; all they had to do was get themselves ready to go to work. The twins were now just over two years old. Things were very different. They were too young to dress themselves and still needed help. They could feed themselves, but what a mess they made. Kevin was pretty much potty trained, and Emily was totally trained. They were able to get into their car seats, but Sarah still had to buckle them in. The twins could say several words that one could understand, but the twins had some kind of language between the two of them. At least it seemed that way because they were always talking to one another. The twins rode to work with Sarah, and she would drop them off at the company's day care facility. Sometimes Sarah would visit them and Margo too. Margo had several people working for her now, but she was a working boss. If you didn't know she was the manager, you couldn't tell her from anyone else working there. She believed she should lead by example.

The meeting with the Harlow time and motion people and Goodson people was scheduled. They were to come up with a better production line flow. Bruce brought three of his people with him. The conference room had a whiteboard mounted on the wall. Jill arranged to have two additional whiteboards delivered to the conference room. Jill got a bunch of extra-large sheets of paper from the print shop and a bunch of different color markers from the supply room just in case they were needed. The plans and blueprints were laid out on the table.

The teams worked all day. Bruce and his people explained the current flow and answered questions the Harlow people had. They went through many different ways to rearrange the workstations. They used the paper from the print shop to cut out pieces that matched the machines and workstations. They used them to move around and came up with a flow they all liked. Bruce and his people were careful not to say what products were being made, and the Harlow people were told not to ask.

The new production line flow required several of the workstations to be relocated. Some of the older equipment and machines needed to be replaced, and a few new ones purchased and installed. Additionally, a new forklift also needed to be purchased.

Sarah was called to join them. They made a presentation to her. She said, "It sounds like you have all agreed on the best way. Will this new flow accommodate new products, or is it custom to the products we are now producing?"

Bruce said, "My team considered that, and we all agreed that it will work for many different products we could potentially be making, even if the new items were more complex to make and assemble. We don't think it would work if we were to make things that were much bigger. The stations just are not built to handle large items."

Sarah asked, "How long will it take to order the new machines, have them delivered, and make the changes? More importantly, how long would the production line have to be shut down?"

Bruce said, "That was not something we had worked on. We were concentrating on the flow itself."

Sarah asked, "Is that something you people could work on now and give me an estimate?"

Bruce said, "We have been working well together so far. I see no reason why we can't."

They all agreed they would work to come up with that estimate.

Sarah said, "Great. I'm going back to my office. Give me a call when you are done."

Bruce and his people made a few calls to see if the new equipment and machines were readily available. Everything was locally in stock and could be delivered within a few days to a week's time. The teams directed their focus on what had to be moved and reinstalled so the new equipment and machines could be installed. They came up with their best estimates to do all of the changes and installations.

It was a couple of hours later when Jill said on the intercom, "They're ready for you to return to the conference room."

Sarah entered the conference room and said, "What were you able to come up with?"

Bruce and the team leader from Harlow gave Sarah their best estimate.

Sarah said, "Thank you for your hard work and for working to get everything finished in one session."

The Harlow people expressed their thanks, and Jill escorted them out of the building.

Sarah said to the Goodson team, "Bruce and I are going to my office to have a meeting. Please remain here in the conference room. I don't think we will be that long."

Sarah and Bruce went into her office. Sarah invited Bruce to come in and sit down. She said, "How are you feeling now?"

Bruce said, "That was some meeting. You were so right from the start. The new flow is going to make such a big difference. Those Harlow people sure know their stuff. Me, I'm feeling so energized right now. Sarah, I owe you so much. I can't begin to tell you how much I have learned from you since our first meeting. My father never invested this much time or trust in me."

Sarah said, "I felt you had potential. All I did was have you focus and apply yourself. Now comes the hard part. I want a detailed implementation plan on my desk within the next two days. I'm not going to give you any hints at the moment. I want to see just how much you say you have learned from me on paper. After I receive the plan, I will call you, and we can go over it. If you leave soon, you won't be getting back that late."

Bruce said, "It is a little late but not that late. We did come prepared to stay the night, but I think everyone will be happy to get home tonight."

Sarah thanked the team for their hard work and escorted them out of the building. Each of the Goodson team members shook Sarah's hand and thanked her.

The implementation plan was emailed to Sarah by the middle of the next day. Sarah thought they must have worked on the plan all the way on the drive back. Sarah reviewed the plan. It was very good and very detailed, including the purchase and delivery time of the equipment.

Sarah called Bruce's office. Polly answered and said, "Mr. Goodson's office, Polly speaking. May I help you?"

Sarah said, "Hello, Polly. This is Sarah. Is Bruce available?"

Polly said, "Hello, Ms. Brown. Let me check."

Bruce picked up the phone and said, "Sarah, you must have received the implementation plan. What did you think of it?"

Sarah said, "Very impressive. Right down to giving paid days off to the line workers while the line is shut down. Would it be helpful or reduce the downtime if your maintenance department had some outside help?"

He said, "My team had a meeting with the maintenance people. After they saw what we were wanting to do, they said they could do it without extra help. Besides, it would take extra time to clear all of the security-sensitive products and secure the area so non-employees could work in there."

Sarah said, "That's a good point."

Bruce said, "All of the equipment and machinery have been delivered, uncrated, and are ready to be installed. The day after tomorrow is Friday. I will shut the line down for Friday and Monday. The maintenance department said they will work the four days and have everything up and running by Tuesday in time for the line workers' return to work. Did you see anything that I missed?"

Sarah said, "Bruce, your plan is very good, and your implementation sounds good too. Keep me updated on your progress."

Bruce said, "Thanks."

The new equipment and machinery were installed, and the production line flow changes were all completed in the four-day timeframe. The workers came to work on Tuesday as planned. It didn't take long before everything was flowing smoothly—such a big improvement over how things had been done for years. All of the workers were pleased with the changes.

Sarah was waiting for the production performance report. After reading the report, she was amazed at what she saw. She checked Ms. White's calendar to see if she had a meeting; she didn't. Sarah went down to her office. Tammy said, "I guess you want me to tell Ms. White you are here?"

Sarah said, "Yes, if you would be so kind to do so."

Tammy pressed the intercom button and said, "Sarah is here to see you, and she seems to be in a very good mood."

Ms. White said, "Send her in."

Sarah opened Ms. White's office door and walked in.

Ms. White said, "So what has put you in such a good mood?"

Sarah said, "I just received the production performance report from the Goodson Company."

Ms. White said, "The numbers must be good to make you so happy."

Sarah said, "No, they are not good—they are fantastic. The reports reflect the first two weeks of work after the new flow and equipment were installed. And the first week was a short one due to the line being shut down on that Monday."

Sarah put the report on Ms. White's desk and pointed to the numbers and the graph. Production was up over 12 percent.

Ms. White said, "That is fantastic."

Sarah said, "I think that number will increase over the next couple of weeks as the workers have more time getting into the new flow and learning more about the capabilities of the new machines and equipment. I'm sure the backlog will start to shrink too."

Ms. White said, "Your intuition to change the flow was spot on. Good job."

Sarah said, "I can't take all of the credit. Bruce really did step up and did a very good job. I'm going to call and tell him he is now officially the president of his company. I will take a trip down there and make the announcement and thank the workers for their hard work."

Sarah called Bruce and said, "The production numbers look fantastic. I would like to come down and thank the people myself. When can you schedule the meeting?"

Bruce said, "I know you are busy, so tell me when you can make the trip."

Sarah said, "My tomorrow is open. Would that be okay?"

Bruce said, "I will set up the meeting for ten. Does that work for you?"

Sarah said, "See you in the morning."

*****

The next morning, Sarah met with the people of the Goodson Company. She said, "The new numbers were excellent, and thank you all for your hard work and support. I have an announcement to make. Congratulations, Bruce Goodson. Come say a few words."

Bruce said a few words about how the changes took place and how proud he was of all the people working at the Goodson Company. After the meeting, Bruce took Sarah on a quick walk-through of the buildings and new production lines. Sarah left and returned back north. It was a long trip for such a short meeting, but she felt it was well worth it.

CHAPTER 52

The Trip to Washington, DC

Jill got a phone call from Tammy saying Ms. White wanted Sarah to come down to her office. Jill passed the information on to Sarah. As Sarah was walking out of her office, she asked Jill, "Did Tammy say why Ms. White wants to see me?"

Jill said, "No, just that she wants to see you."

Sarah said to herself, *I hate it when she doesn't do that. Not giving me a hint as to why she wants to see me. She does that to me all the time.*

Sarah walked down, trying to think what could possibly be the reason that Ms. White wanted to see her. She got to Tammy's desk, and Tammy said, "Ms. White said to just go on in when you get here."

As Sarah walked into Ms. White's office, she gave the open door a couple of light knocks. Ms. White was reading something and looked up. She stood up and said, "Let's sit over here in the lounge area. Have you had your coffee yet? There is some in that container."

Sarah offered to refill Ms. White's cup.

She said, "I'm fine. Go ahead and pour yourself some."

Ms. White was holding a letter in her hand and handed it to Sarah. On the letterhead was the seal of the United States of America Department of Defense. Sarah read the letter. It was an invitation to meet with General Peabody.

Ms. White said, "This is the letter I have been waiting for. It's for the DOD to review and hopefully renew the contract with the Goodson Company."

Sarah looked at the letter and said, "The meeting is in two weeks."

Ms. White said, "That's the government for you—wait, wait, wait, and then hurry up."

Sarah asked, "Does that give you enough time to prepare?"

She said, "With your help, it's plenty of time. Besides, you're going with me."

Ms. White saw Sarah's mouth drop open. Nothing was coming out, just wide open.

Ms. White said, "You told me you had never been to Washington, DC, before. So here is the plan. We will fly out the day before the meeting. We will do some sightseeing in the afternoon and in the evening of that day. If you like, we can do some more sightseeing the morning of day two. The meeting doesn't start until late afternoon. Not knowing just how long the meeting will last, we will fly back home the morning of the next day. There is a lot to see in DC. We will see as much as we can. I have been there many times, so we will do what you want to do. I suggest you come up with a list of things you want to see and do. So what do you think?"

Sarah said, "Two weeks will give us two more weeks of performance data. That presentation you gave to that company to get more business could be tailored for the Goodson Company. You did such a good job and got us a whole lot of new business out of it. I can get you the graph and data information scanned so it can be added to your presentation. Jill and I could create a PowerPoint presentation."

Ms. White said, "Wait a minute, a PowerPoint presentation? I don't know."

Sarah said, "Remember how impressed you were with the one you saw at Harlow? You can do it. You don't need to know how to put the presentation together. Leave that to Jill and me. All you will have to learn is how to go forward and backward through the pages."

Ms. White said, "Enough about the business end of the trip. So what do you think about going to DC?"

Sarah said, "Oh, that part. I have seen a couple of travel shows about Washington, DC, and have wanted to go see it. I guess now I am going to get my chance. I will do some research and come up with some places I would like to see and visit. I will also have to figure out how to break the news to Karl that he will have to become Mr. Mom for a few days. Karl and I will figure out something. We have two weeks to plan for it."

Ms. White said, "I'm sure you will work it out."

Sarah said, "I don't think I should say anything to Bruce about the meeting right now. The way I left it with him was that we in headquarters would take care of the contracts. He was in total agreement with that. I will fill him in after the meeting, and we return with the renewed contract."

Ms. White said, "I like the way you think."

When Sarah went to pick the twins up from day care, she said to Margo, "Could you give me the name of the babysitter you had to watch the twins while you were doing the job interviews? I have an out-of-town business trip. I thought it would be easier on Karl to have someone at the house instead of having to drive all the way over here and then all the way back across town to his office."

Margo said, "Yes, it would be a lot easier for Karl. How long are we talking about and when?"

Sarah gave her the information.

Margo said, "I will call Patty and explain to her what you are needing and have her call you."

Sarah said, "That would be wonderful."

*****

Sarah got the twins and headed home.

Karl was home and had already changed his clothes. Sarah was getting the kids out of the SUV when Karl came out to greet her.

He said, "There's my family."

The twins ran up to Karl to get their hugs and kisses. Karl gave Sarah a kiss and said, "I had a wonderful day. Today was bonus day.

For the second time in a row, I beat George and am again the top senior accountant at the firm. How was your day?"

Sarah said, "That's fantastic news. How did George feel about that? Let me change my clothes. We can talk more about it on the walk. I have some news to tell you too."

These days, the walks were no longer with the kids in the stroller. Either the twins walked along or rode their tricycles. Karl got the kids' tricycles out of the garage. Sarah had changed her clothes and was ready for the walk. The walks were not as long as they used to be when the kids rode in the stroller. They walked slowly as the kids pedaled along on their tricycles.

Karl said, "George said, 'Nice job and congratulations.' I could tell he was a little disappointed he didn't win for the second time in a row. Tell me about your day."

Sarah said, "I'm trying to come up with a way to tell you."

Karl said, "It's that bad?"

Sarah said, "No, nothing like that. I'm going to Washington, DC, with Ms. White on a business trip for a meeting at the Pentagon with the people from the Department of Defense."

Karl said, "That's fantastic. You've always wanted to visit DC. So what's the problem?"

Sarah said, "You will have to be Mr. Mom while I'm gone. I'm only going to be gone for three days. I talked to Margo to see if her friend Patty could babysit here during the day at the house. She was the one that babysat while Margo was doing the day care interviews. This way, you don't have to worry about getting the twins to and from day care. You will still have to take care of them all by yourself in the evening and overnight. You have never had to do it all by yourself before. Let that sink in for a minute."

Karl said, "It's only for a few nights. I think I can manage. Will you have time to see any of DC?"

Sarah said, "Ms. White said we would have some time to do some sightseeing. She said she had been there many times before, and for me to research places, I would like to visit and see and come up with a plan."

Karl asked, "Do you know where you will be staying?"

She said, "The details have not been worked out yet, but knowing Ms. White, we will be going first class all the way. She did offer for Charles to pick up the twins and take them to and from day care in the limo. I said that would have the neighbors talking. Ms. White had a belly laugh over that. Besides, it will give Charles a few days off."

Karl said, "That would have them talking for sure. Especially that one two doors up."

They finished the walk and fixed dinner together. Just as the kitchen was all cleaned up, Sarah's phone rang.

Sarah answered, "Ms. Brown, this is Patty. Margo told me all about you needing someone to babysit your twins. I remember you. You live in that new big house in Pony Express Estates. I will be most happy to babysit for you. Besides, how could I turn it down after hearing Margo go on and on about those twins? She sure does love them."

Sarah said, "Thanks, Patty. Yes, Margo is like a grandmother to the twins."

Sarah ended the phone call and said to Karl, "That was Patty. She said she would be happy to babysit the twins while I'm out of town. Got my kiddos taken care of."

Karl said, "Our kiddos. By the way, how about me?"

Sarah said, "Let's get the twins their bath and put them to bed, and I will give you some TLC in the bedroom."

Karl said, "Emily, Kevin, time for your bath. Daddy has a play-date with Mommy."

*****

It was six o'clock in the morning on the day to go to Washington, DC. Charles, as always, was right on time pulling into Sarah's driveway. They had an early flight, and you had to be at the airport two hours before flight time. Charles pulled up outside of the airline terminal, opened the limo door, and then got their carry-on bags out of the back.

Charles said, "Safe journey."

Ms. White and Sarah went through security, and Ms. White led the way to the airline's executive lounge. She placed her card in the slot, and the door opened.

She said to Sarah, "We will wait in here until flight time."

Ms. White gave their flight information to the receptionist, and they sat down.

Sarah said, "I have always wondered what the inside of these lounges looked like."

Ms. White said, "I'm a lifetime member. It's so much nicer sitting here than at the gate. Help yourself to anything over there at the snack table, and please bring me back a coffee."

Sarah got Ms. White her coffee and got herself an orange juice. A little later, the receptionist said, "Ms. White, it's your boarding time."

Sarah and Ms. White walked to the gate and straight onto the plane. They took their seats in first class.

Sarah said, "This is another first for me."

Ms. White said, "You have never flown before?"

Sarah said, "I've been on an airplane before. Just never in first class."

Ms. White said, "This is probably not the best time to ask, but you did bring the presentation with you?"

Sarah said, "I have it loaded on my laptop computer and a backup copy on a memory stick."

Ms. White said, "And a backup copy too. Sarah, you never cease to amaze me. Do you have that list of things you want to visit or see while we are in DC?"

Sarah got the list out of her briefcase and handed it to Ms. White. She looked at it and said, "We will see how much of this we can do."

Jill and Sarah had made a PowerPoint presentation. Ms. White had edited it. She made some additions and corrections, and they updated the presentation. Ms. White, at first, was uncomfortable using it, but she soon learned how and really thought it would be an asset. During the flight, she used Sarah's laptop to review the presentation to help pass the time.

The plane landed at Dulles Airport. Ms. White and Sarah walked down to the baggage claim area to meet the driver Ms. White had arranged to meet them. Looking around, they spotted a person holding a sign with Ms. White's name on it.

She said, "There is our driver."

Sarah just followed her lead. The driver took their bags and led the way to where the limo was parked. As he opened the door, he asked, "The Watergate Hotel, is that correct?"

Ms. White said, "Yes, the Watergate Hotel."

He said, "I have been assigned to be your private driver for your entire stay. Here is my card with my phone number on it."

Ms. White said, "After taking us to the hotel, give us time to check in, and we would like to do some sightseeing."

The driver said, "My name is Charles. Whatever is your pleasure. I have been asked by my company to be available twenty-four hours a day."

Sarah did a quick look at Ms. White and said, "Charles? Now how did you arrange that?"

They pulled up to the hotel. Charles opened the door, and the hotel bellhop took their bags to the front desk. Ms. White said, "Checking in—Ms. White and Ms. Brown."

The receptionist said, "Your rooms are ready. Here are your keys. The bellman will show you to your rooms."

Their rooms were next to one another. Ms. White said, "Get settled and put on your walking shoes. You think you will need more than a half hour?"

Sarah said, "Half hour? I will be ready."

Sarah called Karl and said, "You won't believe it. We waited in the airport executive lounge until flight time. We flew first class, there was a limo and driver waiting for us when we arrived here, and we are staying in THE Watergate Hotel. I will take pictures of this room and send them to you."

Karl said, "Slow down. You are doing it again. When you get excited, it's hard to keep up with you."

Sarah said, "Sorry. I've got to go anyway. Need to unpack. We have a private car waiting to take us sightseeing."

Karl said, "Private car? Tell me tonight before you go to bed. Enjoy yourself living like the other half."

*****

The half hour was up. Sarah knocked on Ms. White's door. She opened it and said, "Come on in. Let me give Charles a call so he can bring the car around."

Her room was nothing like Sarah's room. It was more than twice the size of hers. They went down to the lobby, and Charles was waiting with the door open.

Charles said, "Where would you ladies like to go?"

Sarah handed him her list and said, "This is my first time visiting Washington, DC. On the list are the places I would like to visit and see. Since you know the city, I figured you would best know how we can go and do as many of these as possible."

Charles said, "I can drive past the monuments and the White House. The ones that you would like to walk around and see, I will just drive around or park and pick you up when you are finished. For the Capitol building tours, it is hit or miss as to how long it takes to get in and how long you take to have your look around. The Smithsonian, you could spend days there. Is there a particular part you have an interest in?"

Sarah said, "The aeronautical and space would be the one. I looked on the Internet to see if I could book a tour of the White House. It didn't look like I could get one."

Charles said, "Let me see what I can do about getting a tour for you in the morning."

Charles drove around the monuments. At some of them, Ms. White and Sarah got out and walked around. Ms. White pointed out some of the points of interest visible from where they were standing. They stopped for lunch, and after eating, Ms. White said, "Take me back to the hotel and drop me off. Sarah, when you are ready for dinner, call me. Charles, see how many more places on her list you can take her to—maybe someplace you think she might like that is not on your list."

Sarah asked, "Are you okay?"

Ms. White replied, "Sarah, I have been here so many times. I just enjoyed watching you see them for the first time. Enjoy your afternoon of sightseeing."

Ms. White then said to Charles, "Take good care of her, and I'll see you around dinnertime."

Charles took Ms. White back to the hotel. He and Sarah spent the rest of the afternoon going from place to place.

Sarah said, "Find a place to park this limo, take off that hat and coat, and join me in going to some of these places."

Charles replied, "That's against company policy."

Sarah said, "So would this be the first time you ever did something against company policy? Besides, I'm not going to say anything, and it's no fun going alone."

Charles said, "You sure have a way with words. It's a deal."

He parked the limo, and they walked, it seemed like, for miles. They returned to the limo, and Charles said, "We still have a little time before dinner. I'd like to take you up to Mount Vernon. I know it wasn't on your list, but it's a place I think you'll enjoy seeing. You'd be trading it for the Smithsonian Aeronautical and Space Museum, but I don't think you would see much in the time we have left before dinner. Maybe next time you're in DC."

Charles took Sarah to Mount Vernon. Sarah said, "This was worth seeing. Thank you, Charles."

It was time to return to the hotel for her dinner with Ms. White. On the way back, Sarah called Ms. White and said, "We're on our way back."

Ms. White replied, "Let's eat here in the hotel."

Sarah said, "I'll let Charles know. Should I tell him we won't be needing him anymore today?"

Ms. White said, "I'll leave that up to you. I do enjoy a drive around DC at night, seeing the buildings and monuments all lit up. If you'd like to do that, I'll join you."

Sarah said, "I'd like that very much. I'll let Charles know."

Charles said, "Call me after you've had your dinner, and I'll come pick you up."

They went to the nicest restaurant in the hotel. Ms. White ordered the grilled salmon, and Sarah ordered the prime rib. It was now dark, and Ms. White called Charles. He said, "Traffic is backed up due to some diplomat coming into town. I'll be there in about twenty minutes. I'll call you when I've arrived at the hotel."

Ms. White said, "Okay." She turned to Sarah and said, "That should give us time to go back up to our rooms and freshen up."

*****

Charles picked Ms. White and Sarah up and drove them around the city. Sarah said to Ms. White, "The evening drive sure is something to see. I'm happy you suggested it. I don't know about you, but I sure am tired. I promised Karl I would call him before going to bed. If you don't mind, I'd like to call it a day and go back to the hotel."

Ms. White said, "Charles, please take us to the hotel."

As Charles was letting them out of the limo, he said, "I was able to get you two White House tour passes for tomorrow morning at nine o'clock. I'll pick you up at eight-thirty if you still want to take the tour."

Sarah said, "I won't ask you how you did it, Charles. Thank you. Ms. White, will you go with me?"

Ms. White said, "I wouldn't miss it for the world."

They went up to their rooms. Sarah called Karl and told him all about her day, all of the places she had seen, and that she and Ms. White were going to tour the White House. Karl told Sarah everything was good at the house and not to worry. He said, "Good luck in your meeting."

*****

At eight-thirty, Charles picked the two of them up and dropped them off at the White House for their tour. After the tour, Ms. White said, "Sarah, I think it's best that we go back to the hotel, go through the presentation, and have some lunch."

Ms. White then said to Charles, "We have an appointment at the Pentagon at three o'clock. What time do you need to pick us up to make that appointment?"

Charles informed Ms. White of the time he would return to pick them up.

Ms. White and Sarah went over the presentation. Ms. White looked like a natural. She pressed the buttons to advance through the presentation. Sarah tried to mess her up by interrupting her and asking her to go back to the previous slide. Ms. White did it flawlessly.

Sarah said, "You're ready. What do you say we go get some lunch?"

They had lunch, and Ms. White said, "I think I'd like to relax until it's time to go."

Sarah said, "Okay" and went to her room. She watched a movie on TV but set her alarm just in case she might fall asleep. She wanted enough time to take a shower and change into the outfit she would be wearing to the meeting.

They arrived at the Pentagon with plenty of time to go through security and get to the place where the meeting would be held. Introductions were made. Only a few in the room were not in uniform. You couldn't count the number of decorations and ribbons on some of their uniforms.

Sarah handed her laptop to the person who would hook it up to the projector. Ms. White said, "The Goodson Company, with which you have a contract, is due to expire next month. My company has purchased that company. As you'll see here on this slide, we've invested over $250,000 to upgrade the capabilities of the production assembly line. On the screen is the latest production and delivery of the parts we've manufactured, assembled, and sent to you. We have no backlog for the products you've ordered and will continue delivering products on schedule or ahead of schedule. We not only have the ability to deliver more product, but we're also in a position to take on additional products to manufacture and assemble. We're running one shift. If we were to go with two shifts, we could easily double what we're doing today."

General Peacock stepped forward and said, "That was a very interesting and professional presentation. My aides have verified what you've presented and tell me they're impressed by the numbers and found them to be accurate. If you could please step outside, I'd like to meet privately with my staff and these other generals. My aide will escort you to a waiting room just down the hall. Thank you. I don't think we'll be long."

Ms. White and Sarah followed the general's aide to the waiting room.

Sarah asked, "What do you think is going on?"

Ms. White said, "I have no idea. Usually, after the presentation, it takes weeks before you ever find out what they've decided. Normally they just say, 'Thank you, we'll be in touch,' and that's it."

They sat there for the better part of an hour before the aide asked them to follow him back to the meeting room.

General Peacock said, "I'm sorry to keep you waiting so long. The DOD has been pushing for more delivery of products like what your company provides. We don't normally do this. Our standard procedure is to notify you by registered mail. What took so long was for our legal department to draw up your renewed contract. Another two years have been added to the expiration date. I have a letter of intent from the United States Department of Defense to do business with White Enterprise, pending contract review by your legal department. You'll need to sign here if you agree. I think we'll want to meet with you again to investigate additional products for your company to manufacture and assemble."

Ms. White looked over the contract and signed the letter of intent. She said, "We'll be returning home tomorrow, and I'll have my legal department review the contract and have it returned to you."

The general said, "Here is an envelope addressed directly to me."

Ms. White called Charles to come pick them up. Sarah and Ms. White walked out of the Pentagon building. Charles was waiting with the limo door open.

She said, "Please take us back to the hotel."

Ms. White gave Charles their flight information and said, "That will be all for today."

Charles said, "I'll be here in the morning to drive you to the airport. Have a good evening."

Ms. White said to Sarah, "I'm heading to the bar. Care to join me?"

Sarah said, "I'm right with you on that one."

They walked into the lounge and sat down at one of the tables. They ordered their drinks. Sarah was sipping, Ms. White was drinking. She was looking around for the server and said she'd like another.

Sarah said, "Congratulations on getting the contract renewed. I have to say that was some experience."

Ms. White said, "Sarah, I don't know you to make an understatement, but that was one. That was so unexpected. I'm still trying to process it. What do you say? Let's have dinner and call it a day? We'll have to get up early in the morning to check out and get to the airport."

Sarah said, "You do come up with some excellent plans."

That made Ms. White laugh, and Sarah joined her. It seemed to break the stress they were having.

Ms. White said, "You need to make another trip down to Goodson to follow up with Bruce. I don't think a phone call will do. Remind him we'll continue to do the government contract negotiations from headquarters."

They had their dinner. On their way to their rooms, they passed another one of the hotel bars. Inside, they were doing karaoke.

Sarah said, "Come on, Ms. White, let's go in and listen. We could have a nightcap. We won't stay long. It could be fun. I've never been. Jill has been trying to get me to go to one. I just never seemed to have the time."

Ms. White said, "Okay, but just one drink, and then off to bed."

The place was packed. They found a place to sit and ordered their drinks. The one singing wasn't bad. The next one was very drunk, and the crowd booed her off the stage. The next was a duet, and they sounded like professionals.

Sarah could tell Ms. White was enjoying herself but could also see she was getting tired. Sarah said, "I don't know about you, but I think I'd like to go to my room."

Ms. White said, "Lead on."

They got to their rooms, and Sarah said, "Thanks for going to karaoke night with me. And thanks for all that you've done for me on this trip. See you in the morning."

Ms. White said, "Sarah, you've earned it, and it's been a pleasure having you accompany me. The karaoke was interesting and enjoyable."

Sarah called Karl, and they talked for about an hour. Sarah said, "I've got to get some sleep. I'll be home tomorrow. I miss the twins so much, and I miss you too."

He said, "See you tomorrow. I love you. Have a good sleep and a safe flight home."

Sarah laid out her clothes for the next day, packed her suitcase, and went to bed.

*****

The morning seemed to come quickly. Ms. White checked them both out of the hotel. Charles was waiting at the hotel door.

He said, "You ladies ready to go home?"

Sarah said, "Now that's an understatement if I've ever heard one."

She looked at Ms. White, and they burst into laughter.

Ms. White said, "Sarah, get in the limo."

Charles pulled up to the airline entrance, opened the door, and then got their bags out of the back.

Sarah said, "Thank you for the DC tour."

Ms. White said, "The next time we come to Washington, I'll make arrangements to hire you again."

She handed him three one-hundred-dollar bills as a tip.

Charles said, "Thank you. It's been my pleasure to drive you. Have a safe trip home."

The flight was on time. They landed and walked to the baggage claim area. There was Ms. White's Charles waiting. They got into the limo, and Sarah said, "Charles was the name of the driver we had in DC."

He said, "Is that so? Welcome back. Sarah, I'll have you home soon. I bet you both are happy to be back."

Charles drove Sarah home. Sarah said to Ms. White, "Thank you for such a wonderful time. Congratulations on getting the contract renewed. See you in the morning. Goodbye, Charles. Thanks for everything."

*****

Waiting just inside the door were Patty and the twins. Karl had not made it home yet.

Patty said, "I see how Grandma Margo loves these twins. They are such good kids. Anytime you need a sitter, call me."

Sarah gave some love to the twins and said to Patty, "It looks like you got a little pool time in."

Patty said, "Yes, while the twins were taking their nap, I sure did enjoy your pool."

Patty left.

Sarah loved on and played with the twins. While she was in DC, she bought them each a little gift. She changed her clothes and put on the softball jersey she loved to wear.

Karl came home at his regular time. Sarah had just about finished making dinner when he came through the door. The twins rushed to him to say hi to their dad.

Sarah said jokingly, "What about me?"

Karl said, "What about you?"

Sarah knew he was just trying to get back at her. He gave Sarah a big hug and a long kiss.

Sarah said, "Go change your clothes, dinner is just about ready."

They skipped the walk tonight. The twins got their bath and were dressed in their jammies. The four of them raced around the house, playing their form of tag. Soon the twins were running out of steam, and it was their bedtime. Karl and Sarah put them in their beds, and Sarah read them a story. Karl went into the living room to watch a little TV. The twins soon fell asleep.

Sarah went out to the living room and said, "I sure could use some attention."

Karl said, "Here or in the bedroom?"

Sarah said, "I'll race you to the bedroom."

CHAPTER 53

Another Visit to the Goodson Company

Sarah returned to her office after her trip to Washington, DC. Jill greeted her with a, "Welcome back. How was the adventure? Did you get the contract renewed? Look here, I got my security clearance. It came in while you were gone."

Sarah said, "One question at a time," and handed Jill a T-shirt she bought for her. It had several Washington, DC, pictures on it—the White House, the Capitol Building, and several of the monuments.

Jill said, "Thank you."

Sarah said, "It was short, but I did get a sampling of DC. After the twins get older, I'd like to take a vacation there. The meeting we had at the Pentagon went better than expected. Ms. White said the government usually takes weeks to approve contract renewals. They did it while we waited. Ms. White is going to have our legal department review it. If everything is okay, she'll sign it, and it will be a done deal. She said that looking through it, the only thing she saw that really changed was the dates. There is also an increase the government will pay if we live up to our end of the contract."

Sarah went down to Ms. White's office. She was sitting in the lounge area of her office, drinking her coffee.

She said, "Would you like a cup?"

Sarah said, "Thanks but no thanks. I just wanted to check to see if you were okay and if there was anything you wanted me to do."

Ms. White said, "Not at the moment. The legal people got back to me and said everything is okay. I signed the contract, and it has been sent off."

Sarah said, "Since it is now a done deal, on Monday, Jill and I will go down to make a visit to the Goodson Company to make the announcement about the contract being extended."

Sarah returned to her office and said to Jill, "I would like for you to call Polly, Mr. Goodson's secretary, and schedule a meeting at one-thirty on Monday with him and a second one with the employees at two. That meeting should not last more than a half hour. You can tell her the meeting will be a status report on the DOD contract. Also, ask her to set up a tour of the production area, now that the new machinery and equipment are in place and you have your security clearance."

Jill said, "Us? As in you and me?"

Sarah said, "Us, as in you and me. Don't forget to add it to the calendar. I'll arrange for a babysitter for all of our kids. We'll leave at nine o'clock. We'll have some lunch down there, have the meetings, the tour, and return. I don't know exactly when we'll get back, but it shouldn't be too late."

Jill said, "I'm on it."

Sarah called Patty, and she agreed to babysit all four of the kids.

Sarah walked over to the old building. Bill had set himself up with an office there. She walked in and said, "Hello, Bill. I've been reading your status reports but have been so busy lately I haven't been able to come see how you're doing."

Bill said, "It's harder than I thought, but I'm gettin' it done. We already have some tenants in their new offices. We have better than 50 percent of the building space leased, and more are coming in every day."

Bill had sheets of blueprint-style pictures of the floor plans. The occupied and free spaces were marked.

Bill said, "How would you like a tour to see some of the areas?"

Sarah said, "Sure, I've been on a few tours lately, including the White House."

Bill said, "You toured Ms. White's house?"

Sarah said, "No, Bill, THE White House. The one in Washington, DC."

Bill said, "I know. I talked to Elizabeth last night, and she told me all about the White House tour you two took. I just wanted to have a little fun with you."

Sarah said, "You talked to Ms. White last night?"

Bill said, "I told you we were longtime friends."

Sarah said, "What does your wife think about you talking with her?"

Bill said, "My wife and Elizabeth are friends too. Have been for years. Every once in a while, they'll have a girls' day out. Keep that between us. Right?"

Sarah said, "For sure."

Bill took Sarah on a tour. Sarah was amazed at how much work had been done in such a short period of time.

She said, "Bill, you sure are a miracle worker. How's it been working with the Harlow people?"

Bill said, "They sure are a bunch of professionals and really know their stuff. It's been a pleasure working with them. There are times I just stand and watch these workers. They're so skilled. Harlow only does subcontract business with the top companies in town. They do have some of their own workers, but they only do the specialty work."

Sarah said, "Thanks for the tour. Is there anything you need from me? Are you getting paid on time? Have you purchased that fishing boat yet?"

Bill said, "Everything is going well. I am getting paid on time, and no, I have not bought the boat yet. Anyway, I don't have time now to use it. Besides, if I milk this project long enough, I can get a bigger, better one."

Sarah said, "Bill!"

*****

It was Monday, and Jill was pulling into the driveway about fifteen minutes early. Patty was already at the house and was playing with the twins.

Sarah said to Jill, "You're a little early. Would you like anything before we go?"

Jill said, "Help me get the kids out of the car. The coffee went through me—I need to go pee."

Sarah said, "You know where the bathroom is. I'll get the kids out."

When she was done, she came back out and said, "Hi, I'm Jill. Thanks for watching my kids. This is Steven, and that's Jack."

Patty said, "Hi, I'm Patty."

Sarah said, "I was going to introduce you two, but you looked like you were going to wet your pants if you didn't go right away."

Jill said to the twins, "Come give your Aunt Jill a hug."

The twins came over and gave Jill a hug.

Jill said, "They are such good kids."

Sarah said, "Saddle up—we need to hit the trail."

On the way down, Sarah explained to Jill the purpose of the meeting and the role Jill would perform. They arrived and found a place to eat.

Jill said, "This is a nice little town."

When they had finished eating, Sarah said, "It's still a little early for us to show up at Goodson. I've driven around town some. This is the county seat. They have an interesting old courthouse not far from here. I'll drive by it."

Jill said, "It does have a different look to it. Not my style, but it still looks nice."

Sarah drove around a little more and then headed to the Goodson Company.

The receptionist said, "Hello, Ms. Brown, you must be Ms. Hill. I have you both on the visitor's log. Ms. Hill, may I see your security clearance ID?"

Jill handed her the card.

The receptionist said, "I'll let Mr. Goodson's secretary know you've arrived. Here are your visitor badges. If you like, you may take a seat while you wait."

Sarah said, "Thank you," and they sat down.

Jill said, "Wow, sure am glad I put that card in my wallet. What is it they do here?"

Sarah said, "You'll see on the tour."

A few minutes later, Polly came through the lobby door and said, "Sorry it took me so long. Hello, Ms. Brown, nice to see you again, and this must be Jill. Finally, we get to meet face-to-face."

Jill said, "It sure is nice to put a face to a voice."

Polly said, "Mr. Goodson has been looking forward to your visit. He's been going over the production reports again and had me straighten his office. Ms. Brown, he is a mess. Please don't say I told you."

Sarah said, "No problem. This should be a friendly meeting, and I don't have any last-minute things for you to do."

Polly said, "The company meeting is scheduled for two o'clock, as you requested."

Polly entered Mr. Goodson's office and said, "Ms. Brown and Ms. Hill are here to meet with you."

Bruce extended his hand to Sarah and shook it, then shook Jill's hand and said, "Pleased to meet you, Jill."

Sarah said, "Ms. White and I just returned from our trip to Washington, DC. We had a meeting with the DOD about renewing the contract we have with them. I am pleased to tell you the government contract has been extended for another two years. That is what I wanted to announce at the company meeting."

Bruce said, "That's great news. I was worried that something went wrong and the contract didn't get renewed. I thought your trip down here was to inform me of the bad news."

Sarah said, "The DOD said they may want the Goodson Company to manufacture and assemble some different products and would be getting back with us in the near future."

Polly said, "It's time for the company meeting."

They all walked down to where the meeting was being held.

Bruce started off the meeting by saying, "Thank you for coming. It is my pleasure to introduce to you Ms. Brown from White Enterprise. She has some news she would like to share with you."

Sarah said, "Thanks, Bruce. The work you and Bruce Goodson have done to the production line flow and the productivity level that has been achieved is remarkable. That was a major factor for the United States Department of Defense in renewing the contract for another two years. You, the people of the Goodson Company, have a good future ahead of you. Keep up your excellent work and support for Bruce Goodson. Thank you."

The group erupted into applause and cheers. Bruce walked out among the people. He shook hands, received words of congratulations, and thanked the people for their hard work.

Bruce said, "You said you wanted Jill to take a tour and see the new production line flow?"

Sarah said, "Yes, she has a secret security clearance."

Bruce said, "The receptionist informed me of her security clearance. Please follow me."

They all put on the safety gear, and Bruce led them into the first building.

Sarah said, "This looks very different."

Bruce said, "I lost count of how many times I've heard how much better everything is. The new forklift is so much better than the old one. I'm working on a deal to trade the old one in and get another new one like the one we just got."

Bruce pointed out the new equipment that was just installed and where some of the old ones were replaced. He pointed out how changes to the flow were made.

They finished the tour, returned the safety gear, and then returned to Bruce's office.

Sarah said to Jill, "Why don't you visit with Polly while Bruce and I take care of a few things?"

Sarah and Bruce went into his office and closed the door.

Sarah said, "Well, Mr. President, you've earned it. Have you talked to your father?"

Bruce said, "I have, but not about the company. I started to tell him about what we were doing with the production flow, but he said he wasn't interested in hearing anything about the company. So we talk about family and other things. Sarah, he is such a horse's ass. I love him because he's my father, but that's about all."

Sarah said, "It's good that you know the boundaries and can keep some kind of relationship with him."

Bruce said, "It sure would be nice if he were to say how proud he is of me and what I've done."

Sarah said, "It would be nice, but Bruce, you know you're doing a good job, and I think so too."

Sarah could see Bruce was fighting back his tears.

Sarah said, "Besides seeing the new production line and making the announcement, I wanted to talk to you about the company's future. You had said you were more of a day-to-day leader and needed help with visions and directions. You did a good job on the flow. Now you need to work on growing the company. I want you to hire a salesperson to get some nongovernmental business. The government contract is nice to have, but I don't want to have to count on it to keep the business going. Have the salesperson find manufacturing and assembling products that will fit into the Goodson product flow."

Bruce said, "Additional business? That might cause us to backlog on our governmental contract."

Sarah said, "Can you think of how you can increase the production without jeopardizing the current workload?" Sarah was giving him time to think and didn't want to tell him what he should do.

Bruce said, "Sarah, we could get more throughput if we went to a second shift."

Sarah said, "And you said you need help in the area of planning."

Bruce said, "Thanks for believing in me. I'll hire a salesperson and work up a plan for a second shift for when we get the extra work."

Sarah said, "You may be surprised that some of your workers would want to work on the second shift. That would give them the opportunity to take day classes at the college or do other things during the day that they can't do now. Having a plan in place before you get the extra business is also planning. Bruce, you're on the right track. Keep me posted, and know I'm available to help you if you need me."

Bruce said, "Thanks so much for everything."

*****

Sarah and Jill turned in their visitor badges and were on their way home. Jill said, "How did your meeting go with Bruce?"

Sarah replied, "Better than I expected. He is turning out to be nothing like his father. He's going to grow that company. Look, there's a place to get some ice cream. Do you want to stop?"

Jill said, "Sarah, you know I'm on a diet and still trying to lose STEVEN WEIGHT, and you go and ask me if I want to stop for ice cream? Hell, yes, I want to stop, I'm dying for a banana split."

Sarah and Jill laughed.

Sarah said, "We are going inside. There will be no eating in my new SUV."

They had their ice cream and soon were back on the road.

When they got to Sarah's house, Jill said, "That was some day. Thanks for taking me along. The tour was very interesting. I got the chance to visit with Polly and got to know her better. I really need to be getting home."

She gathered her kids, thanked Patty, and said to Sarah, "See you in the morning."

Sarah asked Patty, "How did things go today?"

Patty said, "Good as always. The twins were great. They seem to have their own language going. I can't make out what they are saying, but the two of them understand each other perfectly. Steven and Jack were no problem."

Sarah said, "Yes, it's spooky at times how they communicate. Were you able to get any sun?"

Patty said, "I forgot my swimsuit. I did lay out there topless and in my panties. I think I may have gotten rid of my tan lines. My BOOBS got too much sun, and it hurt to put my bra back on."

Sarah said, "You need to be more careful. Thanks for sitting today."

Patty said, "I love sitting for you. Call me anytime. Have a nice evening. Goodbye."

Sarah had just changed her clothes when she heard the garage door opening, and she said to the twins, "Let's hide and surprise Daddy when he comes in!"

The twins hid as best as a three-year-old could. Karl came into the house, and Sarah jumped out, saying, "Surprise!" The kids ran to Karl and gave him a hug. Sarah joined in, and they had a group hug.

Karl said, "There's a lady at the office whose dog had puppies. They are GOLDENDOODLES—part golden retriever and part poodle. They are a very smart mixed breed and are becoming very popular. They don't shed and are hypoallergenic. They are known to be very friendly and good with kids. She said these puppies will grow up to be medium-sized dogs weighing between forty-five and fifty pounds. What do you say?"

Sarah said, "You sound like you're sold on the idea. We can't just have one. The twins will fight over it. Go ahead and get two females."

Karl went out to the car and returned with two of the cutest little tan-colored puppies. One had some white on her back foot. The other had a lot of white on her chest. He said, "I was hoping you would say yes. Emily, Kevin, come see the puppies. They are the new additions to our family."

The twins came over, looked at the puppies, and took to them right away.

Sarah said, "What if I said no or only one?"

He said, "The lady said I could bring them back if we couldn't keep them. She gave me the pick of the litter and said they were so popular she would have no problem selling them."

Sarah said, "Selling them? She wasn't giving them away?"

Karl said, "It's best that you don't ask how much I paid for them."

Sarah pulled out her phone and looked up how much gold-endoodles were selling for and said to herself, *They got the gold part right.*

Sarah said to Karl, "We need to come up with names for these two.

Karl said, "And we also need to get them some puppy food and toys. I brought home some food the lady gave me. I will buy some tomorrow. Right now, they can stay in the twins' old playpen. I will get it out of the barn and set it up in the living room."

CHAPTER 54

Several Months Later

It had been several months since Sarah and Jill visited the Goodson Company. The production flow had improved and reached its optimum level. Reports back from the DOD were outstanding. They had less than a 1 percent failure rate and were indicating they would like to have talks about Goodson Company producing additional products. Only time would tell on that; the government wheels turned slowly.

Bruce hired the salesperson who was already bringing in additional business. Bruce implemented his plan to go with a second shift. He had no problem getting people to work for the company. Word had gotten out that the company paid high wages and had good benefits. Several workers who had been on the same shift for years were happy to move to the second shift. This worked out great as it added experience to the new shift. Both shifts were fully staffed. Government production took a short dip because of the new people but soon returned to normal levels. Bruce also hired several people to staff a research and development lab—something the company had never had before. Sarah's belief in Bruce was paying off.

Bill now had 85 percent of the building occupied or would as soon as the office areas were completed for the new tenants. Bill met with Sarah and said, "My part is just about done. The areas of the building that have not been leased are going to be completed as standard business offices and should not take more than a couple more weeks. That should be the end of my commitment. You should see the fishing boat I bought. Maybe you, Karl, and the twins would like to go fishing with me sometime. We could have a little competition: first catch of the day, biggest one, most caught."

Sarah said, "That sounds all too familiar. I don't have anything on the horizon that you could help me with. Bill, you have been so helpful, and you are so good at what you do. I haven't had to worry about getting this building renovated and ready for lease. You did it all. Thank you. I'm going to see what I can do to get you an end-of-contract bonus."

Bill said, "Thanks, but that would be nice. The extra money would just end up going to the IRS in additional taxes, and I wouldn't see any of it."

Margo was in her element. She was a grandmother to the twins, and the twins loved her. The day care facility had grown to full capacity. The people working there were busy and happy. They especially liked their boss, Margo. Margo took an interest in each of her employees, gave them training, and paid them well. There was little turnover. Margo demanded that the older kids behave and get along with each other. The city inspected the facility regularly and gave it a superior rating.

Karl installed a doggie door and fenced area for the puppies, who were no longer puppies. They were housebroken and had learned to sit, lie down, and a few other tricks. They walked on leashes on the streets, and on the trails, they were allowed to run free. They both had to sniff everything. On their evening walks, Sarah and Karl each walked one of the doodles. At night, the dogs would sleep with the twins. Each dog had bonded with a twin. Emily had hers, and Kevin had his. In the beginning, Sarah wasn't much of a dog person. She was amazed at how smart the dogs were and how much the twins loved them. She ended up being a *doodle* person.

Karl and George were back and forth on who was the firm's best senior accountant. Karl was loving his job, and his clients loved him. He now had seven accountants and bookkeepers working directly for him and still occasionally had to use some from the pool. Business was good. So were the bonuses he was getting.

Ms. White had Sarah handling more of her meetings. Sarah took Jill with her much as Ms. White had taken her when she first started working. Jill would take notes, do research for Sarah, and write up the recap reports. Ms. White still handled the high-level meetings and met with the board of directors. She still held controlling interest in the company. Ms. White had grown the company to the level of her dreams.

Jill got the message that Ms. White would like Sarah to come to her office. As always, Ms. White would never say why she wanted to see Sarah, and Sarah had gotten used to just going without having to know. Sarah thanked Jill for giving her the message and headed down to Ms. White's office.

Tammy said, "Go on in, she is expecting you."

Ms. White said, "Close the door and come on over and have a seat."

Ms. White was sitting in the lounge area of her office. Whenever Ms. White said to sit over in her lounge area, Sarah knew something was about to happen. Ms. White said, "Sarah, one year from now, I'm going to retire. At that time, I will be naming you as President and CEO of White Enterprise. You will be the head of the board of directors. I will keep controlling interest in the company with my stock holdings. You already have most of the skills needed to be President and CEO. Over my final year, I will teach you what you lack."

Sarah said, "I didn't see this one coming. I am so blown away by you picking me to replace you. I thought I would be working with you for many more years. I know I have learned so much from you but never to the level that I could take over the company. You're really young to be retiring. What are you going to do? Buy a fishing boat like Bill?"

Ms. White just laughed and said, "If I were to buy a boat, it would be a yacht. No, I'm going to pursue my love. I'm a professional poker player. I make several hundred thousand dollars a year playing Texas Hold'em poker. I have an invitation to play in the Las Vegas World Championship Texas Hold'em Tournament. The buy-in is

$100,000. You stand to win several million dollars or lose a lot. I would like you to join me."

Sarah said, "I don't know if my heart could stand it. That's a lot of money. I've never been to Las Vegas before. If I were to go, I'd want to take Karl and the twins with me. When is the tournament?"

Ms. White said, "It's not for a couple of months. I think that would be a nice vacation for you and the family. You have been working really hard for a long time. You could use some fun time, especially with the next year preparing to replace me. You might want to take that babysitter you like so much along too. I will pay for everything except your personal expenses. I will arrange for a three-bedroom suite for your family and the babysitter. Talk it over with Karl, and let me know so I can make the arrangements."

Sarah said, "I will get back to you soon."

*****

On the evening walk—Sarah with Sniffer, Karl with Hunter, Emily, and Kevin—Sarah said to Karl, "A year from now, Ms. White said she is going to retire."

Karl asked, "Is she going to sell the company? What's going to happen? What is she going to do?"

Sarah said, "Slow down, you're beginning to sound like me. No, she's not going to sell the company. She will keep her controlling interest, her position on the board as past president, and enjoy retirement. She wants to pursue her love of poker. Did you know you could make thousands playing poker?"

Karl said, "Some make lots more than that. There are poker tournaments all over the country and internationally too."

Sarah said, "So you know about it?"

Karl said, "Yes, there is a big invitational tournament every year in Las Vegas."

Sarah said, "Well, Ms. White received an invitation to play in the Las Vegas tournament."

Karl said, "Only top players get those invitations. She must be really good."

Sarah said, "She invited our entire family and Patty, our babysitter, to accompany her. I will support her by sitting in the guest area while she plays. When she's not playing, I can join you to do whatever we want. With Patty there, she can babysit so we can have some time together. When we do take the twins, Patty could join us or do whatever she wants to do."

Karl said, "Sounds like something I would like to do. We have saved up some money for a vacation. We haven't taken a real vacation in some time."

Sarah said, "I know you are not sitting down, but Ms. White said she would pay for everything: transportation, lodging, and the meals we eat with her. She even said she would treat us to a Las Vegas show. We would have to pay for our own expenses, including Patty's babysitting fee. She will not be babysitting the entire time because you will be there with the twins, and we will be there at night. Ms. White said she would arrange for a three-bedroom suite. She even said she was going to lease a private jet to fly us out there and back."

Karl said, "How could we possibly turn the sweet lady down?"

Sarah said, "That's what I'm thinking. I will check with Patty and let Ms. White know we would be most happy to take her up on her offer."

When they got home, Sarah handed Karl a beer and said, "I have another piece of news to tell you."

Karl said jokingly, "You're pregnant again."

Sarah said, "No. I'm happy with the twins. Besides, this is bigger than that."

Karl said, "I know you're happy with just the twins, but accidents do happen. So what is your bigger-than-that news?"

Sarah said, "You will need to be sitting down for this. One year from now, Ms. White will be announcing me as the new president and CEO of White Enterprise."

Karl said, "Oh yes, that's sitting-down news. I'm going to be married to a president and CEO of a company."

Sarah said, "Déjà vu. I've not seen you like this since the doctor said we were having twins. This isn't going to happen for a year from now. You can't tell anybody—I mean no one—and neither can I.

That is the agreement I have with Ms. White. She said during the year, she will teach me everything I don't already know, and I will be taking on more and more of her responsibilities as the year progresses. It's going to be an even wilder ride than I've ever been on."

Karl said, "Slow down, Sarah. Got to pace yourself."

CHAPTER 55

The Poker Tournament

It was time to go to Las Vegas. Patty was at the house, and everyone was ready to go. Charles came to take them to the airport. He said, "I took Ms. White to the airport earlier, and she's taking care of the last-minute arrangements."

Charles drove the limo right up next to the airplane. They boarded the airplane, and soon they were wheels up and on their way to Las Vegas. Upon landing, a minibus was waiting to take them to their hotel. They were staying in the same hotel where the poker tournament was being held. They checked in, and the bellboy took them to their rooms. Ms. White said, "I'm not scheduled to play until midmorning tomorrow. I would like for all of us to have dinner tonight. I will have the concierge make the reservation and let you know where and when."

Sarah, Karl, the twins, and Patty entered the suite. It was beautiful. It had a large common sitting area with a dining table, two bathrooms, a small kitchenette, and three large bedrooms. Patty said, "Is this heaven or what? The limo ride to the airport, the private jet, the bus waiting for us to bring us here, and now this room."

Sarah said, "Patty, are you excited?"

Patty said, "Oh no, I'm beyond excited. I'm up two levels above excited."

Sarah said, "Karl, I know you will want to go exploring. I'm going to feed the twins, and when they're finished, I'll put them down for a nap. I will stay here with them. Patty, you can go exploring with Karl or go out on your own. Both of you need to be back in time for dinner. Karl and Patty, keep your phones on vibrate. You will never hear them ring if you go into a casino."

Sarah handed Patty $100 and said, "This is an advance on your babysitting. I'm going to order something from room service, watch a movie, and enjoy some BY MYSELF time while the twins nap. Go have some fun."

That evening, they had dinner in the hotel's restaurant on the top floor. The restaurant had huge windows. It was totally clear out, and you could see for miles. The sun was just setting, and the night lights were coming on. What a sight to see. The twins were the only kids in the restaurant. Sarah said, "Are kids allowed to be in here? I don't see any other kids."

Ms. White said, "I told the concierge that there would be two children eating with us, and he said it would not be a problem."

Sarah said, "They are normally very good when we go out."

Patty said, "If they get fussy, I will take them back to the room."

Sarah asked Ms. White, "Are you nervous about playing tomorrow?"

She said, "I have played in so many tournaments I don't get nervous anymore. Besides, there's no time to be nervous. I have to keep my head and study the other players. If you don't, chances are you will lose. These are the best of the best. They've all learned to hide their body language. I know you've heard of a POKER FACE. It is a real thing. You really have to concentrate on every little detail of the other players and also pay attention to your cards. As they say, you've got to know when to hold them and know when to fold them."

They all laughed at Ms. White's humor, as did Ms. White.

The twins were extra good. They all finished their dinner. Patty was the first to thank Ms. White for the dinner and wish her good luck. She said, "I'm going to take the twins back to the room. Enjoy the rest of your evening."

Karl said to the twins, "Say good night and thank you to Ms. White for dinner."

They both said, "Thank you, good night."

Ms. White bent down and gave them both a hug and said, "You're welcome. Good night, sleep well." Ms. White had a smile on her face and said, "You sure do have such wonderful kids."

Sarah asked Ms. White, "When is it your turn to play?"

Ms. White said, "Nine o'clock. Do you want to meet before and have some breakfast?"

Sarah said, "Sure. What time?"

Ms. White said, "Why don't you meet me at that coffee shop just outside of the room where they are holding the tournament at eight-thirty? We can have some coffee and a donut or something."

Sarah said, "I'll see you there at eight-thirty. Thanks for dinner, and have a good sleep."

Karl said, "Thank you, and good luck in the tournament."

Ms. White said, "Thanks, and good night."

Sarah and Karl went to their room. Patty said, "I gave the twins their bath, and they are already in bed. What a day I have had. I'm going to my room to watch something on that big-screen TV before going to sleep. Good night."

Sarah said, "Thanks for taking care of the twins. Yes, it has been some day. Good night, see you in the morning before I go to the tournament."

Karl looked in on the twins. They had a big day, too, and were sound asleep. After his shower, Karl put on the satin pajamas he had gotten for his birthday. With Patty staying there with them, he couldn't very well sleep in his underwear like he did at home. Then he got into bed. Sarah finished her shower and climbed into bed. She had not put her nightie on yet. Karl was busy watching the TV and didn't notice Sarah slip into the bed naked. He said, "If you don't mind, I would like to watch a little TV before going to sleep."

Sarah pulled back the covers, and Karl saw she had nothing on. Karl said, "Let me turn this TV off."

*****

The next morning, the alarm went off. Sarah got up, dressed, and was ready to meet Ms. White. She said, "I will have to turn my phone's ringer off while in the poker room, but I'll have it on vibrate. Call or text me if you need to, but only if you need to. I have no idea how long I will be. I'll give you updates as I can on breaks. Don't worry about me. Work out what you guys want to do. If you take the twins out in the sun, make sure you put a thick layer of sunscreen on them, especially if you take them to the pool. Room service is quick. My lunch was good. I'm leaving now. I love you. Have a fun time. You two be good for your dad and Patty."

Sarah gave Karl and the twins a kiss, and off she went.

Sarah beat Ms. White to the coffee shop. She thought that was a little strange because she was never at the office before Ms. White. Sarah still was looking for that secret bedroom Ms. White had to have there at the company. She saw her walking up with another person, and Ms. White said, "Sarah, I want to introduce you to the one who got me hooked on poker. This is Amy French. She was invited to play this year but passed it up. She just wanted to come and watch this year. Last year, she ended up twenty-fifth in the overall ranking. The two of you can sit together. She can fill you in on how the game is played and how the tournament works. Let's get some coffee and go in."

By the time they got in and through security, Amy and Sarah had to sit a couple of rows back away from the players. Sarah said, "That was some security check."

Amy said, "Security is so they can catch the cheaters before they have a chance to cheat. You won't believe the lengths people will go to cheat in these high-stakes games. Before the players are seated, they are checked for any listening devices or anything else that might be used to cheat. If you look around, you will see cameras everywhere. At any one time, there could be upward of a million dollars or more being bet on a single hand. They are about to start. I will try to fill you in as it goes along, but feel free to ask questions. You will have to keep your voice down. Maybe it's a good thing that we are farther away for now. Let's watch."

Amy explained the basics of how the cards were dealt and when the bets could be placed. At the table Ms. White was playing, players were being eliminated as they lost all their money. Ms. White was doing really well and had won a lot. It was down to just her and another player. The other player went all in. Ms. White had a strong feeling he was bluffing and called. He had an okay hand, and he was bluffing. Ms. White had won her first round. There was a thirty-minute break before she had to play again.

Sarah said to Ms. White, "That was so exciting. Amy explained to me what was going on. You did so well. When that guy went all in, I held my breath. How did you know he was bluffing?"

Ms. White said, "It's something that I can't explain. It's just a feeling I get. I need to go to the bathroom before my next round. See you later."

This time, Amy and Sarah got better seats. Sarah sent a text to Karl, saying, "Ms. White won the first round."

Karl texted back, "Tell her congratulations and good luck on the next round."

Ms. White won that round and the next one too. She would not play again until tomorrow.

Sarah said, "I don't know how you do it. I'm a basket case just watching you. Some of those hands were over a million dollars."

Ms. White said, "Wait until tomorrow when there are only a few players left. Go find your family and enjoy the rest of your day. Amy and I are going to reminisce, and maybe she will give me some coaching and tips."

Sarah sent a text to Karl, saying, "Ms. White is done for today and doesn't play again until tomorrow. I'm on my way to the room."

Karl texted back, "Why don't you put your swimsuit on and come on down to the pool?"

Sarah texted, "Be there soon. Do you have the sunscreen there?"

Karl said, "Yes, and I made sure the twins had plenty on."

Sarah put on her bathing suit. She had a wrap that matched. When she got to the pool, there were a lot of people there. She walked around and found Karl, Patty, and the twins sitting under a shade umbrella. Sarah took the wrap off and asked Karl to put some sunscreen on her.

Patty looked at Sarah and said, "Look at your tummy. You had twins, not a single stretch mark, and a flat stomach to boot. Is that a bit of a six-pack you have going there?"

Sarah said, "Oh, stop. I am just lucky. I take advantage of the exercise facility at the company. More of a stress relief than body building."

Karl put suntan lotion all over Sarah's fair skin. She said, "Who wants to go swimming with Mommy?"

Both twins ran over and said, "I do!"

Sarah took Kevin, and Karl took Emily. They were on their way to the kiddie pool play area. Emily pointed to the big people pool and said, "No, Mommy. Big people pool."

They got into the shallow end of the pool. Both twins had swimming lessons and were good swimmers. After all, they had their own backyard pool and swam all the time. After a while of swimming and splashing, the kids were tired. Besides, it was getting close to dinnertime.

They all went back up to the room. Patty said, "Why don't you two plan on going out to dinner and walking around, just the two of you? Maybe do a little gambling. I will get some room service meals and feed the kids, give them a bath, and put them to bed."

Sarah looked at Karl, and he said, "How could we turn that down? I need to take a shower. I have all of this sunscreen all over my body."

He went into the bathroom that was attached to their bedroom. He took his swimsuit off and stepped into the oversize shower. No sooner did he get the water adjusted, the shower door opened, and in stepped Sarah. She said, "Do you need someone to wash your back?"

Karl said, "What? Are you only going to wash my back?"

*****

They finished their shower and got dressed for dinner.

Patty said, "While you were getting ready, room service delivered the dinners. We just finished, and the kids ate everything. Soon I will give them their bath and get them ready for bed. I told them I would read them a story. I have your phone number, and if anything comes up, I will give you a call. Now go out and enjoy yourselves."

Karl said, "Thanks," and they left.

They didn't have reservations at any of the restaurants, and the wait time was longer than they wanted to wait. Sarah said, "Let's walk on down the strip and eat at one of the other casino hotel buffet restaurants."

Karl said, "I'm okay with that."

They went into one of the casinos. There was a line, but it was moving quickly. They were seated at a table not far from the food. They both piled the food on their plates. Everything looked good, and it was delicious. Both went back for seconds and dessert too.

Sarah said, "I have not eaten like that ever. I need to walk this dinner off. Besides, I have never been here before and would like to see some of the other hotels and casinos."

They started down the Las Vegas strip, stopping in each hotel and casino on the way.

Karl said, "I want to stop at the next place and do a little gambling."

Sarah said, "I don't know how to gamble."

Karl said, "That's okay. We can watch and see what others are doing."

Sarah watched and said, "What I see mostly is people losing money. Those chips are HUNDRED-DOLLAR chips. There's a guy who looks like he knows what he's doing. Look at the stack of hundred-dollar chips he has."

Karl said, "And he just lost over a thousand dollars on that one roll of the dice."

Sarah said, "Come on, let's go. I can't watch this."

Karl said, "Come on over here to the slot machines. I'm going to put $40 in this 50-cent slot machine. You can place one, two—up to five bets. You see the lines there on the screen? Depending on how much you bet, you have a chance to win on one or more lines."

Sarah said, "How much do I win?"

Karl said, "That depends on how many of the same symbol are lined up in the row or rows you bet. See up here, there is a list of the different symbols and how much they pay if you land on them. This is your bet button, this is the max bet button, and this is the spin button. You see the machine has $40 I just put in there? As you win, that number will increase, and as you lose, that number will decrease. This button is the magic button. Use it to cash out. It will spit out a piece of paper with how much you have left in the machine. Later, we will take that over to the cashier, and they will pay you the amount on the ticket. Any questions?"

Sarah said, "I think I understand. Aren't you going to watch me or play the machine next to me?"

He said, "No, I might bring you bad luck. I will be in this area. Come find me when you are done playing. I will come back after a bit and see how you are doing."

Karl left Sarah to play. He went over to try his luck at a couple of different tables. He won a little but lost more than he won. He understood the basic concept of the games but lacked the strategy to win any amount of money. After he lost the amount he was willing to lose, he just watched for a little while before returning to the slot machine where he left Sarah.

He said, "How are you doing?"

Sarah said, "I'm down right now."

Karl looked at the amount on the slot, and it showed a little over $1,000.

Karl said, "You are down?"

Sarah said, "I was up to just under $2,000."

Sarah pressed the max bet button and the spin button. When the symbols stopped, lights, bells, and buzzers went off. She had just hit a big jackpot. The slot pit boss came over.

She said, "Do you want to continue to play or would you like to cash out?"

Sarah said, "I would like to cash out."

The pit boss said, "With the amount you have won, you will need to fill out some paperwork. Would you like to have the IRS share deducted?"

Sarah said, "What are my total winnings?"

The pit boss said, "About $5,317.50. You can have the full amount in cash or amount in a cashier's check or any combination you like. You will need to follow me over to the cashier."

Sarah said, "I would like the $317.50 in cash and the balance in a cashier's check after taxes."

Karl said, "Wow, that was some winning. Now what would you like to do?"

She said, "How did you do?"

Karl said, "Not so good. I lost the entire $100 I had set aside for gambling."

Sarah said, "I guess it's easy to do. Glad you stopped at your limit. Let's take one of those city tour buses. I'll pay."

Karl said, "Whatever you say, Ms. High Roller."

*****

They found a tour bus stop and got on. There was a tour guide talking about the history of Las Vegas and about each of the hotels as they passed by. They got off the bus at their hotel.

Sarah said, "Let's keep my winning between just the two of us."

Karl said, "That's probably best."

When they got to the room, Patty and the twins were all snuggled together on the big couch in the living room. They were all asleep. Patty woke up and said, "Did you have fun?"

Sarah said, "We ate buffet food in a place down from here. Then we walked further down the strip and looked inside all of the hotels and casinos. We finished the night taking one of those double-decker tour buses."

Patty said, "Sounds like you had fun. Did you gamble? And how did you do?"

Karl said, "I lost, and Sarah won. Don't want to talk about it."

Patty couldn't help but laugh at how Karl said it.

Sarah said, "I will carry Emily, and you can carry Kevin. Let's put them in their beds."

Sarah said to Patty, "Thanks for suggesting that we go out while you watched the kids. I'm going to go to bed. I don't know what time

Ms. White will be playing tomorrow. I need to get to sleep. Good night."

Just as they were getting into bed, Ms. White sent a text to Sarah. "Eight-thirty in the morning, the same coffee shop as before."

Sarah texted back, "See you in the morning. Have a good sleep."

*****

Sarah was at the coffee shop just minutes before eight-thirty. Ms. White was already there, drinking her coffee and eating a bagel. Sarah got an orange juice and a muffin.

Ms. White said, "Amy should be along shortly."

As soon as Amy got her hot tea, they walked in. Ms. White entered through the *Players Only* entrance. Amy and Sarah went through the guest security screening entrance as before. They were early enough to get good seats. Soon all of the seats were taken as more people were showing up.

Amy said to Sarah, "Last year, I didn't make it this far. Elizabeth is doing an outstanding job. I have played against most of the players left. They got here and this far in the competition because they're good. Right now, Elizabeth is ranked eleventh by her winnings. It will be interesting to see just how far she will go."

Sarah asked, "How far do you think she will go?"

Amy said, "That's hard to know. The players at the table she is at now are the best in the business. She is up against a tough bunch of players."

They watched as the dealer dealt out the first set of cards.

One by one, players were being eliminated. It was down to the last three players at the table. Ms. White was the next one to be eliminated. Her winnings earned her fifth place overall. She got up from the table and walked over to where Amy and Sarah were seated.

Ms. White said, "Sarah, how do you say it? That was some wild ride."

Sarah laughed out loud, and the judges told her she had to be quiet.

Ms. White whispered, "Let's go."

369

Once they got outside of the room, Amy said, "Elizabeth, for your first time here in Las Vegas, you did an outstanding job. Do you know you ended up ranking fifth?"

Ms. White said, "I did? I guess I was still in shock. I should have gone with my gut and folded on that last hand."

Amy said, "That same guy knocked me out last year. He is tough. Hey, there is always next year."

Ms. White said, "Why don't we all go out and take the dam tour? I've never been, and I heard it's something to see. I also got us all—you included, Amy—tickets to see the *Cirque du Soleil* performance this evening."

Sarah said, "Let me round up my tribe and meet you in the lobby."

Ms. White said, "Maybe we should have some lunch before we go. I will get with the concierge to arrange transportation out to the dam and back."

Sarah said, "The buffet might be the best place to eat."

Ms. White said, "The buffet it is. Amy and I will meet you just outside the buffet entrance."

Sarah went up to the room. Everyone was still there and just about to go out on their adventure. She said, "Great, you all are ready to go. Ms. White was eliminated. She ended up ranked in fifth place. All of us are going to eat some lunch at the buffet, and then we all are going out to take the Hoover Dam tour. Ms. White is arranging transportation for us now."

Patty said, "Me too?"

Sarah said, "Of course, you too. But that's not all. Ms. White got us all—you too, Patty—tickets to see the *Cirque du Soleil* performance this evening. Let's go eat."

This time, Karl and Sarah didn't overeat like the last night. When they all finished, Sarah said, "I think it's best if I take the twins up to the room and see if they can go to the potty before we go. It shouldn't take long. Come on, kids, let's go potty."

*****

When she returned, the bus was ready to take them to the dam. They all liked the tour. Even at the young age of the twins, they really enjoyed it too. On the ride back to the hotel, the twins fell asleep. Sarah asked Ms. White, "What time is the performance? And where do you want to meet?"

Ms. White said, "Amy and I are going to eat in the restaurant at the top of the hotel. We will meet in the hotel lobby at seven-thirty and take the shuttle over to the hotel where the performance is being held."

Sarah said, "We will be ready, right, guys?"

Karl carried Kevin, Sarah carried Emily, and Patty carried the bag containing the things the twins might need on the outing. They put the twins in their beds for a nap. Patty said, "If it's okay with you two, I would like to go down to the pool."

Sarah said, "That's okay with me. Be back in time to eat dinner and get ready to go to the performance."

Patty said, "Roger that."

She changed into her swimsuit and was off.

Sarah said to Karl, "Well, we will be going home tomorrow. Is there something you want to do before we leave?"

Karl said, "Patty went to the pool, the twins are down for a nap. Let's put the DO NOT DISTURB sign on the door."

And off to the bedroom they went.

*****

That evening, they all had dinner and saw the performance. The twins were amazed at all that was going on. Ms. White enjoyed watching the twins as much as watching the performance. The twins stayed awake as long as they could. The performance was not over yet, and Emily crawled up on Ms. White's lap and fell asleep.

Sarah said, "Let me take her from you."

Ms. White said, "Don't you dare."

When the performance ended, Ms. White handed Emily to Sarah and said, "I can't tell you how happy I am right now."

Sarah had to fight back her tears hearing Ms. White say that.

On the way back to their hotel, Ms. White said, "It's back home and reality tomorrow. Everyone needs to be in the lobby and ready to go by ten o'clock."

*****

The flight home was just as nice as the flight to Las Vegas. There was one flight attendant to take care of their needs. Everyone was thanking Ms. White and saying how much fun they had and what they liked best about the trip. When the plane landed, Charles was there with a minibus that would hold everyone and all of the luggage. Charles dropped Ms. White off at her house. They all said thank you and goodbye. They had the entire weekend before having to return to work.

Sarah said, "See you on Monday."

Charles drove to Sarah and Karl's house. He helped with getting the luggage out of the back of the minibus. Sarah gave Charles a big hug and slipped a couple of hundred dollars in his pocket and said, "A little something from Las Vegas for you."

Charles said, "Sarah, you know Ms. White takes good care of me."

Sarah said, "Let me give you a little loving too."

Charles said, "Thank you," and gave Sarah a hug.

Patty said, "I can't thank you guys enough for taking me along. I had the time of my life. This is something I will be talking about for some time. The way Ms. White lives is something else. I need to find me a rich husband so I can live like that. Before I go home, I need to go to the bathroom. That was a long flight back."

When she was done, Karl gave her $200 and said, "Thank you."

Patty said, "This is too much. Remember, I already got $100 when we got there."

Karl said, "You earned it." Karl said to Sarah, "I have just enough time to go pick up Hunter and Sniffer before the place closes."

Emily and Kevin, hearing their dogs' names, said, "Daddy, we want to go."

They all piled in the car to go get the dogs.

CHAPTER 56

The Year Leading Up to Retirement

A memo was sent out to all company employees. The memo was to announce the promotion of Sarah Brown to Senior Vice President of Corporate Planning and Development. The memo went on to give a brief history of Sarah's accomplishments and the work she had done with the new and old buildings and the growth of the Goodson Company.

The year leading up to Ms. White's retirement was filled with meetings and trips. Ms. White and Sarah had come up with a plan to help Sarah transition to replace Ms. White upon her retirement. Sarah was taking on more and more responsibilities, ones that Ms. White had usually done. In Sarah's new position as Senior Vice President of Corporate Planning and Development, she would be integrating the companies into divisions in the White Enterprise organization. Sarah and Jill were going to the meetings with Ms. White when she was meeting with the company executives of the companies that she had purchased. They were also attending sales meetings to get more business for White Enterprise. Ms. White was making the presentations, and Sarah and Jill would take notes.

It wasn't long before Sarah and Jill were going to all of the meetings without Ms. White. It was Sarah who was making the presentations now. Ms. White wanted to grow the company bigger before she retired, both by acquiring companies and new business. Sarah was doing due diligence on companies that Ms. White had targeted to acquire. Sarah even put together the plans to purchase one of the companies. She went with Ms. White on trips abroad to get some foreign and several other trips all over the country.

Soon Sarah was doing these trips by herself and with Jill. Ms. White was very pleased with Sarah and how quickly she learned the skills needed to fill her responsibilities as the president and CEO of White Enterprise when that day came.

As Senior Vice President of Corporate Planning, reporting directly to Sarah were the day care and exercise facilities, along with the Goodson Company. Sarah came up with a new organization and responsibility chart for White Enterprise. Ms. White and Sarah had a meeting to discuss the proposed changes that Sarah wanted to make. Sarah laid out the organization chart on Ms. White's conference table and said, "We need to hire more sales staff. I will have them reporting directly to me for now. All of the companies you own will become divisions and will take on their company name followed by a Division of White Enterprise name. Our Senior VPs of Manufacturing will have a new title of Executive VPs of Manufacturing. The presidents of those companies will become Senior VPs reporting to our Executive VPs. There will be some of these company presidents who will not like these changes. Some will retire or seek jobs elsewhere. We need these changes to become one company, not a bunch of separate standalone entities.

"As for the ones who do not want to be part of White Enterprise, they will be replaced by promotions from within or hired from the outside. When everything is in place, we will have a strong company going forward. The different Executive VPs of Manufacturing will be making business calls to the various companies. For now, I will work directly with the senior VPs, the VPs, and the directors in each manufacturing area, along with the Harlow Company's time and motion team. Together, we can work toward upgrading and improving our productivity levels, much like we did with the Goodson Company. After the plans are in place, the executive VPs will be responsible and held accountable to implement and manage their area.

"All of the different accounting departments will report to the senior VP of finance here at HQ. This way, all of the divisions of

White Enterprise will have the same accounting principles and standards. The development of financial reporting will be much easier and timelier too. Each of the divisions will need to convert their accounting software to the accounting software we use here at HQ, if they are not already using the same system.

"The different HRs will report to headquarters. All divisions will have the same standards and code of ethics of White Enterprise. Local issues, the hiring and firing, will stay at the local level of each division within their existing HR departments."

Ms. White said, "What you have done here is showing me how much control I have had over everything. I should have relied on my staff more. I guess those who have called me a control freak were correct. They will need to step it up."

Sarah said, "You are a strong leader. You have taken your father's company from a small company to what White Enterprise has become today. Let's just say you did it your way."

Ms. White said, "Sarah, you sure have a way of saying things. I am leaving this company in the best hands one could pick. The plan you have come up with, well, I don't see any way I can improve upon it. I will help you make it happen."

Sarah said, "Thanks. You know better than anyone else that I'm going to need help to get this done. I hope everyone will see the future this company has. I may call upon you to do some arm twisting with some of these old folks who have issues with me messing in their turf."

Sarah called Bruce and said, "Bruce, good news. You are being promoted to VP in White Enterprise Corporation."

Bruce said, "Good news? VP? I'm President!"

Sarah said, "Bruce, would you just get off your ego trip for a minute and listen to me? You look at it as a demotion. Don't you see you are being accepted into the White Enterprise Corporation? The only thing that has changed is your job title. Your responsibilities will be the same. Instead of being a president of a small company, you are going to be a VP of a large corporation."

Bruce asked, "Will you still be my boss?"

Sarah said, "You will be reporting to one of our Executive VPs of Manufacturing. I will still be here for you. We have come too far together for me to just kick you to the curb. Are we good?"

Bruce said, "Everything you have done for me has been in my best interest. You have helped me grow personally and helped me bring this company to its full potential. Not only did you mentor me, but you have also been a friend. For that, I will always be thankful."

Sarah said, "This promotion will not take effect immediately. I will let you know when it's official. Like I said, what is being changed is your title, not what you are doing. I will keep in touch. Don't say anything until it's official."

*****

Ms. White called an executive meeting. She took Sarah's new organization chart and presented it as her own, as Sarah suggested. She explained to the senior VPs about their title change to Executive VPs and their additional responsibilities under the new organization. She said, "Sarah, in her capacity as Senior Vice President of Corporate Development and Planning, will be working closely with each of you during this transitional period and beyond. I trust you will give her your full support as you have given me."

Sarah said, "With my new responsibilities, as you can see on this chart, I will report directly to Ms. White. I am not your boss, but I will be a major coworker. Reporting to me will be the sales staff along with the day care and exercise facilities. With this centralized sales force, we will be going after new business for all manufacturing areas, not like it is now where the salesperson only goes after business for the division they currently work for. One sales call could generate new business in several of our manufacturing facilities. I will need your help with getting the salespeople up to speed on what the capabilities are in the areas of your responsibility. We are needing new customers to grow our bottom line. The current production lines need to be looked at from a time and motion evaluation to see if maximum product flow and efficiency can be achieved. Evaluation of equipment needs to be done, replacing older models with new, more efficient ones. New equipment will be added as needed. That is something that needs to be worked on with you and your people.

"The Executive VP, Senior VPs, and VPs will need to be doing face-to-face meetings with the divisions they are responsible for. Your travel budgets will be increased to cover your expenses. We all know that Ms. White has been doing these visits for you. It's now your turn to do it for yourselves. Ms. White is going to change her focus from the day-to-day to acquiring additional companies, not just in the area of manufacturing but investigating other areas too. I will be assisting her as part of my corporate planning duties. People, plan on your area to grow. We will need to work together, helping each other. This is a new day for us all. At the end of this year, we will look back in amazement at how much we have accomplished. Ms. White and I will be happy to answer any questions you have."

One of the senior VPs asked, "Ms. White, why are you getting out of the day-to-day business now?"

Ms. White said, "I have been working too many hours doing the day-to-day operational side. I need the time to research and procure additional companies to add to our corporation. That's where the fun is for me. I want to increase my efforts there. The only way I can do that is for you to take on more of the day-to-day duties. Probably should have done it years ago."

Another question was asked, "When will this organizational change take place?"

Ms. White said, "The organizational changes will take effect immediately, as will your new job duties."

The next question was, "Will all of the companies have their company name changed?"

Ms. White said, "The companies will be titled with their company name followed by a Division of White Enterprise. It's good business for them to keep their names.

"Sarah has already contacted Bruce Goodson. He is on board and is waiting to be contacted by his new Executive VP. The rest of the companies Sarah knows and has met with these folks. She and you will need to meet with them face-to-face and explain the new organization structure. These meetings should be scheduled as soon as possible. If there are no more questions, I guess we can all get back to work."

*****

The very next day, Sarah and Jill, accompanied by Matt, one of the Executive VPs of Manufacturing, went on the introduction visits. The closest one was on the other side of town and had been Ms. White's competitor for years. Being so close, the visit was done in a short period of time. The meeting went well with the president and staff. They liked hearing all of the improvements that could be made. They didn't feel the title change or reporting structure was that big of a deal.

Most of these meetings were very well received, especially when the executives found out that they would be receiving major funding for production line improvements and upgrades. At each stop, each Executive VP gave a presentation on the format for reporting and production line statistics. They all knew what had been done at the Goodson Company and were excited that they would be a major part of doing that with the other companies, now being called divisions. A couple of the company presidents didn't like the idea of being VPs to headquarters and not presidents anymore. They chose to retire or leave to get a job somewhere else. Change is not always easy. Most of the visits required a long day trip. A few were a short airplane ride. Soon, all of the divisions had been visited.

There was some pushback from some of the accounting departments of several divisions having to report to headquarters and having to change how they had been doing business for years. With some explanation of the overall benefits of a centralized system, they soon agreed it would be better. The heads of finance would be reporting to the senior VP of finance at headquarters instead of their current company's president. One of the divisions was already using the same software package as headquarters. Accounting functions are much the same all over. It was the difference in how the data is currently being reported to how it will be done in the future. Learning the software was the easy part. The hardest part was the data conver-

378

sion from their accounting system software to the one they would be using.

All of the organizational changes had been completed. Some of the new production line flows and equipment changes had been completed or were under installation. Increases in productivity for the ones that had been completed were up on average of 20 percent. The most important plus was there were fewer accidents, and the people were very happy with the changes. Matt and the other executive VPs were enjoying their new duties. They all were making regular visits to the divisions.

The White Enterprise CFO was extremely happy that all divisions were using the same accounting software. The reporting he had to do for the board of directors was so much easier, along with all of the state and federal government reporting. Let's not forget the stockholders.

Sarah's sales team had all been given information and training on what each division was manufacturing. One of the things that Sarah insisted that each salesperson do was spend eight hours working or observing each division's production lines. In doing so, they had a better understanding of what the capabilities were and could match that to new customers' needs in a particular manufacturing area. The sales team already at Goodson was now reporting to Sarah instead of Bruce.

The amount of new business the sales team brought to the corporation was outstanding. The hundreds of thousands spent to upgrade the production lines was well worth it. The profit continued to add to the profitability of White Enterprise. The stock continued to rise. Dividends were issued. Members of the board were investigating a stock split. They, needless to say, were very happy with what was going on.

The year that Ms. White said she was going to take to turn over the corporation to Sarah was coming to an end. What Sarah had done during the year was better than Ms. White's wildest expectations. Sarah had built good relationships with all of the members of the executive staff. The corporation's morale was the highest it had ever been.

Ms. White told the board of her intentions to retire, and she was going to name Sarah as her successor. She said, "I will keep my seat on the board as past president. Sarah's accomplishments over this last year have been beyond outstanding. I nominate Sarah Brown to be the next President and CEO of White Enterprise."

The board voted unanimously to have Sarah Brown to be the president and CEO of White Enterprise.

A notice was sent out that there would be a corporate meeting held at the White Enterprise Convention Center. Jill said to Sarah, "What is this meeting all about?"

Sarah replied, "It's about Ms. White's retirement. You can't say anything to anyone until after the meeting."

Jill asked, "You are going to replace her, aren't you?"

Sarah just nodded.

Jill continued, "So this is what this year has been leading up to? Why didn't you say something about it before?"

Sarah said, "I wanted to several times, but I had to keep my promise to Ms. White that I would not tell anyone, including you. Besides, if I had messed up, we would not be having this conversation."

Jill then asked, "Does this mean I'm the administrative assistant to the president and CEO of White Enterprise?"

Sarah gave Jill one of her looks and said, "Yes."

*****

At the meeting, Ms. White made the announcement. "I am retired effective immediately. Ms. Sarah Brown will be replacing me as President and CEO of White Enterprise."

Sarah stepped to the podium and said, "Ms. White has brought so much to this company over the years, even before my father retired. She has worked endless hours in various areas of the company, learning it from the ground up. Her father made her work for every promotion she ever received. Her common sense and business knowledge have made this company, White Enterprise, what it is today. Her achievements are nothing short of phenomenal. Ms. White has been given many awards for her achievements. She has generously sponsored many of the city's activities and events. She is well respected in this industry and in our community. There will be a retirement party held in this very hall on Friday. You all are invited. Join me in wishing her much happiness in her retirement. Thank you."

There was a thunderous applause from the employees. Ms. White was swamped with well-wishers, as was Sarah.

After the meeting, Sarah and Ms. White walked to Ms. White's office. Ms. White said, "This is your office now."

Sarah started to cry.

Ms. White said, "I hope those are happy tears."

Sarah replied, "Only half of them are. The other half are for the times I will miss being by your side. It sure has been one hell of a ride."

Ms. White said, "Sarah, you sure have a way with words."

CHAPTER 57

Where Are They Now?

Mr. White: He was so proud of what Elizabeth had accomplished. Shortly after Ms. White's retirement, he died in his sleep. His funeral services were held at the White Enterprise Convention Center. The funeral procession was over a mile long.

Ms. White: She pursued her love for playing poker. The following year, she won the World's Texas Hold'em tournament in Las Vegas. She was having the time of her life. She and Sarah went to lunch every third Wednesday of the month and talked at least once a week on the phone.

Bill: After working many contract hours, he bought his dream bass fishing boat. That boat had every fishing gadget one could have installed on a boat. He entered many fishing tournaments and proved that no matter how many gadgets you have, that's not going to guarantee you'll catch fish.

Jill: She was promoted to be the administrative assistant to the president and CEO of White Enterprise Corporation. They never did try to have that girl. She was still Aunt Jill to the twins.

Tammy: She left the company when Ms. White retired. She got married to the one she was living with, and they moved out of state. She and Jill still kept in touch.

Bruce Goodson: As Sarah had hoped, Bruce was nothing like his father. The Goodson Division became the top division in White Enterprise under Bruce's leadership.

Margo: Happy as one could be. She was definitely Grandma to the twins. The day care facility was awarded the best in the city.

Charles: He remained Ms. White's driver.

Ben and Andrew: They got married. It was the biggest wedding one could imagine. Sarah, Karl, and the twins attended the wedding. She thought the entire gay and lesbian community was in attendance.

Patty: She babysat the twins a lot since Sarah was now the president and CEO and was traveling more. She is still looking for that rich guy to marry.

Ted and Billy: Phase 2 of Pony Express Estates was completed, and they started working on phase 3. Plans were being made to build a school in the subdivision.

George: He is happy in the position of Senior Accountant. He turned down a promotion because he enjoyed what he was doing—working with companies. He continues to be the top senior accountant time and time again.

Karl: He was named a full partner. Julie, Karl's boss, left and started her own accounting firm. Karl became Julie's replacement. George was now working for Karl. He was okay with that. George said, "I'm still on bonus, and you are not. Ha ha!"

Emily and Kevin: They were growing up way too fast. They were in school.

Hunter and Sniffer: Hunter with Kevin and Sniffer with Emily. Oh, how they all played together. They spent hours exploring the trails of Pony Express Estates.

Sarah's dad: He was in his own world now. Sarah and Karl took the twins up to meet their grandfather. He didn't even recognize Sarah. Still in good health as one could be at his age, Sarah said he just might outlive her.

Karl's chair: It got a new home. It now sits in Karl's workshop out in the barn. After Sarah hauled Karl around to several stores and what seemed like trying a hundred chairs, Karl finally picked a chair he liked. But if you went looking for him, you could usually find him out in the workshop sitting in that old chair of his.

Sarah: In her first year, she was awarded the Best First Year President and CEO and earned a spot in the *Who's Who American Business Journal.*

The cow picture: Sarah had it moved into her President and CEO office. The cow picture has a new frame and hangs on the wall where Sarah can see it.

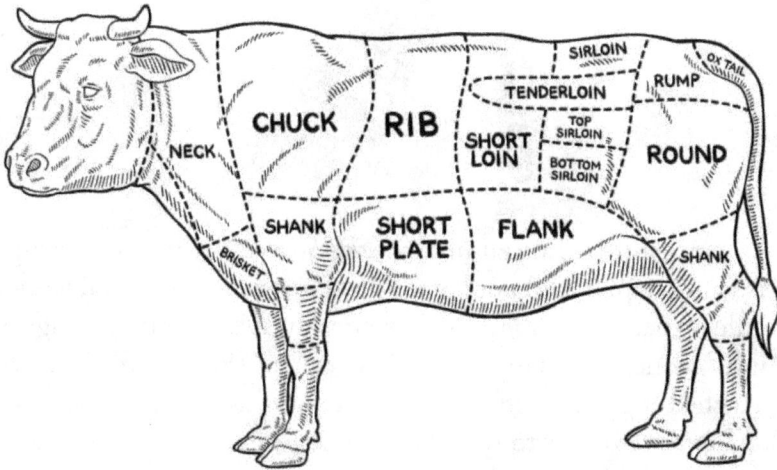

ABOUT THE AUTHOR

Gary Tatem is a first-time author. *Sarah's Story* came to him through dreams. The chapters did not come all at once but over several weeks. He would either wake up, go to his computer, and start typing, or wait until the next morning. The chapters kept flowing until *Sarah's Story* reached a natural ending. He was amazed at how the story unfolded and was eager to see what came next. After the story came to an end, so did the *Sarah's Story* dreams.

Mr. Tatem started his adult career in data processing as a programmer. Later, he joined a software company in the customer education department. Teaching how the software worked, he traveled to many companies in several different countries. After leaving the world of data processing, he and his wife took a midlife retirement. They purchased a motor home and traveled the United States full time. Needing to settle down and have an income, they purchased an RV park. He has since sold the business and is now retired in Texas, where every day is a weekend day.

www.ingramcontent.com/pod-product-compliance
Lightning Source LLC
LaVergne TN
LVHW040851131224
799040LV00008B/63